SACRAMENTO PUBLIC LIBRARY

3 3029 04038 2939

**SACRAMENTO PUBLIC LIBRARY
828 "I" STREET
SACRAMENTO, CA 95814**

A Safe
Place for
Dangerous
Truths

A Safe
Place for
Dangerous
Truths

Using *Dialogue* to
Overcome
Fear & Distrust
at Work

ANNETTE SIMMONS

AMACOM
American Management Association

New York • Atlanta • Boston • Chicago • Kansas City • San Francisco • Washington, D.C.
Brussels • Mexico City • Tokyo • Toronto

This book is available at a special
discount when ordered in bulk quantities.
For information, contact Special Sales Department,
AMACOM, an imprint of AMA publications, a division of
American Management Association, 1601 Broadway, New York,
NY 10019.

This publication is designed to provide accurate and authoritative information
in regard to the subject matter covered. It is sold with the understanding that
the publisher is not engaged in rendering legal, accounting, or other professional service. If legal advice or other expert assistance is required, the services of a
competent professional person should be sought.

Library of Congress Cataloguing-in-Publication Data

Simmons, Annette
    A safe place for dangerous truths: using dialogue to overcome fear & distrust at work
    / Annettte Simmons.
        p. cm.
    Includes bibliographical references and index.
    ISBN 0-8144-0479-0
    1. Dialogue analysis. 2. Communication in small groups.
    I. Title.
    P95.455.S5   1999   99-13992
    302.3'46—dc21   CIP

© 1999 Annette Simmons.
All rights reserved.
Printed in the United States of America.

This publication may not be reproduced,
stored in a retrieval system,
or transmitted in whole or in part,
in any form or by any means, electronic,
mechanical, photocopying, recording, or otherwise,
without the prior written permission of AMACOM,
an imprint of AMA Publications,
a division of American Management Association,
1601 Broadway, New York, NY 10019.

Printing number

10 9 8 7 6 5 4 3 2 1

Contents

PART 1: Dialogue Defined

PART 2: With All That Going Against You: The How-To's of Dialogue

Without Pointing Fingers • Let Them Make the Connection • "This Way ⇨ to Dialogue" Signs • Choosing
Mind-Sets • Now or Never

12   The Socratic Method   147

Socrates—More Than One Voice • Don't Give Them
Fish—Help Them Learn How to Fish • A Midwife
Assists • Experience Is the Best Teacher • Hiding From
Reality • The Wrong Questions • Awakening Perplexity •
Asking Good Questions • Finding the Spirit of Inquiry •
Believe They Can Do It • Awaken the Desire • Let Them
Discover Their Barriers • Avoiding the Hemlock Response

13   Egoless-ness   159

How to Become Unnecessary • The Seduction of Being in
Front of the Room • In the Presence of Your Equals • Body
Language • Don't Hold That Thought • Cockiness: An
Early Warning System • The Fear of Looking Uninvolved,
Uninterested, or Unimportant • Common Ego Trip-Ups

14   Storytelling   169

When Nothing Else Can Break Through • A Common
Experience • Dangerous Truths • Stories That Stimulate
Introspection • Developmental Stages • Oral Language •
The Magic of "Irrelevant Detail" • The Greatest Sin: A
Boring Story • The Power of Stories

15   Modeling   181

Walk Your Talk • Facilitate Yourself • But Didn't You Just
Say . . . ? • Let Me "See" • From Either/Or to Both/And •
When You Screw Up

Acknowledgments

The works of Chris Argyris, David Bohm, William Isaacs, M. Scott Peck, Linda Ellinor, and Glenna Gerard have profoundly influenced my own work, and I am grateful to have been influenced by their hearts and minds. Thanks to Juanita Brown, Nancy Dixon, Jeff Insco, Joe Phelps, and Elizabeth von Clemm for enriching dialogues about dialogue. I am grateful to Jim Farr for the opportunity to experiment and explore these concepts in the early days. Many thanks go to the many individuals who may or may not have shared my passion for dialogue but were willing to experiment within their workgroups. Thanks, too, to the workshop participants who demonstrated faith in the early days of my attempts to share what I had learned with others. Your patience and feedback kept me going and made the book better. Thanks to Sherry and Brandy Decker, Cheryl DeCiantis, Alan Downs, Cindy Franklin, Kenton Hyatt, Doug Lipman, and David Williams for being such good friends and always ready with moral support. Thanks to Adrienne Hickey, my editor, for her support and excellent suggestions.

Introduction

Sometimes the only safe place for dangerous truth is in the bathroom . . . *after* checking for feet, of course.

Only then it is safe to talk. After the meeting, after everyone has said exactly what they were supposed to say, agreed to the action plan, and allocated tasks with due dates, comes the real truth:

"What a waste of time!"

"I'm not taking *that* back to my people—they've got to be kidding!"

"Don't worry about it. It will fall apart long before your piece is due."

Sometimes the meeting is debriefed like a play: "How about when Mark did that 180-degree flip? I thought I was gonna die! He will agree with anything she says," or "Can you believe they still won't face the fact that Amy can't do the job?"

It never occurs to us that we are wasting each other's time (and our own) by not telling the truth *in* the meeting rather than after it. Even when this thought does occur to us, we have many reasons why telling the truth just won't work.

Why not? Why can't we tell the truth? It's *dangerous*, that's why.

It's dangerous for many reasons. Most of those reasons have to do with wanting to keep our jobs. But at what price? Holding back the truth means holding back other things, such as enthusiasm and commitment. Why can't we create a place safe enough where we *can* tell the truth—where we *want* to tell the truth?

It would have to be a very safe place. People would need to trust one another, and they would have to care enough to take the risk. They would need to believe the result was worth the risk. They would have to want to learn from each other, even if it meant admitting their own ignorance, fears, and shortcomings. And they would have to throw the politically correct suck-up routine in the trash where it belongs. Never happen?

I don't think we have a choice. If information and knowledge are now the most important raw resources we have, then we have to start doing a better job of getting it to the people who need it. Bottlenecks in our informal information systems squeeze the flow of knowledge down to a trickle, creating a drought of creative ideas and good decisions. If we are to remove the bottlenecks, we need to understand that the barriers to this vital flow of information are in our minds, not in our technology.

Eight years ago, I stumbled upon a process called "dialogue" in Peter Senge's book, *The Fifth Discipline*. From there I studied William Isaacs's Dialogue Project at MIT, Linda Ellinor and Glenna Gerard's work with The Dialogue Group, the work of quantum physicist David Bohm, M. Scott Peck's work on community building, and contributions from many, many others. I embraced the idea that we can apply a formal process to create a place where it is safe enough to tell each other the truth—safe enough to say what needs to be said. In 1994, I wrote my thesis on dialogue. To satisfy my personal quest to pump a little authenticity back into the workplace, I used my thesis as an opportunity to develop a process and experiment with innovative methods and techniques. My goal was to find a process that would radically change the norms of a group so that people could increase their capacity to face dangerous truths head-on and address the apparently unsolvable and definitely undiscussable issues that were tearing them apart.

My first efforts resulted in a baptism by fire. It isn't easy to get people to have a real dialogue. They are avoiding the truth for what they consider to be damn good reasons. But once I did get people to take the risk, the results were beyond my wildest expectations. When a group faces the facts, drops the pretense, and tells the truth, the euphoria of rising to the occasion connects the group and fills everyone with energy. That euphoria is addictive. Facilitating dialogue is very gratifying work.

My hope is that your efforts will go beyond my research and my experiments. I don't want anyone to get the impression that I think there is a "right" way to do dialogue. There are many paths to dialogue. This is not intended to be the definitive step-by-step guide to dialogue. It is one guide, not *the* guide.

I can only provide a series of snapshots of dialogue (taken from my particular view). There are oversimplifications and gross generalizations. It is up to you to shade in the contours and terrain specific to your application. In the spirit of dialogue, I encourage you to consider the assumptions that guide your approach to facilitation. I suspect that many of your old assumptions won't fit. I also invite you to reflect on what drives your desire to take groups to such a deep level of conversation. Taking a group to a place where people face dangerous truths is not a decision to be taken lightly. This can become, in the words of a workshop participant, "intense facilitation."

The book is written in three parts. In the first part, I dialogue about dialogue. I walk all the way around the concept of turning dialogue into a formal process, what it might look like, feel like, taste like. There is enough information to give you a chance to decide whether you think it is a good idea or not.

Part Two introduces a clear structure and a step-by-step "recipe" for dialogue. The clarity is false. Dialogue is too complex for a recipe. I don't expect you to follow this recipe. In fact, I beg you not to follow it word for word. To me, it is like cooking. When I cook, I consult up to three recipes as a starting point. Then I may toss all three aside and concoct my own that fits with what I have in the pantry and the guests who are coming over. It's the same with dialogue. This recipe is offered as a starting point. If you are the kind of person who likes to "see" someone do it first, there is a simulated example of this recipe in the Appendix. It is presented not as a script to memorize, but to stimulate your own ideas.

Part Three describes seven facilitator skills—but they go beyond skills. They encompass the underlying personal qualities that help you encourage others to dialogue. It takes a special state of being to take a group to dialogue. When you read these sections, you will see what I mean. The last chapter is designed to provide a transition from the false clarity of "this is how to do it" to the real-life experiences you will encounter on your own path to dialogue. I share with you the experiences and opinions of several other people who have successfully forged their own paths to dialogue. As we review what they think it takes to facilitate dialogue, we abandon our temporary illusion of clarity and rejoin a more realistic and complex world where the answer to the question, "How do you do it?" is—"It depends."

Finally, I believe you must hold two basic philosophical assumptions to facilitate dialogue. The main one is that people are basically good. If you think people are bad at the core (e.g., greedy, exploitative, mean), there is no point in dialogue. Dialogue only reveals what is at the core. For me, the greatest payoff of dialogue has been to watch over and over again a group's revelation of how "good" it really is. During dialogue, the "bad" falls away like unnecessary armor.

If you believe that people are good, then the second philosophical assumption is easier to put into practice. No one can or should try to control the process of dialogue. We may facilitate but never direct or control. Dialogue is completely unpredictable. To impose a desired outcome is to corrupt the process. Dialogue is like dance. No one owns the concept. No one invented it. Too much critique will shut it down or stunt the creative process. We reinvent it every time we do it. And, yes, sometimes it looks and feels a little awkward—but it always brings out the best in us and makes us feel alive.

PART 1

Dialogue Defined

Chapter 1

Why Dialogue?

Between falsehood and useless truth there is little difference.
As gold which he cannot spend will make no man rich,
so knowledge which he cannot apply will make no man wise.

SAMUEL JOHNSON

SHOOTING IN THE DARK

In one survey, 93 percent of people have admitted to lying regularly at work.[1] *Ninety-three percent!*

If we want better communication, don't you think this is a good place to start?

We don't simply need to improve the flow of information at work. We need to improve the quality of the information that is flowing. People aren't telling the truth. And it corrupts our systems. It distorts feedback loops. Low-quality information breeds low-quality relationships, low-quality processes, and—surprise, surprise—low-quality products and services.

How often do you tell the truth at work? A better question might be, how often do you believe what you hear? Most of us do not out-and-out lie. We simply hide behind partial truths; prepolished, politically correct routines; or sins of omission that distort perceptions and fracture an organization's ability to adapt.

We end up basing important decisions on a series of doctored opinions, data, and information—each delivered with a missing piece or an accumulating "spin." How can we expect to meet our deadlines, keep our customers happy, or ensure quality with bad data? Engineers call it stacked tolerance. When a tiny tolerance of plus or minus a thousandth of an inch stacks up, the combined effect can destroy the integrity of a system. Every piece is just a little off "true," and the result is that the group of pieces, as a whole, ends up a lot off "true." In terms of communication, we might even say the group ends up discussing falsehoods instead of the truth.

We run the risk of building our strategic plans, allocating our resources, and making other major decisions based on faulty information. Sounds like a recipe for failure, doesn't it? We can't make good decisions if we aren't telling each other the truth. And how in the world can we build a team that works well together when we can't even talk to one another?

Too many people think it is futile to speak the truth at work. They think that to be honest and authentic is to commit career suicide. They believe that only a fool would "call it like it is." And so they compromise. They keep quiet about "delicate" issues. They avoid the touchy points. And soon enough, subjects that are undiscussable exceed the discussable. All that is left are the inane, superficial, and repetitious details that monopolize our workplace conversations. If you've ever sat in a meeting that was a complete waste of time, you were probably surrounded by people unwilling to speak the truth.

THINKING NEW THOUGHTS

It is time to rewrite old rules that filter out the disturbing yet vital truths. What a wasted resource! Those truths, considered dangerous, actually have the power to challenge our workgroups to think new thoughts and generate new ideas. We need to build a safe place where these dangerous truths can surface. We need to make it okay to question, wonder, and reflect. Only then can our organizations begin to achieve the level of responsiveness and foresight necessary for long-term success in today's business environment. Our mills of creativity require the grist of truth telling to produce new ideas, innovative products, and ingenious shortcuts to accelerate delivery times. Half-truths only inspire half-hearted efforts and mediocre results. It is the genuine exchange of meaningful truth that gives birth to enthusiasm, passion, and excellence. It is the experience of genuine dialogue that can transform and develop the full extent of a group's potential into reality.

Dialogue has the power to change a group of strangers into friends and a collection of individuals into a team. Dialogue builds coherence around diversity and trust where suspicion and cynicism threaten to fragment an organization. The process of dialogue is the vehicle through which knowledge is shared. It is how an organization "thinks." Dialogue is the observable neural networking of the organizational mind. And it is sorely lacking in our organizations. Why? Dialogue demands of participants a willingness to tell the truth and, just as difficult, a willingness to listen to the truth (or someone's version of it).

How can you make it safe to tell the truth? Turning dialogue into a formal process is one way you can help a group rewrite its communication norms. When given a time and a place to practice, people have an opportunity to experiment and test new communication protocols that would remain little more than good intentions in the rush of daily activity. If you feel called to take a group beyond current levels of performance, then the process of dialogue presented in this book articulates a path you can adapt and replicate with any group. Dialogue is not a magic bullet. It takes time. It involves risk. And sometimes you will wonder if it is worth it. But it sure beats the heck out of looping back through the same old conversations that doom us to make the same mistakes and limit us to achieve only marginal improvements.

THE "REAL PROBLEM"

When a group fails to address difficult issues, something has affected its members' willingness to see and tell the truth. It could be a turf war, an ego battle, a tyrannical hierarchy, old fears of retribution, or learned helplessness translated into apathy. At one level it doesn't matter. When coworkers will only speak privately about the "real problem," then dialogue has become taboo in the larger group. The "real problem" is code speak for the one thing that needs to be fixed, yet everyone is too scared to mention it for fear of retribution, losing personal ground, or being shot as the messenger of bad news. It may concern an individual's performance, a system that isn't working, the boss's pet project or department that is totally dysfunctional, a deep injustice in allocation of rewards or resources, or some other tough issue. The "real problem" is the one that everyone either pretends isn't there or impotently addresses with the same old solutions that didn't work last time.

We have to stop avoiding the real problems. They contain either the seeds of unique opportunity or the seeds of our demise— regardless, we want the capacity to talk about them before the opportunities wither and die or these little seeds grow into Godzilla-like failures. Part of our problem is that as it becomes more necessary, it also becomes more difficult to "face the facts." More decentralized levels of authority demand new skills that enable whole groups to address problems. The business of business requires us to continually address and resolve conflicts. It was hard enough when our leader had sole responsibility to make the "tough decisions." Now that we have to do it as a group—well, no wonder people avoid the "real problems."

Traditional hierarchy protected us from this dilemma. In the old hierarchy days, we could look to a leader to make the tough decisions. Even now, some of us still blame "leadership" for our inability to face the real problems. But the truth is, we are all to blame. Anytime we skirt an issue, pretend we didn't hear, or engage in an adversarial win-lose debate, we avoid the hard work of a genuine dialogue about the real issues. Today, we find ourselves facing enough complexity, moral dilemmas, and stressful time constraints to make "taking sides" a losing strategy. We scream that we need better leadership, but leaders can't save us now. We are going to have to learn how to lead ourselves. And to do that we have to know how to dialogue.

We need skills that help us resolve paradoxical conflicts as a group. For instance, is the customer still king when he treats an employee (your greatest asset) unfairly? Who is most important? It is no longer either/or, but both/and. We have to learn how to stop taking sides and make decisions together, to piece together a bigger picture from apparently contradictory input, and to resolve seemingly unsolvable dilemmas as a group. For the organization to "think," we first have to learn how to think and reason together in groups. It's a tough order when you've got a group that finds it difficult to agree on what to have for lunch.

DIALOGUE SKILLS FOR DANGEROUS TRUTHS

We need new skills to help groups talk through tough issues without escalating into arguments, declining into debilitated silence, or mindlessly deferring to a "leader" the group can later subvert. Decentralized leadership means sharing the difficult issues as well as the easy ones. What used to be one person's inner conflict now exponentially increases in complexity by the number of people involved, their values, beliefs, and opinions. Sure, with more input we have the potential to make much better decisions, but not if we kill each other in the process or, conversely, give up and take a vote. No wonder leaders don't walk their talk and share the big decisions—without the skills of dialogue and collective thinking, the risk of a free-for-all or a second-rate decision is ever-present.

When you introduce dialogue as a formal process, you have an opportunity to develop your group's skill in dealing with dangerous truths as a group. Right now, most of us working in groups don't know how to talk to each other—much less tell each other the truth. Most of us find it hard to have a productive dialogue with a spouse—forget the bozos in R&D or the Gen-X freak with the T-shirt that says "Ignore Authority." Sure, we can talk to people like us—people who understand the importance of what we think is important. Those are people we can have a conversation with. But these other people—why, they don't have a clue what is going on. They aren't listening to us, so why should we listen to them?

I'll tell you why. First of all, they know something you don't know. Simply because they are in a position to see what you can't see. And second, you can't do your job without them. If you don't figure out some way to talk with these people, you can't get their cooperation, you can't achieve your objectives, and you won't reach your goals—which is totally unacceptable.

LEARNING SCHMEARNING

All of this garbage about a learning organization will remain just that—garbage—if we don't grasp the fact that learning is a social process and what we really need to learn comes from the people we work with. They hold our missing pieces and we hold the key for their understanding. Unless we get better at swapping what we know for what they know, we will find ourselves continuing to make avoidable mistakes, missing market opportunities, and responding too late to threats.

If it were easy, we wouldn't still be griping about needing better communication—we would be doing it. So why not start by stepping back and taking some time to rethink how we talk to each other?

When people don't do what they agreed to do, when someone tells you one thing and your coworker something else, when the truthful talk occurs in the bathroom after the meeting—that's when we have to admit our current theories about communication are failing us.

Ten and twenty years ago, there was time to set people straight after a misunderstanding. That was when we had lag time between communication and its impact. We don't have lag time anymore. Today, we have to communicate in real time, speedily passing on knowledge from one remote arm of the organization to another because the world just changed and people need to know what happened. Knowledge needs to move fast enough to recalibrate people's thinking so the organization can respond to change as fast as it happens. Learning is completely dependent on the organization's ability to communicate.

REENGINEERING COMMUNICATION

The level of communication in your organization is the result of the combined norms, habits, and protocols that have evolved over time. For what once may have been a very good reason, there are certain issues that your communication norms have labeled undiscussable. Forbidden subjects may include admission of ignorance, fundamental disagreements with the boss, or bad news about low quality or slipping deadlines—the very issues that beg for open communication and a learning environment.

Other norms encourage avoidance by passing the buck, blaming, flying into crisis mode, or simply hoping that the problem will go away by itself. These habits provide the welcome distraction of activity, even if it is wheels spinning away from the hard work of talking about tough issues. If making a decision about a $600 million environmental cleanup program seems impossible, the team can simply move on and restructure the division. A new "reorg" offers immediate satisfaction—clean lines, nice square boxes, and maybe even the opportunity to reallocate environmental issues into someone else's area. Problem solved, right? Wrong.

If we need to restructure anything, it is our communication habits. Facilitating the process of dialogue will help you reengineer the norms, habits, and conversation protocols your group employs to avoid or block free access to information feedback loops. Solutions—

indeed your workgroup's success—depend on the free flow of knowledge between individuals unencumbered by old norms that prevent honest dialogue. Old habits need to be replaced with new habits that facilitate communication. We need habits that build links between people's hearts and minds through which knowledge and information can freely travel.

Real communication (dialogue) changes people. It changes our beliefs, changes our minds, and ultimately changes our actions. This is the essence of learning: taking in the new and swapping it for the old. We can't afford to allow outdated norms to prevent our access to the tough issues and to the knowledge of others. We need to learn how to dialogue—to talk to each other in a way that ties us together and links our minds and hearts so we can learn, think, and act as a cohesive system rather than a big pile of people, computers, and products dumped into a building.

IF PEOPLE WERE COWS

If people were cows, traditional group-process methods could do the trick. We could use these processes to negotiate mutually exclusive goals, merge conflicting opinions, and force people to face the scary stuff by herding them with structure or a facilitator/shepherd. The structure of the process or the facilitator would cut off wanderers, barricade "irrelevant" issues, and conform certain individual behaviors (e.g., dominators, hecklers) as he herds the group members into a big corral called Agreement. However, people are not cattle, and while they may follow along a group-process cattle chute to some prefab corral, the minute a discussion is over, they will walk to the gate, let themselves out, and go right back to the patch of pasture they prefer.

The price of using these kinds of group processes to facilitate communication is that people don't really communicate. They may think that they are communicating, but no one emerges changed from the experience. They just pretend to be changed long enough to get out the door. The resulting difference between what is agreed on, through these sorts of processes and what is actually implemented breeds distrust and causes people to label most group "communication" a waste of time. In fact, much of what we have been taught about facilitating communication is a waste of time. Some of it is even counterproductive.

It is time that we stopped blaming people for not "getting" what we try to teach them about communication and started using processes that make sense and offer visible improvements. Dialogue is such a process. It offers new skills so a group can design and build its own corral of agreement—a place so suitable to the group that everyone enters willingly and enthusiastically, without sacrificing creativity and risk taking. Rather than depend on the cattle chute of structured process, today's workgroup needs to know how to genuinely communicate.

COLLECTIVE LEARNING DISABILITIES

The advantages of learning as a collective include the attractive notion of not making the same mistake twice, or not making a mistake at all if you can learn from another's experience. A group that can learn easily has a greater potential for finding creative solutions to problems and the opportunity to leap forward and grab opportunities before the slower-witted and less aligned think to act.

However, learning as a group is difficult. Research demonstrates that groups suffer "process losses" when performing collectively. Ten smart people in a group don't necessarily translate into a group that is ten times as smart as the individuals in it. Untended, groups usually waste available intellectual resources. Most groups perform well below the capacity of the smartest member. If you've ever felt you might have done better on your own rather than with a group, you may have been right. Even if you aren't the smartest member of the group, at least some of your IQ is probably wasted due to "process losses."

Without any intervention, group performance almost always falls below the collective intelligence of the combined group members (forget synergy). It is not quite so bad as the lowest common denominator—groups usually perform above the mean intellect—but let's just say most groups could be doing a much better job of using their available intellectual resources.

There are two reasons for these process losses:

1 Groups usually have a low tolerance for the frustration of uncertainty. And the one thing that is required in order to learn is to consider what you don't know (i.e., to embrace uncertainty). When a group's tolerance for frustration is low, then learning is going to be low as well. Learning can be frustrating. If a group won't tolerate frustration, its members limit their ability to learn. Likewise, facilitation tactics that seek to remove frustration—failing to distinguish between necessary and unnecessary frustration—will diminish a group's capacity to learn. To learn together, a group needs to be willing to, at times, practically wallow in uncertainty.

2 Along with this unwillingness to face the frustration of uncertainty, most groups suffer from a tendency to rush to consensus. The "let's do something even if it's wrong" impulse cuts short the process of reflection and introspection necessary for learning to occur. To learn, groups need time to think. When a group is impulsive and rushes to agree/act, it risks avoidable errors and predictable consequences. The speed of the workplace has accelerated to the point where perceptions of urgency tyrannize groups into treating all decisions as urgent. When that happens, groups risk bad decisions and fail to learn from past experience.

Dialogue addresses both of these causes of process loss. Groups develop tolerance for increased levels of frustration and learn to suspend their rush to consensus long enough to fully explore unexamined options and issues. They learn to hold the ambiguity and risk a few extra minutes of inaction in return for a more creative thought process and more thorough consideration. The primary dynamic that supports a group in developing this higher state of collective thought is an increase in coherence.

COHERENCE

David Bohm, a quantum physicist, has been credited with reviving our interest in dialogue as a learning tool. He used the metaphor of coherent and incoherent light to describe the effects of dialogue. Incoherent light is the light coming from an ordinary lightbulb. Diffused, the light is without shape or focused direction. It just goes everywhere at once (sound familiar?). A laser is coherent light—wavelengths in sync to the point that a small amount of light can cut through steel or hit a microscopically small target. Dialogue is the process by which we, as members of a workgroup, get in sync. It is how we develop coherence.

With coherence, a system can maintain integrity at the same time it flexibly responds to threats and addresses opportunities. Old thinking sought to mandate coherence through a demand for obedience or consistency. In a traditional hierarchy, if everyone does as told, the system's integrity is ensured. But the system can only be as smart as its leader. The quality movement touted consistent process as the way to tighten variance and reduce deviation. Yet in the bargain, it runs the risk of limiting itself to incremental rather than breakthrough improvements.

For a system to have both alignment and the capacity for breakthrough learning/creativity, it needs a more flexible source of coherence than obedience or consistent process. Since creativity is, by definition, "out of control" and learning is unpredictable (if you could predict it, it wouldn't be learning), we need to develop a new source of coherence that operates outside the old limitations of obedience or consistency.

The coherence developed through dialogue is a mutual attraction that connects diverse and unpredictable individuals together in a system. Coherence is evident in a group with high mutual respect, high levels of trust, and the accompanying familiarity that goes along with respect and trust. A coherent group has established links of informal communication along which new information and vital feedback (positive and negative) flow. A coherent group doesn't need defensive routines that avoid dangerous truths. A coherent group welcomes new input, adapts quickly, and redesigns itself without the bickering or apathy that may threaten to fracture an incoherent group.

GROUP SELF-AWARENESS

Dialogue builds coherence by assisting a group in becoming self-aware. Shakespeare's advice to "know thyself" is good for groups, too. Just as an individual who is self-aware exhibits a higher capacity for dealing with unpleasant realities or disorienting opportunity, so does a group that is self-aware. Perhaps most important, a self-aware group knows its strengths and its potential, taking advantage of and creating its own opportunities. High-performing groups have developed a level of familiarity that speeds up reaction times, facilitates rapid communication, and accelerates implementation.

When a group is unaware, its members don't see their weaknesses or their counterproductive communication norms. As you attempt to help a group build new norms, one of the first steps will be increasing the group's self-awareness. Since you can't change norms, the group must do that for itself. Dialogue is a path whereby you can jump-start a group through the process of collective introspection that leads to group self-awareness and ultimately change.

COLLECTIVE INTROSPECTION

How do you get a group to see what it needs to see? First, the group members need to set some time aside for that purpose (don't underestimate the difficulty of this first step, but let's come back to it). The second step will depend on their willingness and ability to stimulate genuine dialogue. The rest of this book is dedicated to increasing your skills in creating that willingness and developing the group's ability. If we look at dialogue as a process of collective introspection, we begin to capture the nature and the power of the process. Introspection is a conscious unraveling of the tightly held beliefs that frame our reality. When we engage in introspection, we revisit our actions and beliefs with the express purpose of discovering beliefs that no longer represent reality and that no longer help us get what we want. The time we grant ourselves to reflect and reconsider fuels our ability to leap into a higher level of understanding. For some of us, time in the shower is the only time we stop "doing" long enough to think. The shower is the only place where we have enough time to reflect. It is not coincidental that this is also the place where we have some of our best ideas.

Although it might inspire new heights of creativity, I don't recommend encouraging your workgroup to shower together. But the concept is the same. Dialogue is a process for collective introspection that allows a group enough time to reflect as a unit. Individual insight is useless when you need collective action. Anyone still dripping from the shower, wondering how to get everyone else "on board" with his newest idea, knows that. The trick is to generate insight at the group level. When you can stimulate shared insight, shared action flows as if by osmosis.

SHARED ACTION

Ultimately, shared action is the big payoff for true dialogue—working with each other instead of against each other in an unpredictable world. One historical example of dialogue can be found in an ancient tribal method for beginning a hunt. For two days the entire hunting party would come together to sit and talk. That's it. No play diagrams of Xs and Os. No strategic plans or agendas. Just talk. After two days the hunting party sets out—no longer a fractured group of individuals but a cohesive whole. When an animal was sighted, the members of the hunting party acted in symphony, coordinating their efforts, not from a strict action plan but from a shared sense of understanding and deep familiarity.

A friend of mine had a chance to see this in action. She was asked to consult with a tribe in Alaska that was facing big decisions on self-government. She said they spent the entire first two days "just talking." Not idle chitchat, but at times deep disagreements. Her traditionally trained consultant's mind wondered where the agenda was. Who was the leader here? Where was the plan? Lucky for her, she kept those thoughts to herself. On the third day, the group was ready for her to facilitate the decision-making process. She was amazed at how smoothly the group reached agreement and concluded its business. They were in sync. The dialogue had sifted violently opposing opinions into bigger-picture views that could coexist. "Just talking" transformed either/or arguments into both/and possibilities.

If your goal is to take a diverse group of intelligent people and turn them into a cohesive, high-functioning group capable of rapidly responding to unpredictable threats and unforeseeable opportunities, then read on. The process of dialogue promises the magic you seek.

NOTE

1. As cited in James Patterson and Peter Kim's *The Day America Told the Truth* (Englewood, NJ: Prentice Hall, 1991).

Chapter 2

How Hard Can It Be?

The quest for certainty blocks the search for meaning.
Uncertainty is the very condition to impel man to unfold his powers.

ERICH FROMM

WHAT'S THE BIG "D"?

At one level, dialogue with a little *d* is nothing more than a deeper level of conversation. The attraction of creating the concept of dialogue with a big *D* is that it gives us an opportunity to turn it into a group process—a training ground. For purposes of this book, when we talk about dialogue, we specifically mean the big concept of building a group process.

To formalize dialogue is to give ourselves a chance to practice it as a group, get better at it, and build our skills so they will be there when we need them. We can't practice communication skills in a training room—all we can do there is learn theory. Learning how to deal with morons in general is just not as useful as learning how to deal with the moron who keeps interrupting you in meetings or the one who says one thing and does another. Skills that help us deal with real people and real problems are developed in real situations.

When you make dialogue a formal process, you create a "real situation" where a group can step back from doing/deciding and take time to think and reflect. The discipline of arresting our compulsion to focus on outcomes for a few hours helps build the thinking muscles of the group brain. The ones who participate—the group of individuals in the room—learn the skill. Anyone who can't make it, needs to be absent for a few hours, or is not invited (those in the "anyone but them" category) misses practice. In your situation, a dialogue group

15

may include five people or thirty-five. The bigger the better—it increases diversity of input, builds bigger pictures, and generates more creative thought. Sometimes the group needs to be small, but ultimately the more people there are practicing dialogue, the more people are learning the skill.

Like a choir practicing harmony, we need to practice with the ones whose performance we depend on. For an experienced choir, practice not only improves current performance, it hones deeper skills useful in tackling whatever unpredictably difficult piece of new music comes its way—either with the current group, individually, or with a new group. Dialogue is not just an experience that bonds a group; it is a skill developed through practice that will be there when you need it, wherever you are, whomever you are with.

FINDING A CHOIR TO PREACH TO

Sounds great if you are in the enviable position of having a choir that wants to practice. But if, like most managers or internal/external consultants, your "choir" is more likely to skip practice than listen to your preaching about dialogue, you need a few tricks up your sleeve. Your first trick will be to sell your group on the concept of spending up to a day in a room together relearning how to talk to each other. I've searched high and low for a way to do this faster, but as of this moment, changing the communication norms of a group remains a very big job. For the first pass, you need a half-day to back everyone off old habits and introduce new ones, two hours for dialogue, and at least an hour of reflection to anchor your gains afterward. The full day happens just once. After that, you shouldn't need more than a couple of hours of practice once a month to build your group's skill.

It also helps to explain to your group that dialogue is not a skill to be used every day, all day. Thinking, reflecting, questioning your assumptions, and listening to alternate points of view are good in the appropriate dose. It is unrealistic to think we can always be open, empathetic, and reflective. We have work to do, after all. It is a question of balance. Any workgroup seeking a sustainable level of innovative performance needs to develop skills both in doing and thinking. When our hyperefficient schedules virtually ensure we have no time to think or to just sit and talk, we must make the time. To commit to dialogue is to commit to taking time out to think.

Which brings us to a dilemma: If you are a manager and want to take the time to "think" with your group, it is difficult to simultaneously perform the "doing" task of facilitation. I don't recommend trying to facilitate your own workgroup to dialogue—it interferes with your ability to be an equal participant in the dialogue. Some people do it, but as a rule it is nice to use an unbiased observer/facilitator when you attempt dialogue for the first few times (after that, your group should learn to facilitate itself). If you are a functional manager, try to find another manager who will swap with you so that you can facilitate each other's group. HR managers or external and internal consultants are much better positioned to facilitate dialogue for workgroups that don't report directly to them.

It is difficult to facilitate a process and participate in it at the same time. If you don't have the opportunity to find someone who will perform the facilitator role for your group, all is not lost. You can adapt this process to a participant/facilitator situation. I know one manager who uses two hats labeled "facilitator" and "participant" to distinguish her roles. Even if you never take dialogue to the status of a formal process, the sequencing of this one-day format and the seven facilitator skills presented in Part Three will be useful in any situation where dialogue is needed. My goal for this book is to stimulate your creative ideas, not necessarily to get you to use mine.

SELLING DIALOGUE

When you ask people for a day of their time, they are going to have many questions. You need good answers. First, they will want to know what you want to do. Do not try to explain everything you know about dialogue. Unless you are incredibly articulate, you will end up rambling. Language isn't up to the task of defining dialogue. It is too many things all at once. There are dozens—probably hundreds—of books that contribute original thoughts on the process of dialogue. Plato started it with the dialogues of Socrates, and the rest of us keep adding our inadequate ramblings to describe a process that in the end must be experienced to be fully understood.

Dialogue is simultaneously a connected state, a set of conditions, an exploration, a learning process, a series of exchanges, a set of communication norms, a transformation of minds, even a philosophy.

If we go too far, we end up with touchy-feely definitions such as: Dialogue is the evolution of thought, the transformation of hearts and minds, the loosening of cherished beliefs, and so on. All are accurate, but guaranteed to generate eye rolling and wristwatch glancing the first time you introduce it to a bunch of executives or a workgroup. When you describe dialogue to people, you need only persuade a group to try dialogue. The experience of dialogue will do the rest. So keep it simple and sell the benefits.

GO BIG PICTURE AND BENEFITS

It helps to use metaphor to describe dialogue. Metaphor makes it easier to introduce a concept as mercurial as dialogue. When you want to entice a group to dialogue, it is important to start with a shared big picture first. If you start with the specifics, there are too many trees. People get lost and end up looking at different trees. If you start with a map of the forest, then everyone has a new framework for the details. Individuals have a new file in their mind labeled "dialogue." Without a common understanding of the whole, each detail you present is relegated to the files labeled "we tried that before," or "sounds like that other communications course."

Find a metaphor that inspires and intrigues. One of the great things about metaphor is that it gives you a shortcut to describe big concepts. Dialogue is a very big concept. When viewed from a distance, the big picture of dialogue can evoke any of the following metaphors.

A Wave State

Dialogue is a process through which we shift our minds and thoughts from a particle state to a wave state. Just as light can be both particle and wave, so can our thoughts. As long as thoughts act like distinct particles, there is no flow. Our minds are separate and disconnected. Shifting to a wave state allows a group to find a frequency through which they can communicate. Getting on the same wavelength is the goal. Our words make implicit thoughts explicit. Dialogue helps us to use language to hear the disharmonies in our perspectives and begin to blend those disharmonies into harmony. It doesn't force us into one monotone but produces blended notes that complement rather than contradict and cancel each other out. We get "in sync."

A Vulcan Mind Meld

Dialogue resembles Mr. Spock's Vulcan Mind Meld in *Star Trek*. Spock had the telepathic ability to connect to an alien's thoughts and mind so he could understand the alien's intention and better interpret its actions. Our coworker can be as alien to us as the Klingons. Dialogue offers us an opportunity to link our minds and blend what they know with what we know for a bigger picture and better understanding. Until the UFOs land and we get the power of telepathy, we are stuck with language as the most efficient communication process available. Without telepathy we must articulate our thoughts for each other (much harder than it sounds) and listen (you already know how hard that is) so we can build a shared understanding of each other's intentions, better interpret each other's actions, and more easily find alignment.

The History of a Chair

Consider the chair in which you now sit. Look at it. Touch it. It was once a thought in some designer's brain. You are sitting in a thought manifested into reality. The thought was shared, interpreted, drawn into a set of plans, and manufactured in some factory into the chair you feel under you. Likewise, the current reality of your workgroup—products, sales, problems, arguments, habits, all of it—is a manifestation of what were once only thoughts. If you can change the thoughts of the group, you can manifest a different reality more to your liking, ideally. You can use dialogue to create reality by changing group thoughts. Dialogue changes the thoughts of those who participate. And thoughts are much easier to change before they become physical reality.

Feeling the Elephant

The old parable about the blind men and the elephant is helpful in explaining dialogue. Each blind man can only "see" his part of the elephant: One man thinks that an elephant is long and slim; another thinks the elephant is flat, wide, and leathery; and yet another thinks it is round and stout like a column. They disagree on everything, and yet each one is technically right (sort of like the situation with your IT and marketing departments, or the Singapore and Atlanta offices). Dialogue is a process where we transcend the disagreement and keep talking until each of us connects our pieces of reality so we can see the whole elephant, together. In a traditional debate, the one most articulate, most persuasive, or most persistent wins. But dialogue gives us the skill to suspend old concepts of right and wrong and paint a collaborative bigger picture inclusive of what seems to be mutually exclusive points of view. Instead of labeling "us" as right and "them" as crazy, blind to the obvious, or refusing to see, we find out that they know something we don't. When we collaborate, we can see the whole elephant.

The Kama Sutra of Conversation

Dialogue is like sex in a way—there is the coming together, the shared contribution, and the creation and birth of something new. If you want to go the birds and bees route, dialogue is the unfurling of tightly held beliefs so that they may cross-pollinate and produce a healthier, hardier hybrid set of thoughts and beliefs. Depending on where your priorities lie (you can't do this metaphor without risking puns), there are distinct advantages to developing your skills in this area. Just as the Kama Sutra teaches the finer points, so can attention to detail and diversity heighten a group's skill in dialogue. Practice makes perfect, right? It just depends on what you want to be good at. And people seem to crave what dialogue has to offer. There is something deeply satisfying about the connections created during dialogue. We experience being together instead of being alone.

REMEMBER A TIME WHEN

All of us have experienced the deeper, transformative quality of a genuine dialogue. If you can get a group to remember a time when everyone was in dialogue, the group will instinctively understand the space you want to create. Ask a group to remember a time when group members felt safe enough to tell the truth and knew that others were also speaking their truths.

Ask if they remember the funeral of a loved one, for example. At a funeral, the quality of conversation slows down and deepens. Shallow, familiar conversations are replaced by new conversations with a lower pitch. We resonate to deeper bonds. It is as if death automatically puts our lives in a larger perspective where we spontaneously reflect on what is important to us. The superficial is stripped away. Tired old arguments give way to lasting reconciliation. People see things differently. Petty disagreements look ridiculous when death shifts our perspective. Dialogue changes what we see.

Dialogue may also occur spontaneously after a crisis, before a long separation, or after one. At my house when an old friend stays over, conversation over morning coffee turns to dialogue. There is a deeper quality of mutual reflection. We talk in terms of years or decades as well as last week. One person told me of a workgroup that in an effort to avoid traffic arrived to work more than an hour early each morning. In those early hours, in a quiet office, they sipped coffee and reflected on everything from lawn care to kid care to the latest work project. In those quiet hours, they spontaneously engaged in dialogue. By their own reports, it radically improved their ability to work together. Often if you ask a group to remember a time, people will respond with excellent examples and a "so that's what that was" reaction.

A CREDIBLE PROCESS

When introducing dialogue to a group, it helps to build credibility by referencing the thoughts and definitions of others. Many wonderful people have written about dialogue and how to create it. My first experiments were shaped by their work, and I endorse their contributions to you. Peter Senge (author of *The Fifth Discipline*) and William Isaacs (who directed the Kellogg-funded Dialogue Project at MIT) have written extensively about the process of dialogue. Senge said he could not "imagine building a learning organization without the practice of dialogue at its very center." Isaacs's work demonstrated the power of dialogue to bring groups (including hostile union and management groups) together and to heal communities fractured by racial tensions.

David Bohm, the quantum physicist, is frequently credited with our renewed interest in the process. His writings give a broad overview to dialogue. Bohm targeted bigger world problems, such as environmental issues, war, and even world hunger. Any process developed to tackle that level of dangerous truth is bound to be useful for what ails our organizations.

Dialogue is gaining momentum as a bona fide tool at work. In an issue of *Fast Company* magazine, the "Best Practices" section describes an "agenda-free talkfest" that has demonstrably lowered turnover and improved productivity at a computer company struggling with exponential growth. Led by a psychologist, the process is described as "group therapy, minus the dream analysis and primal screaming." Sounds like, well, dialogue. You can bet most executives and employees participating didn't give a fat rat about the underlying principles of why this "agenda-free talkfest" worked or how it worked. They just knew that once they "emphasized that no one would be punished for being honest, the floodgates opened," profits quadrupled, and turnover was cut in half. With those sorts of results, who cares about the philosophy behind the process; we just need to learn how to get people to do it. Once the group is willing to try this "dialogue thing," stop explaining and move directly into ground-level strategy. Designing your intervention will require that you map the current communication habits of the group.

MAPPING THE MENTAL TERRAIN

What are the communication habits of the group? Where are the bad habits? You need to know so you can preempt negative habits in your setup. Specifically, you are looking to map the counterproductive habits in dealing with conflict and negative feedback. Negative feedback, even though it is an invitation to learn, is usually treated like a disease. Conflict either becomes a spectator sport or is swept under the rug. When truths become dangerous, communication goes haywire. Ask people to describe specific situations (much more revealing than opinions) that demonstrate how the group has handled conflict and bad news in the past. It won't take long to build a map. More than likely, you will run across one or two of these common habits that plague workgroups.

Code Speak

Some organizational cultures develop convoluted patterns of complex routines so they can pretend they are facing the facts while avoiding reality. When a culture has a "shoot the messenger" routine, people don't directly address dangerous truths. So they develop a code language—a pig Latin for adults. "The roductpe is ailingfe and we are caredse to illke it." When a group tiptoes around retiring a product instead of directly addressing the implications for the soon-to-be-jobless product manager, when "I'm concerned about Frank's performance" really means "I'm about to fire Frank," communication suffers. If people routinely do not say what they mean, they have a code-speak habit.

B.S.

In some organizations, the more dangerous the truth, the more people tend to pile it higher and deeper. And the more time is wasted in meetings and useless conversations. At its best, dialogue is a "B.S. Free Zone." No, you can't completely eliminate B.S. in the work environment. It has its place. If we tried to resolve all conflict, we wouldn't have time to do any work. However, the automatic and mindless habit of treating all conflict as a trigger to duck and weave, confuse and confound, or use smoothing smoke-and-mirrors explanations indicates a B.S. habit. At that point, no one believes anyone. When an organization develops a culture that celebrates the B.S. artist, it invites the resulting distortions right into meetings, strategy discussions, and the decision-making process. The B.S. habit creates B.S. decisions.

Denial

When you hear someone say, "We don't need dialogue; what we need is . . ." followed by the changes other divisions need to make, the people who should be fired, or the extra resources that will solve all problems, then you are probably dealing with denial. As if a group can trade in its current reality for a new one without better communication! Sometimes you will face a group in deep denial about its communication problems. People deny the problem and then deny that they are denying it. Humans share a wonderful ability to shut out what might be too disturbing to consider. They ignore it and hope it will go away. The dangerous truths are stepped over with bland reactions; it's like saying "What dead body?" When a group has the habit of denial, the people in it either reject dialogue completely or decide too easily to give it a try. For the ones that decide too easily, be forewarned that as dialogue removes the cloak of denial, disowned conflicts will flood the room. Make sure the group is equipped with new thought and communication tools to weather the impact and transcend the exposed conflict.

Kissing the Problem

When I was in Hungary, a fellow consultant explained how negative patterns prevented action in her group. In a marvelous Hungarian accent with two fingers brought to her pursed lips, she said, "In Hungary, we have a tendency to want to kiss-s-s the problem." She described her group's enthusiasm in hashing and rehashing problems without ever actually addressing any of them. Many groups in the West like to "kiss-s-s" their problems, too. Big problems become an altar for observance at meetings. One governmental employee told me how his agency, beleaguered by frustrating legislation, developed patterns that looped around and around the problem. They began meetings with an almost-scripted catechism of complaint. They stroked and tended their problems like familiar friends who supported their inaction and confirmed the impossibility of progress.

MAKING DIALOGUE USER-FRIENDLY

Once you have an idea which habits are sabotaging communication, you are ready to take the group down a path toward dialogue. When faced with ingrained habits, you can't just snap your fingers and make dialogue happen. Each individual knows how to dialogue, but a group of individuals usually needs help if they are to use what they know with a familiar group. The goal is to, step by step, lead the group further and further away from old habits and toward new ones.

People need shortcuts, memory devices, and cheat sheets to help them remember to use what they know about dialogue. Problem is, once we begin to reduce dialogue to specific steps, we introduce a false clarity that has the potential to distort the process. Like learning ballet (or football, to be gender equitable), the process must become a set of drills and movements, meaningless alone, but each teaching us a part of the whole. Dialogue can be chunked into a collection of smaller skills and routines that build up to a whole. Proficiency in the steps doesn't necessarily mean we can dance, play football, or dialogue—but how else are we to learn? There are a thousand ways to do this. What you have here is a straw man of steps offered to stimulate your own ideas.

We start with an education in basic group dynamics designed to reposition conflict as a valuable resource. Commonly used avoidance routines and negative behavior patterns are discussed so they are preempted before they occur. New, more productive communication norms are introduced, culminating in a set of group-selected agreements or rules designed to shift the group away from the old and toward the new.

The goal is a collaborative process of unfreezing, changing, and refreezing language and thinking norms in a way that enables the group to safely surface and explore conflicts, challenge old thinking, and forge new, more creative thinking patterns. The resulting interactions encourage a process of collective "self-awareness" and all the benefits that offers.

Chapter 3

The Five Stages of Dialogue

Let a human being throw the energies of his soul into the making of something, and the instinct of workmanship will take care of his honesty.

Walter Lippmann

GROUP DYNAMICS 101

Dialogue is a group process. Fundamentally all groups are believed to proceed through several predictable steps. Research over the last few decades reinforces the view that groups display developmental stages. The most popular way to look at these stages follows Taylor's "Form, Storm, Norm, and Perform" model. To describe dialogue, I add a new stage in between Storm and Norm that has a developmental twist to it.

It helps to understand the developmental phases of a group so we can value each interim step as much as the step that produces the end results. Some stages get a bum rap because it doesn't look like much is happening or the stage is uncomfortable. But skipping a stage corrupts the process as much as baking a cake at 500 degrees for thirty minutes instead of 250 degrees for an hour. Sure, there are things we can do to help a group progress more efficiently, but there are certain natural laws we do well to observe. Giving a group a minicourse in group dynamics helps the group resist the urge to make value judgments on the usefulness of any stage and try to skip it or rush through.

Most theorists agree with Taylor's model. Initially, a group is superficially smooth and concerned with inclusion, then conflict and contradictions appear. Next the group makes some agreements about handling that conflict, and finally the group sets out to perform some

27

task, concluding this task with good-byes and rituals of closure. Allowed to progress naturally, these stages will normally be negotiated using traditional interaction strategies that repress conflict, ostracize deviant members, and resort to simplistic methods that speed agreement (e.g., majority rules, status wins, compromise). These interaction strategies become norms, are translated into invisible habits within organization culture, and are rarely revisited. Your job, should you decide to accept it, is for an intact group to reinitiate the process and create new norms, or for a new group to facilitate a mindful journey through the stages.

CONFLICT AS A RAW MATERIAL TO INNOVATION

Every organization has norms to handle conflict and negative feedback. It is a fundamental part of the organization's culture. Conflict disturbs the system, and systems seek equilibrium. If the system takes the disturbance in (the product isn't selling) and allows the disturbance (an uncomfortable meeting) to disrupt the current thought patterns (what now?), that creates an opportunity to develop into a higher-order system (modify the product). Ignore the conflict and the system doesn't change or learn.

When norms develop by default rather than by design, they focus on either eliminating the conflict or diverting energy in a blame routine, thereby missing the opportunity to learn. Few organizations have developed norms that use conflict as a raw resource. Finding out what you are doing wrong, what you don't see, what you haven't figured out yet is the first step toward innovation and improvement. Mined properly, conflict is a source of creativity. Without conflict there is no need to innovate or to develop.

Conflict is the opportunity to move to a higher level of performance. Without conflict everything is smooth and will continue to run exactly as it has always run. (Which isn't always bad, by the way.) Only when we are forced to accept an order too large for our capacity, deliver a feature that was not designed into the product, or cut costs and improve service at the same time do we get creative. We are forced to stop doing things the way they've always been done and move up to the next level. Conflict is an opportunity to learn something new.

Certain conflicts are built in to business. Unavoidable and unresolvable, they include quality versus quantity, employee satisfaction versus customer satisfaction, development versus delivery speed. When the hierarchy protected us from these conflicts, decisions were made by leaders who struggled internally with the conflict, leaving others, even entire divisions, free to "take sides." One of the unexpected by-products of distributed decision making is distributed conflict. Thanks to years of cultural conditioning under hierarchical structures, the people in our organizations have not developed good skills to handle conflict as a group. The old routines of "taking sides" or deferring to "leadership" are all most of us know. The only response is to cry, "We need better leadership." What people want is for someone to save them from the uncomfortable experience of being faced with a conflict and not knowing what to do. Those days are over.

Any group struggling to allocate too few resources among too many products is in the grip of a sticky conflict. No one can claim to predict the future. They cannot quantify the massive amount of subjective information available into something that means the same thing to everyone. And several key participants are so attached to being "right" and looking good that they see the conflict as a contest they need to win. Under this much stress a group will probably default to conflict avoidance or "duke it out" norms and will come up with an inferior solution or abdicate to a leader (which, if the leader is brilliant, is fine). Even a group committed to participative decision making can find itself stuck in the old norms of taking sides, denial, using code speak, spouting B.S., or kissing the problem—old patterns that deny the group the opportunities that conflict offers.

Dialogue is one way to get a group to redesign its norms so that conflict and negative feedback become a resource for knowledge. Learning as a group requires a completely new set of group skills— the skills of thinking as a team. We must develop a collective willingness to risk uncertainty and stay with it until we learn something new. One of your best tools in facilitating this process is your ability to prepare a group for the trip. If they know what is coming, they are more likely to stick with it when it begins to feel uncomfortable.

A PICTURE IS WORTH A THOUSAND WORDS

Symbols, icons, and diagrams help us communicate in shorthand. If a picture is worth a thousand words, then we need more pictures. The proliferation of whiteboards in our offices and meeting rooms demonstrates that. It is our response to too much information. It is easier to communicate with markers and to draw the problem. Pictures help us see.

When someone hops up and draws a diagram on the whiteboard, the group suddenly has a common focal point. Even though we all project a slightly different meaning onto the picture, for that moment, we all experience the same stimulus. With language, too many different definitions can exponentially fragment each individual's understanding. Different interpretations contribute to misunderstandings. People can think they agree and not even know they disagree until their actions go in different directions because they held different definitions for the same words.

To help your group develop similar interpretations so that behavior flows in the same direction, I'll use some pictures to help you explain dialogue to a group. I've been using them for years and they work on flip charts, whiteboards, and cocktail napkins. Try them out and see what a difference it makes to use a picture.

FORM, STORM, NORM, AND PERFORM WITH A DEVELOPMENTAL TWIST

Dialogue seems to have five basic stages. Here, each of the five stages is accompanied by a diagram that symbolizes the group dynamics occurring during that stage. Of course, groups don't really progress in such an orderly fashion. Sometimes they flip-flop, get stuck in a stage, skip one, or double back. Some groups stay in the politeness and pretending stage until chaos overcomes them and they scurry back to politeness and pretending. But most groups that reach genuine dialogue seem to progress through these five stages.

Politeness and Pretending

Each person walks into the room with a personal view of reality. In Figure 3-1, each pattern with an arrow represents an individual belief system. Beliefs systems are developed from personal experience and are, by definition, closed-loop systems. For instance, pretend that the figure eight in the top right corner represents the IT guy's belief that he knows exactly what is wrong and, moreover, knows exactly what to do about it—buy more hardware. His thoughts loop back to the same outcome over and over. The ellipse below symbolizes the equally firm view of the marketing VP that "what needs to happen is that marketing needs a decent budget and better access to customers so we can do our job." The square represents the finance manager's view that none of these people realize the implications of last quarter's loss

FIGURE 3-1
Politeness and Pretending

and all of them need to stop using valuable resources to pursue "emotionally based decisions on pet projects." The CEO (triangle) is tired of hearing it and simply wants these people to "stop squabbling and stick with the strategy they outlined last month." Their beliefs are minisystems that loop through the same thought process over and over again, separated from and independent from influence by the others.

The lines covering the belief systems represent the fact that each of these people walks in with their own closed-loop opinion but none of them wants to be too forthcoming, too soon. Different groups play it out differently, but conflict is usually beneath the surface in the first stages of a dialogue. People engage in some version of the behaviors of politeness and pretending before the juicy part happens. Groups engage in certain social rituals before conflict is allowed to surface.

Sniffing Behavior

We have a natural reaction to group situations. We want to be either part of a group, in control of a group, or way the hell outside the group's control. We all go about it differently, but these strong dynamics affect the first few things that happen. Familiar groups cycle through stages with an ever-narrowing set of politeness or pretending patterns, but they still do some sort of preliminary "before we get down to business" dance.

When a bunch of strangers come together for the first time, they initially go to great lengths to keep things smooth and happy or at least "in control." Individuals withhold their opinions either to be polite or to suck the other guy into "showing his hand first." They pretend to agree and will try to cultivate whoever is perceived to be the leader. A colleague of mine calls this "sniffing behavior" (rich metaphor, don't you think?). Without conscious thought we revert to primitive routines of circling, finding the alpha dog, and general posturing. In lovey-dovey cultures that can develop in the helping professions, norms of courtesy and decorum (I'm more centered than you are) contribute to the pretending behaviors. For whatever reason, critical beliefs and opinions are hidden. The lined overlay symbolizes the habits and norms we hide behind.

What Problems?

This stage can be misleading, particularly with sophisticated groups that can fake honesty so well even they believe they do not have conflict. A group may deny individual differences and appear to quickly reach a stage of cohesion and aligned values, but this is rarely possible. Any group deeply committed to its goals, passionate about the job, and dedicated to getting there as soon as possible will have conflict. The group that thinks it's one big happy family is the group that is so terrified of the dangerous truths that it clings to politeness and pretending. In a changing environment, real alignment is only possible through regularly surfaced conflict and recalibration of the group. But it doesn't help to rush this first stage.

Don't fool with Mother Nature—groups need this first stage and it suits you too, if you want to reach dialogue. This is the time to introduce the models, rules, and structure of dialogue. You have an open window to reach agreement on these things while the need for inclusion is strong. Politeness and pretending will not last forever. You don't want it to last forever. I've been with groups where it did seem to last forever, and they never got to the heart of their issues and left disappointed and bored with each other. Nothing of much interest happens during the politeness and pretending stage. Only when the norms are peeled back and the hidden patterns or agendas are revealed do things start to get interesting.

Chaos

Ready, set, riot. Turf battles, personal causes, unresolved conflicts, anger, prejudice, differing ideologies, the need for control, festering injustices, not to mention all the conflicts built into the process of business can become exposed during this second stage. They don't all pop up at once, thank goodness, but the conflicts exist. You need only help them emerge.

FIGURE 3-2
Chaos

    Creating a safe environment is the best strategy to surface individual differences and dangerous truths. Extroverts usually go first. And, if they can get a word in edgewise, the introverts will begin to reveal their views as the discussion continues. Everyone has a different piece of the puzzle. At first glance, pieces can seem diametrically opposed. Just as each blind man touching the elephant is convinced that his part of the elephant is "reality," so are the individuals convinced that the view from their vantage point in the organization is the truth (the figure eight, the ellipse, the square, and the triangle in Figure 3-2). Once revealed, the conflicts, if they are juicy ones, will increase the heart rate and heighten energy levels.

Adrenaline Rush

Conflict, if left untended, usually becomes a contest. Group members may attempt to convert each other or fix each other. The emotion of disagreement fuels a struggle for supremacy of one view over another. In our quest for certainty we will tend to choose one view as right and label all others as wrong, or individuals will secretly continue to believe they are right and everyone else is wrong. Left alone, the differences that surface at this stage clash and clang against each other until someone wins or the group collectively regresses to the smothered silence of politeness and pretending.

    This is the first point at which dialogue redirects old norms. Dialogue allows a group to hold the conflict in full view yet suspend the power struggle. Instead of debating to the death, participants become as focused on learning about other vantage points as they are in explaining the view from their own vantage point. The different points of view don't have to make sense—yet. Conflicting data is allowed to surface, contradictions are welcomed, and for a while the group has one big fat mess of confusion on their hands.

When people are really committed to the group's goals, you will see strong emotions attached to their views. That's good. There are no passionless dialogues. Emotions provide fuel for excellence. They have emotion because they care. They are frustrated that others don't see what they see, and they are beginning to suspect that what they see is inadequate in some way. In dialogue, the main feature of chaos is that no one is on firm ground anymore. The process will not only reveal conflicts between group members but also conflicts that operate within individuals—internal conflicts.

Contradictions in what we say we believe and what we have been doing become as obvious to us as they have been to everyone else. We come face-to-face with the difference between what we wish were true of ourselves and what seems to be observably true judging from the evidence of our behavior. We begin to see that we have been using baseless assumptions and outdated thinking. The conflict roars inside us as well as between us. Yes, there will be a certain amount of emotion in the room.

Ohmigod Let's Pretend Again

The goal during the chaos stage is to encourage exploration into the conflict and resist the urge to escape uncertainty. When it works like it is supposed to, chaos creates uncertainty for everyone. As a group becomes more experienced with dialogue, the chaos stage will be warmly welcomed as the birthplace of creativity. This is the stage where you find out you don't know as much as you thought you did. Instead of feeling dumb, people begin to realize they've got an opportunity to learn.

However, the first few times people would rather have bamboo shoots shoved under their fingernails than deal with big internal conflicts or face conflict without trying to win. Many groups run back to politeness and pretending and breathe a collective sigh of relief at having escaped a close call. Others degenerate into fighting. Your goal is to help them last the distance without taking any of the escape routes. If curiosity is strong enough, or the results of the conflict are too awful to continue to bear, a group will hang with it long enough to move to the next stage.

Discarding and Redefining

If the group does not retreat back into politeness and pretending or turn chaos into a boxing match, magic begins to happen. Long pauses of silence begin to occur. People begin to speak more slowly. You are witnessing the deconstruction and redesign of belief. The group has entered the stage where "I give a little and you give a little." In Figure 3-3, you can see the individual belief systems opening up and shifting. Each individual allows the conversation to affect them—to permeate past their defenses and transform long-held beliefs or cherished certainties. They reflect. They discard old beliefs and redefine others.

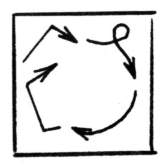

FIGURE 3-3
Discarding and Redefining

As individuals, most of us take time to reflect and reconsider the way we see the world. "Looking out the window time" is what one of my friends calls it. We pick a time and take refuge from the pressures to do, perform, respond, or explain and we just sit and think. This is the time where we acknowledge nagging evidences that what we are doing is not working anymore. Or we stop pretending that we understand and face our ignorance. On the outside it doesn't look productive. But on the inside there is a lot going on. Time spent in reflection gives us a fresh perspective. This is what happens in the discarding and redefining stage, if we let it happen.

Pregnant Pauses

Each formerly firm view becomes increasingly malleable as it develops into a new perspective that incorporates aspects that were not visible to that individual before the dialogue. The MIT stories of union and management dialogues in the steel industry give us a clue as to how dramatic these shifts can be. I imagine each side of the conflict walking in, certain, among other things, that the other side would exploit it if given the opportunity. Each side "knew" what kind of people they were dealing with and had some strategy of working an angle, bullying, or stonewalling that would've kept them bouncing back between chaos and politeness and pretending, ad infinitum.

Instead, they used dialogue to move into the discarding and redefining stage.

Union and management revisited what they "knew for certain," matching it against the real people sitting across from them. They acknowledged that rather than bull-headed extortionists these were people who, just like them, wanted to do a good job, were genuinely trying to be fair, and felt the same anxieties they felt. The new data didn't fit their old beliefs, and once they let it in, their old beliefs began to open up and develop into new beliefs.

In nondialogue groups, the process of chaos reveals a limited selection of beliefs and opinions from which the group will choose to reach "agreement." They will choose the square or the triangle and simply impose it on top of the others. In dialogue, a group uses old beliefs as a resource to generate a new set of beliefs shared by all who created them. In Figure 3-3, the figure eight, ellipse, triangle, and square are reformed into something new. That is the creative force of dialogue. But first, the old must make room for the new. The previous stage of chaos will have begun to disconfirm many beliefs, and the group must be encouraged to continue to detach itself from certainties and assumptions that may prevent it from generating new collective thinking with the group. M. Scott Peck calls this stage "emptiness." William Isaacs refers to it as the "crisis of collective pain." Both acknowledge the courage necessary to successfully negotiate this stage.

Staying the Distance

The worst part of this stage is that everyone finds a place where they were wr-wr-wr-wrong. We *hate* to be wrong. It doesn't look good, it doesn't feel good, and Lord knows, if we have to admit we are wrong, we'd much rather do it in private. This is the stage groups most wish to escape. This is the point where someone will say, "Well, we are obviously not getting anywhere" and vote to stop. Pity. If they could just last the distance, the payoff is to learn. Sometimes, to learn big. This is where learning disabilities and process losses can sabotage true dialogue.

Groups have a strong tendency to rush consensus. At some point a group will begin to seek common ground. Many of the beliefs that need to be discarded will be beliefs used to protect a participant from feeling responsible for the problems of the group. Releasing these beliefs is not a process that can (or should) be rushed. Rushing risks superficial insight that won't stick after the dialogue is over. People need the time and space to forge and polish new beliefs. While the previous stages displayed visible group interactions, this stage of discarding and redefining operates as much on an invisible individual level as it does on a group level.

Our beliefs represent a series of conclusions we have reached throughout our lives. We can see them as steps up a ladder. One group of people may learn, for instance, that to work hard is good. Working hard means lots of activity. Then they conclude that activity is good, without realizing each assumption takes them further and further away from their original observation. Operating from the general assumption that activity is good can cause people to undervalue inactivity (thinking) and overvalue activity, even when it is mindless. They then approach all problems by generating lots of activity, filling their lives with activity, escaping into activity, and judging people who aren't active as less dedicated.

Yet another group of people may build their ladder of beliefs against another wall. They learned that success is a result of careful planning and thoughtful (inactive) consideration. When forced to work together, the two shout at each other from the top of their ladders ("Lazy!" "Impulsive!"), trying to get the other one to come over to their side. It is impossible. Only when both climb back down their ladders and gather at the starting point can they find common ground. Once they do that, they can choose to create a new set of beliefs that allows them to create a new ladder, together.

Discarding and redefining is the stage where people are climbing back down their ladders of beliefs. For many it's frustrating because instead of "getting somewhere" it feels as if they are going backward. In a way it is, but if the group can stay the distance, it will be richly rewarded.

Resolution

This is the payoff stage for the group. After the conflict, the confusion, and the emptiness, the group finds new beliefs that lift it above old differences to a higher level of understanding. The group has created from the collection of old beliefs a new collective belief system that can be shared by the entire group. It did not exist previously. The group built it together. In Figure 3-4, it is represented by a new,

**FIGURE 3-4
Resolution**

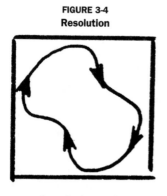

larger, more inclusive belief loop flowing through all and built from the contributions of each participant. It incorporates the diversity of the original perspectives and builds an inclusive, bigger-picture perspective shared by the group. The shared experience of dialogue built a common understanding that connects the group. Meaning flows through the group, and individuals have a sense of being part of a whole, rather than existing in different worlds. They know more than they knew before and experience the joy of creation.

Euphoria

In practice, resolution can seem like a lightning flash of insight or a deeper sense of peace. There is a euphoric element to it. Individuals see each other with new eyes. After years of unresolved conflict, bad feelings, and adversarial tactics, the relief of peace is palpable. A woman in one of my dialogue groups used the word *peace* to explain her experience. She felt the source of most conflict is usually some sense of personal injustice. She said that dialogue gave group members the chance to address that sense of injustice and get over it, go beyond it, and find peace. The journey is different for everyone, but it almost always stirs up emotions like belongingness, trust, and even affection and excitement.

Group members feel understood and better understand each other. They might not agree, but that is suddenly okay. They have found something more important to agree on. There is a deeper alignment between group members that tolerates individual differences. When the group has reached this stage, everyone is operating on common ground. They have developed coherence that will hold them together today and tomorrow. How powerful this experience is, and how frequently the group returns to it, will determine how much of this common ground will be transferred into the day-to-day lives of group members.

A group that reaches resolution is primed to operate at a much higher level of alignment than ever before. The group members have connected in a way that will cause them to reach similar conclusions. They have developed a familiarity that smooths their way through day-to-day conflicts and accelerates reaction time out in the field. Because of their collective experience, each individual has become part of a cohesive whole.

Collective Learning

The trick to collective learning is for all group members to learn their piece of the new whole. Dialogue connects a group's divergent experiences so that all members of the group can reflect together on all the pieces of the puzzle. Resolution is when the pieces fall into place. Sometimes the picture isn't so rosy. Rather than euphoria the group may feel a little depressed. It happens. Some of our workgroups face big issues that are so daunting they have unconsciously chosen to ignore or avoid them. The new belief that they create through dialogue may be some form of collective awareness that "we are in deep doo-doo here." As uncomfortable as it may be, it is a more empowered view than the hyperanxiety or defensive positivism that may have preceded this awareness. At least from now on, they aren't so alone in their sneaking suspicion that all's not right. Now they can work together to deal with reality rather than collude to ignore it. A burden shared is not only lighter but more likely to be resolved. After a group has finally faced its demons and told the truth, it is a great relief for everyone involved.

Whether euphoric or grounded, the resolution stage connects individual group members through a common understanding of something new. You can't know in advance what it will be. You can't manipulate group members to understand what you want them to understand, or the understanding they reach might turn out to be a common perception of you as a manipulator. However, my experience tells me that a group that is willing to dialogue has enough goodwill to guarantee the stage of resolution will be a step forward rather than a step backward.

Closure

No one can dialogue for too long. It is hard work and it is exhausting. The mental energy used in dialogue is equivalent to Olympic training sessions for a world-class rowing team. The heightened awareness necessary to tune in to team members and the rhythm of the group, and

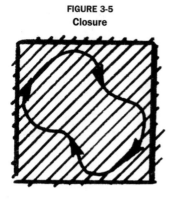

FIGURE 3-5
Closure

to monitor all of your own judgments and generate the energy necessary to enter the zone where you row (i.e., think) as a team—well, it just plain ol' wears you out. Dialogue is "power thinking" for a group. The defenses are down and brains are cranked up to maximum levels. We can't dialogue all the time. If you try, you end up over-working the group, and people will respond by either learning how to fake it or avoiding it altogether.

Cool Down

Besides, dialogue is a place for reflection, not action. Too much time spent in dialogue can decrease a team's ability to act. It could create a paralysis by analysis response, and the team might become a group of navel gazers where no beliefs are firm enough to create action. Dialogue needs a beginning, a middle, and a clear end. Closure is the point where we go back to the norms that serve us well in our day-to-day social interactions. Figure 3-5 shows this concept by reapplying the overlay of lines representing social norms we reassume as our defenses go back up to operating levels. And the new beliefs we created descend into our mental operating systems beneath conscious awareness.

One of the characteristics of dialogue is that the process creates a safe place to explore one's assumptions. Group members will, hopefully, retain an increased ability to reproduce the dialogue skills of mental flexibility and tolerance whenever they wish. Yet critical "certainties and assumptions" that were temporarily suspended must be reassumed before going back into day-to-day reality. Dialogue is about willing uncertainty. Work demands a certain level of certainty to create action.

Closure is particularly critical for intensive dialogue sessions. Reaching resolution can be a powerful experience, and separation may be difficult. Sufficient time should be allowed for expressing feelings and for readjusting to roles outside the group. Over time, the skills of dialogue will creep into conversations outside of the formal process, but the transfer is much more successful when people understand there is a time and place for dialogue.

Saving the Magic for When You Need It

The theory behind creating dialogue as a formal process is that you can make a distinction between the process of thinking, learning, and understanding and the process of doing. The processes require such different behaviors and thinking styles that it just makes sense to use dialogue as a special time and place set aside for reflection. This will save the magic of dialogue for when you need it. In Kurt Lewin's "unfreeze, change, refreeze" model, closure is the time when the group refreezes and solidifies whatever new beliefs were created during dialogue.

The new awareness shared by the group connects people in a way they were not connected before. People have better access to each other as colleagues. Work doesn't snag on petty differences—they have been handled or at least discussed. Collective action will become smoother. Closure is the end of reflection and the jumping-off point for collective action.

FALSE CLARITY

The idea that there are five distinct stages of dialogue is only a hypothetical model, an idea. It is not a fact. There are no facts when it comes to dialogue. However, if we agree to approach dialogue as a formal process with certain expectations, it gives us a better chance at achieving dialogue. Expecting these five stages sets a group up to succeed. A group that expects a little "Politeness and Pretending" uses the first stage to make agreements and then will actively seek to leave it. They begin to look for the next stage, "Chaos." When Chaos comes, people aren't as uncomfortable as they might have been without the preparatory descriptions. The description of "Discarding and Redefining" prepares a group for the discomfort of the "groan zone" so they know there is meaning to their struggle. "Resolution" is a promise that the hard work will pay off. "Closure" allays the group's fears that this heightened level of listening and understanding is going to be expected all the time from now on.

When you present the five stages, (see Figure 3-6) you make it clear that no one is asking people to change everything all at once. There is no implicit agreement that they must suddenly become this understanding all the time. Just for now, just for here, and with these people. The bargain is that, afterward, individuals can go back t

FIGURE 3-6
The Dialogue Process

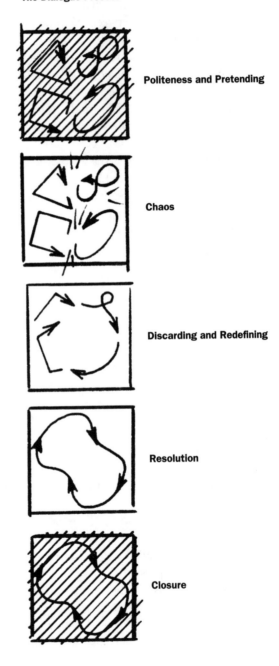

Politeness and Pretending

Chaos

Discarding and Redefining

Resolution

Closure

being the bitch from hell or the company scrooge—no problems. But if they happen to discover that a display of understanding seems to get them better results—hey, it's a free world. (I have no problems using a bait-and-switch strategy with dialogue.)

The stages provide a shared set of expectations that begins to build mutual perceptions of safety, so the group is more confident that it can face whatever dangerous truths it may have been avoiding. And the group has definitely been avoiding something. A dangerous truth is a truth (usually someone else's) that seriously challenges the way people see their world or the way their world works right now. That is what makes it dangerous.

Chapter 4

When the Group Doesn't Wanna Go There

The truth is a snare: You cannot have it, without being caught.
You cannot have the truth in such a way that you catch it, but
only in such a way that it catches you.

SØREN KIERKEGAARD

O ne snag with dialogue is that at some point during the
process a new learning might turn your world upside down.
It is possible you will gain an insight that could require you
to completely redesign the way you see a part of your world or
change the way you interact with others. This is always a risk when
you engage in the process of learning. Even though you can be
assured that this mental redesign will incorporate a higher level of
understanding than you have right now, the potential disruption is
daunting. Like renovating a house, it can be inconvenient to add
that new wing. Stretching your mind through dialogue may widen
your picture tenfold, but it puts your belief system "under construction" for a little while. Your mind will have a few concerns. Wisdom
ain't all it's cracked up to be. It has this nasty habit of expanding our
personal responsibility.

EXPANDING PERSONAL RESPONSIBILITY

Einstein said that we cannot solve a problem with the same thinking
that created it. Dialogue is one way to create new thinking. And
while we say we want new thinking, when we get close to the point
where we realize that means us, we wimp out. We default to old

norms. We defer or smooth over conflict and get the hell away from any kind of realization that we might be part of the problem.

It is impossible to have a genuine dialogue without becoming more aware of your interdependence with other people. I had a yoga instructor, Rodney Yee, who explained, "You do not need to build relationships, you need only see the relationship that already exists." When a workgroup sits down to dialogue, its members are already in relationship. The process merely reveals and examines those relationships—good and bad.

I had a retail client where the group was divided into two geographical areas—north and south. They were happy being divided into two. It was easier. There was an "us" and a "them." One group could focus on "our" work, "our" customers, and "our" stores without too much concern for "their" problems. All fine, except that the two areas were duplicating efforts, developing in different directions, and sending customers mixed messages. They needed to find common ground and make some agreements. Each blamed the other for their problems.

I think deep in their subconscious they knew that if they didn't engage in dialogue, they could continue to blame all their issues on the other side. In fact, we had to schedule this meeting several times before everyone could attend. It's amazing how many unexpected emergencies happen when a dialogue session has been scheduled.

When they finally did dialogue, the justifications, the blame, the conflicts—all came out into the open. As you would expect, in the light of day, many of the assumptions and beliefs just didn't hold up. The southern office found it difficult to gather evidence that the people in the northern office were "just lazy," and the northern office was having a heck of a time holding on to the notion that these other people were "a bunch of brain donors." They realized that not only was the "other side" full of bright, well-intentioned people, but they were in this together and solutions would include changes by everyone. Blame, our favorite shield against personal responsibility, is rendered impotent in the face of dialogue.

Dialogue inevitably will expand participants' sense of personal responsibility. When you add that to the expectation that new learning may be disruptive, it is understandable that groups will avoid the hard work of dialogue. A steady diet of us changing is not what we were looking for. Our tastes lean toward everyone else changing and realizing we were right all along.

The bargain of dialogue is that we all agree to be changed together. It is a "one, two, three, go" jump into the learning process. But there are always some who back off at the last minute. When you introduce a group to dialogue, the best defense is a good offense. Predicting for a group of people exactly what they will tend to do instead of dialogue can have the effect of preempting the predictable escape routes groups will (quite unconsciously) travel to avoid dialogue. Educating yourself and the group allows the group to be more conscious of the escape routes so you can work together to stay on the dialogue track.

RESISTANCE IS NATURAL

Dialogue can be a wild ride. Once the roller coaster starts rockin' and rollin', there are going to be some people who want off. They don't like not being able to see around the corner or the feeling that the ground just dropped away from beneath them. Don't think of them as wimps. Different roller coasters affect different people. There are issues that would get too close for any of us. When you are the one who wants off, you just want off; you don't see yourself as a wimp. You just don't want to go there.

The phrase "let's not go there" is used often these days. There are many subjects we don't want to visit. When a certain subject has the potential to discharge a Jerry Springer–style free-for-all, we leave it alone. We don't want to calmly discuss racism, sexism, abortion, or the president's sex life (most of us don't, anyway). Been there, done that, boring. We are tired of these conflicts and the futile loops back through the same old conversations. We know how it is going to turn out . . . so why bother?

At work there are similar conflicts that stir up emotions. They too have been overworked for so long that people choose a side and avoid revisiting their opinions at all costs. The option of finding a resolution to these sorts of dilemmas was dismissed so long ago that it doesn't occur to anyone to try again. They are abandoned as futile. These are the very conflicts that you will find at the root cause of most business symptoms that plague a workgroup. These are the dangerous truths.

These conflicts frequently surround unresolvable paradoxes of business. Consider the employee satisfaction versus customer satisfaction conflict. If the customer is king, does she get to treat employees like dirt? And what about employee satisfaction—how far does that go? Can employees blow off a little steam whenever they need to? Business conflicts such as this one play out in work disagreements that set people up to think they are in conflict, personally, when in fact the conflict is inherent.

While the conflicts may be unresolvable, it does not prevent people from reaching resolution. In a sense, their protests of "why go there; we will never resolve it" are true. Without an experience of dialogue, they can't yet see that the resolution comes from seeing both sides of a conflict, not necessarily resolving the conflict itself.

A strong reluctance to visit these unresolvable conflicts is another reason people will avoid dialogue. And to complicate things further, these unresolvable conflicts may or may not be business issues.

SOUNDS LIKE A PERSONAL PROBLEM

When you agree to dialogue, you invite disclosure of deep levels of conflict. The process strips back the superficial and reveals core issues. I have worked with groups where the core issues included personal issues as well as business issues. We may have been able to separate our personal lives from our professional lives ten years ago, but the new demands of business require our whole being. When we bring our whole being to work, business becomes more personal. Ignoring that fact severely limits your ability to build cohesion with a group.

One time I was working with a group having a devil of a time coming up with a group vision. The process I was using usually generates tons of energy and excitement, but it was falling flat with this group. People mouthed the words that they thought they were supposed to say, but no one was "into" the process. Apathy is usually a sign of an unresolved issue. I realized that before we could go forward, we would have to step back. I suggested a dialogue session. It took several sessions before the conflict was revealed. And when it finally came to the surface, it had nothing to do with business—except for the fact that it was destroying this workgroup's ability to perform.

The dialogue finally revealed that four years ago the wife of one of the managers had an affair with another (since fired) manager.

Irrelevant? Hardly. The hurt feelings and distrust created when this manager realized that everyone in his workgroup knew about the affair and had chosen not to tell him were still there, festering. In fact, these sentiments had spread throughout the group. Since other people felt guilty, they avoided contact with this manager, which just made things worse. The behaviors on both sides had damaged trust to the point where even new people, unaware of the original situation, were affected.

The point at which the dialogue revealed this deep conflict was painful for everyone present. There were even tears. But for the first time in four years they talked about it. People shared their perspectives and gained a much deeper understanding that four years ago each of them was only trying to do the best they could to protect the others. Nothing was resolved. There is no right or wrong, should have, shouldn't have resolution for this sort of conflict. There is only the opportunity to realize that with a bigger picture both sides made sense.

Most conflicts aren't quite this sticky—although they almost always carry some sense of injustice by a significant element of the group. Unexamined feelings of injustice always disrupt the ability of a group to work as a team. Facing a conflict is the only way to rechannel disruptive energy into motivating energy. The longer it stays beneath the surface (i.e., telling them to just get over it), the more powerfully disruptive it can become.

Issues that arise in dialogue may include personal feelings of betrayal, perceptions of unfair compensation, blame, different values around work versus quality of life, varying opinions about the business mission, differing interpretations of core values, or judgments about others' integrity and character. When true feelings are revealed, you may have a dangerous truth on your hands. The very idea that people are going to admit they carry, for instance, the assumption that one faction of the group neglects family and expects the same from others, or that a certain VP is more interested in personal glory than the organization's success, is scary. Groups have a sixth sense when they are getting close to this point and, without a conscious decision to face the fear and plunge in anyway, will usually collude to escape the discomfort. Lucky for you as a facilitator, groups seem to choose the same escape routes over and over again. All you need to do is mark the exit doors.

PATHS OF LEAST RESISTANCE

Groups are predictable to an extent. The theorist Bion suggested there are four predictable strategies that groups use to avoid facing the kind of conflict exposed during dialogue. As a facilitator or as a group member, it is important to know in advance the escape routes that a group might take. Once you are into dialogue, it is usually too late to point out that the group is heading down one of these escape routes. A particularly effective technique in encouraging dialogue is to prepare the group to be "self-referencing" by discussing escape strategies in advance. Having a clear description and a memorable picture of the most common avoidance strategies helps a group to learn how to facilitate itself to dialogue.

THE FOUR GROUP ESCAPE STRATEGIES

When these four tendencies are discussed up front, your group is forewarned of the pitfalls of group process. They may not always succeed in resisting the escape routes that beckon, but they have a better chance than if they remained unmarked. The four strategies are:

 Flight avoidance

 Fight avoidance

 Pairing avoidance

 Dependency avoidance

The figures I use in this chapter are "icons" meant to illustrate the concepts and to serve as an easy reference or reminder for the group. If you establish these escape-strategy icon drawings early in the process (I tape the drawings on the wall). it gives you wider latitude to reference them later.

THE "FLIGHT" AVOIDANCE STRATEGY

The flight avoidance strategy is the "Get the Hell Outta Dodge" route (see Figure 4-1). Things start to get deep and groups begin to

look for an escape hatch. Someone
has the guts to speak a dangerous
truth; the group as a whole takes a
sharp intake of breath and eyes dart
around in a physical expression of
the group's search for a way out.
This is not usually done at a conscious level. Groups unconsciously
conspire to flee from dangerous
truths and tough issues. For many
groups this is accomplished simply
by pretending that the conflict does
not exist. People just ignore the elephant on the table. Some people
insist there are no conflicts in their group. They are doing just great
(teeth clenched), thank you. The truth is, if a group wants to do good
work, if people have limited resources, and if any of them gives a
damn about the outcome, then they've got conflict.

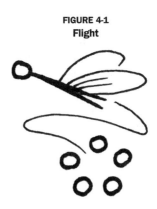

FIGURE 4-1
Flight

People are pretty creative when they don't want to face an
issue. During chaos and particularly during the discarding and
redefining stages (see Chapter 3), groups will turn to the safety of
structure to ease the stress. "Let's split into subgroups," "Let's vote,"
or "Let's review this and come back to it later;" all seem preferable to
the uncertainty of dialogue. These kinds of traditional group-process
solutions will relieve the stress of a group. And when a group has to
make a decision now, these solutions are useful. However, dialogue is
not for making decisions now. It is the one time when we agree to
think rather than decide. The stress of thinking outside the box is to
be valued rather than avoided. Escaping into structured process is
escaping the hard work of dialogue.

Taking a vote and escaping into a "majority rules" solution
simply leaves a group with a majority of people who are happy
because they got their way and a minority waiting to prove the decision was stupid. The structure of the traditional group process is a
Band-Aid and rarely offers the opportunities to learn or the lasting
resolution that results from genuine dialogue.

Some people escape by leaving the room—their cell phone
rings, they have to make a call, or they just check out mentally. They
look out the window, count ceiling tiles, or begin to have a fantasy
about . . . whatever. There are many ways to escape the real problem.

Sometimes a group will turn on one member as a scapegoat to receive the group's frustration. They pretend all the blame can be laid at the feet of one unfortunate individual and fly into a feeding frenzy. Any distraction will do.

Blatantly ignoring a group member's expression of emotional pain is common. I see this happen often. Some brave soul steps up to the plate and tells the truth—"I feel like giving up" or "No one believes in our leaders anymore"—and after seconds of palpable silence the group either pretends that he never spoke or makes redirecting comments. They smooth over it saying, "Well, we all feel nervous at times" or "We can't afford to focus on personal issues right now." Everyone gets the message that this is a "don't go there" subject, and they fly off like a bunch of pigeons scattered by a thrown object.

Luckily, when a group has been briefed about the flight avoidance strategy, it often happens that one or two of the pigeons will come back to investigate. When they do, the group usually finds that facing the issue is much more satisfying and much more productive, in the end, than avoiding it through flight. In the situation where the guy admitted to feeling overwhelmed, once others in the group stopped avoiding the conversation, they found that everyone was feeling overwhelmed. The courage to speak openly about their fears galvanized the group in facing them together. The situation they were facing was overwhelming. They couldn't change that, but the dialogue that ensued changed them. It created a sense of solidarity that diminished the feelings of being overwhelmed and stayed with them as they tackled other obstacles. Had they continued to flee from telling the truth, they would never have reached that level of teamwork.

THE "FIGHT" AVOIDANCE STRATEGY

FIGURE 4-2
Fight

If you can't "Get the Hell Outta Dodge," you can always start a barroom brawl (see Figure 4-2). A good fight is a great distraction from having to do the less glamorous hard work of dialogue. A well-placed jab at the HR manager's new compensation plan is returned with a potshot about sales being 50 percent below budget, and soon the fight is on. Emotions flare, and even if the fight is "civilized," it is not dialogue. Chaos can look and feel like fighting. The same emotions come into the room. Speaking about dangerous truths almost always starts the adrenaline pumping. The difference in dialogue is that people don't let the emotions hijack their brains and push their fight buttons. Fight is just another avoidance strategy. Fighting is mindless pursuit of a "win."

A good test for this is to measure the level of persuasion being displayed. If members are trying to convert, coerce, or fix each other, they have set up an adversarial relationship. Fighting sabotages open inquiry and avoids facing the underlying issues. In a fight the participants are motivated to conceal any information that might help the "other side." This motivation is in direct opposition to the motivation to learn. When a group is in dialogue, all relevant information is welcomed—whether it proves you right or not. When a group is fighting, big chunks of relevant information may be concealed, discounted, or discredited in the mindless pursuit of being right. In a fight, the objective is to win. Winning means "destroying" another's case. But what if the loser had some good points? If the loser turns out to be a lousy debater but a brilliant observer, her observations are lost. The group ends up learning only what the successful debaters want the group to learn. Learning is distorted. It is cut short—particularly for the ones engaged in the fight.

Some group members come with deeply ingrained habits of interrogation, where verbal violence is an automatic response to conflict. It can even be a source of entertainment. The emotional charge from a "good debate" pumps them up and makes them feel alive. It is as refreshing as a good tennis match. For some groups, the excitement of tense battle is addictive. They develop a shared habit that dominates interactions. They have norms that cause them to favor duking it out whenever there is a conflict. The exhilaration—plus the relief of breaking a deadlock (even if there are dead bodies, even if it is an inferior solution)—has reinforced fighting as a successful method of resolving conflict. They don't see it as an escape but as a solution. Worse, people who don't fight are perceived either as wimps or as indifferent, and their contributions are lost.

A fight can be openly aggressive or passively aggressive. Little sniper shots or guerrilla attacks devolve dialogue into a fight. It is to be expected that the group will have little skirmishes here and there. Some fighting is inevitable. Too much allows a group to escape from true dialogue.

THE "PAIRING" AVOIDANCE STRATEGY

Dialogue can make your brain hurt. When you are doing it, you are forcing your brain to embrace mutually exclusive alternatives, hold paradoxes, question everything, and listen intently to people you don't agree with. Your neurons could easily be in danger of overheating. The brain is stretched like a rubber band holding together just a little too much input.

FIGURE 4-3
Pairing

No wonder groups are going to search for an avoidance strategy. Anything to simplify, reduce down, or relieve the uncertainty. Particularly satisfying is a short little conversation with someone who agrees with you. Leaning over and whispering a funny sidebar seems like a harmless way to vent a bit of frustration.

However, dialogue requires the participation of all group members. Particularly in factional groups, members will escape into the comfort and relative simplicity of interaction with one person instead of the entire group. This is the pairing avoidance strategy (see Figure 4-3). The "pairing" two have effectively withdrawn from the group, and the rest of the group, whether glad to be rid of the two or feeling left out, cannot get on with the process of dialogue. The process requires the participation of the entire group; pairing divides the group into two groups—one group of two and then the rest of the group.

Pairing often occurs when a member is not willing to "go public" with an opinion, perhaps a dangerous truth. The individual can satisfy the need to speak but avoid the responsibility of speaking to the entire group. Like the other avoidance strategies, it feels better, but it isn't dialogue. Dialogue requires full participation with the whole group.

Pairing is not only verbal and does not require the pairing two to be sitting next to each other. Frequently there'll be individuals who will get so frustrated with the process they scan the group for a pair of sympathetic eyes. Once found, the avoidance can take the form of a nonverbal pairing. One eyebrow arched high, a "get a load of this" head nod, or the old standby eye rolling is enough to make contact and detach the individuals from the rest of the group.

The avoidance breaks the group into two groups. It breaks the cohesion of the group. Perfectly natural and almost unavoidable— it is still important to heighten your group's awareness of how pairing will dilute the strength of their dialogue.

THE "DEPENDENCY" AVOIDANCE STRATEGY

As you will discover in the next section, one of the recommended rules of dialogue is to have "no leader." If one person leads the group's thinking, then the group doesn't gain the benefit of diversity that dialogue offers. The entire process is

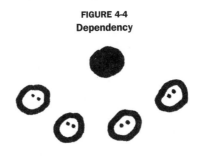

FIGURE 4-4
Dependency

based on equal and full participation of all group members. Allowing a leader sets up the corresponding role of follower. Followers are not using their full powers to dialogue. This is the avoidance strategy of dependency (see Figure 4-4).

Following is not creating, at least not in its fullest sense. Leading is wholly creative. Dialogue requires everyone in the group to be a leader—to contribute vision, wisdom, and direction. The cacophony that is initially created when everyone leads may be turbulent, but it is the birthplace of collective vision, wisdom, and direction that one brain, no matter how smart, cannot concoct on its own. It may be simpler (and faster) to depend on a leader to do the thinking for a group, but it isn't dialogue.

Most workgroups have a leader already. This person may have formal or informal authority that influences the thinking and decisions of the group. People defer to this person. Either she has led the group well in the past and they trust her judgment, or they have found it futile to disagree with her. Either way, they have developed some habits of dependence. They no longer put the full force of their intellect into making their own judgments. In a hierarchy, it doesn't do much good to have a dissenting opinion, so why exert the effort of coming up with one? They may even be afraid to disagree. In this sort of situation, any efforts to create dialogue can be limited to the leader's opinions mirrored back to him and looped again and again through the leader's pattern of thought. B-o-r-i-n-g. Functional, maybe, but not creative.

Thus is the heritage of the hierarchy. If you want to create true dialogue, you will have to find a way to disengage the habits of leader/follower for the duration of the dialogue. (Disengaging them completely is usually not in the best interests of the organization.) Otherwise the group will seek a leader and escape into dependency. Most groups would prefer that someone do their thinking for them. Even radical dissenters depend on a leader as a counterbalance for their polar position. To always take the opposite point of view is no more creative than following. Dialogue is about thinking for yourselves as a group—one of the hardest group activities to tackle.

Refusing to lead is the only way to help the group avoid the escape of dependency. Sure, a group has to stop trying to follow, but the leader's habit of giving direction is such a powerful stimulus that dialogue will rarely occur unless the leader refuses to lead. So many leaders complain that their group just won't "step up to the plate." They "don't want to take the responsibility" of thinking for themselves. They "tried that before" and the group preferred to just follow. No kidding. I want to ask these guys: How long did you give this group to change a norm that has been instilled in them since kindergarten? Shedding the habits of dependency takes a bit of time.

When denied the guiding force of a leader, a group usually gets frustrated and looks more than a little lost. This is a good sign, but most leaders interpret the frustration as a problem they step in to fix. Wrong. A leader must create a vacuum that draws the members into the process, not rescues them from it. Dialogue requires a measure of feeling lost. It is part of the creative process. It isn't a fun part, but it is necessary.

Almost always, a group denied the opportunity to depend on a leader will then look to the process itself for guidance. They ask, Are we doing this right? When it begins to feel uncomfortable they think, This isn't dialogue. When you are the facilitator, their eyes will implore you to step in and give them guidance. A facilitator with an ego (and who among us is free?) will be tempted to show them the way. However, a better response will be to encourage them to brave the breach and the uncertainty by guiding themselves, and each other, and resisting the urge to escape into dependency. Continued resistance to a request for leadership will eventually cause the group to accept responsibility and start providing their own leadership.

WHEN THE EGO DOESN'T WANNA HEAR IT

No matter how open-minded you think you are, when you hold a deep conviction that you are right, a challenge to your ironclad view will stimulate defensive-thinking patterns. Sophisticated, even subtly disguised as progressive, these patterns distort incoming data so that it fits your current beliefs. Since the purpose of dialogue is to examine and challenge beliefs, it is important to understand the strategies we tend to use to resist challenges and protect our status as "right."

Human beings like to be right. It is programmed into us as a survival mechanism. If we were to question everything, we wouldn't survive. Sticking with the familiar has been a strategy well rewarded by evolution. Our brain has, since birth, been generating a list of beliefs about which we are "right." These are the things we know to be true. We stick with what we know—and we get to be successful.

Challenge those truths and the ego reacts with vigor. A challenge to our beliefs is a challenge to our ability to be successful. For a successful sales manager, entertaining the concept that internal competition may now be doing more harm than good is as dangerous as testing the assumption that snakes bite. Who in their right mind would want to test that assumption? What has worked has worked, and as far as the ego is concerned, it will continue to work. What is true is true. There are no rewards for being wrong. The manager is likely to want to stick with what he knows.

Except—all of a sudden—the pace of change has sped things up. If we bother to look, the frequency with which we are wrong is also increasing. We find out that we are encountering new truths at an unprecedented rate. This week we are wrong about something we most definitely were right about last week. Our habit of trusting what we know can do more damage than good. Our egos need to learn to embrace uncertainty, to welcome the discovery of where we are wrong—but the ego just doesn't wanna go there. Uncertainty is too much of a strain. So we hunker down and stick with our beliefs. New data be damned; there are a few truths we aren't willing to revisit. They form our anchor in the storm, and we escape into primitive thought patterns that protect us. We want the black-and-white world we have designed, and we reject the entertaining alternative views that may dissolve our world into shades of gray. The price is that we allow certain mental muscles to atrophy.

DEVELOPING MENTAL AGILITY

These defensive thought patterns operate as barriers to new patterns of thinking, as barriers to learning. They are automatic defensive reactions of the ego preserving its present view of reality as "right." This limits us to thinking in closed loops. Our brains are stiff and inflexible, unused to the mental exercise of dialogue. To develop a higher level of mental agility, all individuals need to stretch and strengthen their ability to think—to break free of the thinking ruts that trap us.

To open closed loops, most of us need to limber up a bit. There are four thought patterns we seem to rely on so heavily that our other mental muscles are weak. When an individual tries to break out of old thinking patterns, the mind will resist. Unless we use our awareness to override default thought patterns, they will inevitably prevent new insight. These defenses can be quite functional in day-to-day life. They give us a reliable foundation of quick action and automatic responses. Constantly exploring new thoughts would cripple our ability to act.

We need the agility to do both. Even though most of yesterday's thoughts and decisions and actions will work fine repeated again tomorrow, some won't. Dialogue is about finding the ones that won't. In dialogue, we consciously choose to temporarily disengage these reliable thought patterns and force ourselves to think outside the box.

THE FOUR INDIVIDUAL ESCAPE STRATEGIES

The individual escape patterns that operate as barriers to dialogue are invisible. They happen inside someone's head. The only way to avoid them is by individual choice. If everyone in the group recognizes these strategies, they can steer themselves away from them. An understanding of these common defensive reactions before dialogue encourages awareness before the fact. After the fact, people are usually so attached to being right that they take offense at any implication from you, their facilitator, that they are being closed-minded.

While there are many variations on a theme, there are four main avoidance patterns that tend to sabotage an individual's ability to reach genuine dialogue. These were derived from a longer list of "tacit thought patterns" developed by William Isaacs of Dia Logos. The figures are offered as icons for easy reference and as memory devices. You might want to make up your own or make up new names for these. Your purpose is to help a group become more aware of the patterns people use to avoid "thinking." Different groups of individuals have different patterns. However, these four are quite common:

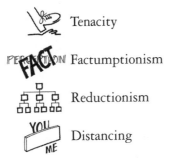

Tenacity

Factumptionism

Reductionism

Distancing

Like the group escape strategies, when these four tendencies are discussed up front, the group is forewarned. Understanding specifically how the mind will escape dialogue is much more useful than simply telling a group to "be more open-minded." When you help them pinpoint the cause of closed-mindedness you empower them to develop enough open-mindedness to dialogue.

TENACITY

"Digging your heels in" is one way to describe tenacious thinking. Tenacity can be a wonderful quality. It denotes someone who sticks to his guns and is consistent and reliable—my mother calls it "stick-to-itiveness." Our society values consistency as an attractive trait. Consistency does not, however, always contribute to productive dialogue. Learning

FIGURE 4-5
Tenacity

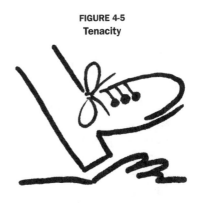

requires inconsistency. One of my favorite bumper stickers reads: "If you haven't changed your mind lately, are you sure you still have one?"

Any individuals who automatically react to a challenge by mentally digging their heels in abruptly stop the learning process. They shut down input. Frequently they will say the same thing over and over again (usually getting louder) as their egos seem to expect that if they say it often enough or loud enough, it will not only become true, but everyone else will begin to agree. Introverts are harder to pick. They may look as if they are listening, but introverts can be just as tenacious in their thinking. They can completely shut down input—letting any disturbing new facts roll off them like water off a duck's back. A tenacious mind is closed. Any dialogue that might change protected beliefs is avoided. When someone retreats into a tenacious thinking pattern, the result is an opinion completely protected from the modifying influence of dialogue.

Without realizing it, people will value familiarity and consistency over accuracy. They will resolutely reject new data that threatens an existing belief. Prejudice, dogma, and other preconceptions are examples of tenacious thinking routines. Open attack usually strengthens this sort of rigid thinking. The thing is, people aren't holding tight to old beliefs simply to be bull-headed. They need that belief for some reason. Try to snatch it away and their grip tightens. It is much better to create an environment where they can examine their white-knuckled grip and wonder if tenacious thinking is in their best interest. In a safe environment, willing and genuine inquiry into the assumptions behind a tenacious thought will loosen it up. With a little forewarning of the tenacity pattern, people can examine the possibility that they have been digging their heels in on the wrong issues—possibly because they were treating assumptions as facts.

FACTUMPTIONISM

When we confuse assumptions with facts, we are on shaky ground. What is the old saying about assumptions? They make an "ass" out of "u" and "me." Not necessarily. There are many perfectly good assumptions. Take the assumption that people like their personal space, for instance. Challenge that one at your peril. Or how about the assumption that, in America, people are going to drive on the right side of the road. At one level it is an arbitrary choice. There is no law of the universe that requires us to drive on the right, but the whole system works much, much better when we agreed to treat that particular assumption as a fact. In real life, it is often functional to raise an assumption to the operational level of a fact, to no

FIGURE 4-6
Factumptionism

longer question it. The "fact" that we drive on the right side of the road is much better than leaving it open to situational interpretation.

Assumptions give structure to our lives. They give structure to the systems we call organizations. Treating assumptions like facts enables us to operate at higher and higher levels of complexity. It gives our brains an operating system that supports day-to-day applications. There is a powerful force at work in maintaining the use of assumptions as fact when we interact. Even the definitions of the words we use represent a useful collection of assumptions. Once we can assume what certain phonetic sounds mean, voilà—we can communicate.

At some point we forget that the assumptions we use were once choices based on perceptions, not facts (see Figure 4-6). All of our assumptions, all of our beliefs, were once "best guesses" based on limited data. Except the chosen few among us who are omniscient and all-knowing, none of us has ever made an assumption based on all the facts. All of our facts of life—"Time is precious," "If you want to kill an idea, give it to a committee," "Let the boss be right," "White people can't dance"—aren't facts at all. They are assumptions based on perceptions from an inherently limited viewpoint and an inadequate amount of data.

We are programmed to confuse perceptions with reality. People use primary perceptions as data for new perceptions. "This won't work" is always based on an assumption (i.e., it didn't work last time) in place of factual data (i.e., trying it out) as the basis for the conclusion. Since no assumptions are literally true, each one will contribute varying degrees of inaccuracy to the perceptions built upon them. Most of the time the assumptions are more true than false and things work great. However, our assumptions also operate as constraints. They box our thinking into limited options.

We forget how powerful we are. Since the assumptions we choose form the basis for our reality, we can change reality by changing our assumptions. Sounds like radical stuff. Too bad we can't tell an assumption from a fact anymore. Your first step will be to help the group override its habit of treating assumptions as facts. That means developing the ability to see old choices that have become invisible (and prefer to remain invisible). Be prepared. The strain of shifting your internal thought process down a notch, so that facts are treated like the assumptions they really are, is similar to the eyestrain of "seeing" the 3D picture of a photo mosaic drawing.

The sheer volume of processing the image cranks the brain up to the point where people make the same funny faces they do when they are trying to see those 3D pictures. The head moves forward, brows furrow, eyes squint and widen—sometimes people will mouth the words of the person speaking. No wonder. They are deconstructing their own reality in real time. It takes effort to examine all of the assumptions we have put in place. It also means that the simplicity of reductionism gives way to an exploding complexity.

REDUCTIONISM

The human brain's limited capacity for conscious thought makes it necessary for us to segment reality into chunks in order to think about it (see Figure 4-7). We segment teams into roles, work into tasks, an organization into departments, a state into counties,

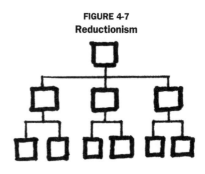

FIGURE 4-7
Reductionism

and people into races. We draw artificial lines to simplify the complexity and then we pretend as if they are real. And when someone comes along with a different representative picture of reality (i.e., they don't see what we see or how we see it), we act as if we think they are blind. Like two kindergartners arguing over whose picture is a cat— we forget that neither drawing is a cat. A cat is a cat. A picture is a picture. Likewise, an organizational chart is not an organization. It is a representation—and usually not even a good one. A better representation of reality would be a network diagram based on frequency of interaction, but we are slow to let go of old habits.

An organizational chart is a reductionist picture, oversimplifying relationships and function. Our tendency to oversimplify complexity is one of the thought patterns that causes huge difficulty in our ability to learn. Evidence of that is found in the "organizational chart de jour" phenomenon. How much time is being wasted trying to force new realities of highly complex relationships into line drawings? These guys forget that the objective is not a better organizational chart but a better organization.

Like the other thought patterns, reductionism is necessary in day-to-day functioning. The concept of holistic thinking is fine and dandy, but the reality is our brains just aren't big enough to constantly think about the big picture. The old saying about "when you are up to your wazoo in alligators, it is hard to remember you are there to drain the swamp" says it perfectly. When you have to meet a deadline, your programmer has the stomach flu, and someone from accounting needs a printout now, your response that "that's not my job" may be functional. Yet in the big picture, you might see it as your job. Viewing all competing priorities with all the information (one of your biggest customers needs it badly) might cause you to see the situation differently. We need balance. For most daily activity our minds simplify what we "see" in order to keep things manageable. That works fine, but it also means that without a conscious effort to see more, we will tend to see less.

One of the more dangerous patterns of reductionism happens when people confuse individuals with departments or other groups and make judgments about their intent, character, or integrity. Generalized statements such as "They never listen" and "They always take this position" are oversimplifications that distort the reality you are trying to examine through dialogue. Interrupting the habit of reductionism will greatly enhance the richness of the picture available for dialogue. Of course, it might show you something you'd rather not see. At that point you will probably need to monitor your habit of distancing.

DISTANCING

Dialogue stops dead in its tracks when someone gets stuck in the "That's not my problem or not my job" trap. Whoever is speaking is distancing themselves from the group (see Figure 4-8). Imagine it as a picture: "Here's me, and there's the problem—and way over there is where you are." Again, this is a response that may be perfectly natural and quite functional when work needs to be done. If we tried to take responsibility for every problem, we would drive ourselves crazy and everyone else, too.

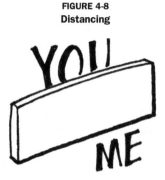

FIGURE 4-8
Distancing

Likewise, when group members try to fix someone or solve someone else's problem, then they are excluding (distancing) themselves from the solution. You end up with a room full of people telling each other "what you ought to do is . . ." Come to think of it, most of your meetings are probably conducted in a room full of people telling each other what they are doing wrong and how to fix it. That's why we need dialogue. It is the one time when everyone agrees to consider how they might be contributing to the problem. The group steps back far enough so that everyone can see the connections.

Now we come back to discussing personal responsibility. One of the personally dangerous truths we avoid is the truth about what we, as individuals, could be doing to fix a problem. Those who hide, reframe, or deny this dangerous truth cut themselves and the group off from solutions. Anyone who has spent more time griping about our federal government than taking action to improve it hides behind the defensive thought pattern of distancing. To come together as a collective force strong enough to solve such a big issue, each individual must first see himself or herself as part of the collective. And trust me, the ego most definitely does not want to go there! It is easier to attack an external enemy than address the one within.

Acknowledging shared responsibility is risky to self-image, not to mention our current levels of playtime. It almost always involves accepting something negative about one's self and indicates extra effort needed to address it. Distancing is a personal defense mechanism that frankly keeps us sane and stuck at the same time. We can't drop this defense all of the time. But if we want to tackle the bigger problems, we must drop it long enough to dialogue.

When an individual removes the blinders he uses to distance (protect) himself from the problems he can't solve by himself, he usually gets to see there is something he can do if everyone else would do their part, too. This is where thinking as an individual is distinctly different from thinking as part of a group. The thought habits of distancing operate like walls separating individual group members. Every individual has control of their wall. Yet the group usually follows an "I'm not bringing my wall down until you bring yours down" pattern. Talking about the pattern of distancing and making some agreements about limitations give the group an option to bring down the walls on a "one, two, three, go" basis. When that happens, you can start to link individual brains and do some real power thinking through dialogue.

BRAIN TRAINING

Even Olympic-class athletes don't train all of the time. They spend most of their time living their lives. One of the important aspects of dialogue is making the distinction between the kind of thinking that works most of the time and the kind of "power thinking" practiced in dialogue. This is a critical concept. You don't have to operate at this exalted level of megaprocessing, heightened receptivity, and 360-degree views all of the time. It wears you out. Eventually it erodes your ability or willingness to do it at all. No one wants to do wind sprints all of the time.

For people to make a time and a place where they can safely discuss dangerous truths, they have to know that most of the time they can just live their lives. This is why so much of communication training doesn't stick. It was presented as something people should do all the time. Frankly, I don't have time for reflective listening when I have a deadline. I don't want to examine my assumptions all the time. No one does. Even those psychotherapist types (not the professions—I'm talking about those overly earnest regular people who feel everyone's pain) can't pull it off. If they aren't pretending to us, they are pretending to themselves. I love to listen to the language that develops when people try to hold an attitude of dialogue for too long. At the consulting firm where I first began this work, we developed phrases (me included) to hide our daily levels of closed-mindedness. While we would never say "yes, but . . ." (too defensive), we would say, in an understanding tone, "I hear what you are saying and . . ." It meant the same thing, but it sounded so much more open-minded. If you try to dialogue all the time, you end up faking it. Either that or you don't have much time left to create action.

I'd venture to make a bet that even the Dalai Lama wants to just get on with it at times. Real dialogue is not getting on with it. It is taking time out to stop getting on with it, and to reflect on whether "it" is something you want to get on with at all.

PART 2

With All That Going Against You: The How-To's of Dialogue

Chapter 5

Before You Begin

The discovery of truth is prevented more effectively, not by the false appearance things present and which mislead into error, not directly by weakness of the reasoning powers, but by preconceived opinion, by prejudice.

ARTHUR SCHOPENHAUER

Once you have a clear idea about what dialogue isn't—the potential escape routes and barriers that prevent it—then you are ready to take action to help your group discover what dialogue is. Let's be up-front about it. This is "lead a horse to water" territory. You have little overt power to shift a group's norms away from traditionally narrow communication and thought routines. That's the bad news. The good news is that formal authority isn't useful in bringing about dialogue anyway—so who cares.

CORNFIELD AND A SHOTGUN

The metaphor that I tend to use when explaining this process is based on a story my father once told me about driving the deserted roads of the rural South. This was back when he thought he was invincible and slept only three or four hours a night. The way he tells the story, one minute he was driving down the road and the next minute he woke up so deeply buried in a cornfield that he couldn't see the road from where his car sat. (Our entire family is given to exaggeration. It's a Southern thing.) He didn't know how he got there or how to get out. I think many workgroups have gone without rest and reflection for so long that they feel just as lost.

So they sit in this cornfield arguing over which way they should go, even though no one can see more than three feet in front of them. Without the ability to see above the stalks, they end up arguing or ignoring each other. They spend valuable time trying to support shortsighted opinions rather than working together to rise above the stalks and get a better view.

Setting the scene for dialogue is like building sturdy scaffolding right in the middle of the group lost in the cornfield. You build the scaffolding so high and make it so easy to climb that when the time comes, the group forgets to argue and people ignore their difficulties long enough to climb the scaffolding so they can see. Once they all see the same view, the likelihood that they will set off in the same direction is greatly increased. The question is, How do you distract a group from these emotionally absorbing, limited-view debates (or advanced stages of apathy) and refocus everyone's efforts into climbing up to see a bigger picture?

It is all in the setup. There are certain agreements you can make and details you can arrange before the group attempts dialogue that will make a big difference to your group's level of success. If you take the time to think through when, where, who, and for how long, and include vital opinion leaders in your planning stage, you have a much greater chance for success. The best opportunity for you to influence a group's ability and willingness to dialogue is before you even start.

CAN'T MAKE 'EM DRINK

You can't force someone to reflect on her decisions or basic assumptions. This is something that is done completely of one's own free will or faked for your viewing pleasure. I now realize that in my early days of facilitation, I often believed a group "really got it" when people were simply telling me what I wanted to hear. Sponsoring a group's genuine reflection takes a very light hand.

Even in the most extreme situations—as extreme as brainwashing—coercive force doesn't work. Successful brainwashing methods use strategic leniency to cajole deeper reflection out of those who would prefer to simply fake it. In-depth studies done by psychologists investigating the brainwashing tactics used by the Chinese communists in the Korean War focused specifically on what caused some of the American prisoners to abandon their core values and to so deeply repent imagined "crimes" that they signed genuine confessions. The Chinese didn't want fake confessions and they could tell the difference.

These psychologists found that those prisoners initially treated with leniency, allowed to air grievances, and encouraged to reflect in "self-analytical contemplation" in group discussions were far more likely to be influenced by the doctrines of the Chinese than the captives kept in solitary confinement and force-fed Chinese doctrine. No mistake, the groups included self-flagellating "plants" to model the process of reflection for the targets, and there were terrorist tactics that generated plenty of fear. But even the Chinese communists discovered that to change the way a person thinks and feels requires group process, open space, and time for individual reflection.

My only point in quoting this research is to demonstrate the power of group discussion and providing "room to think" against humiliation, punishment, brute force, or other extreme coercive actions that have their own correlates in corporate life. I realize it is a risk to quote this research. How can we even compare the two? Both situations focus on shifting core beliefs. The critical difference is that through dialogue, people choose the beliefs they want to change and what they want to change them to. In brainwashing, beliefs are chosen for them. Yet the successful methods are similar. If you want to shift the beliefs of your group—to get people to take more responsibility, take more risks, or embrace the global organization—the vital secret is to use open discussion and reflection rather than force. Force doesn't work.

"They are going to have to change" and "They have to see" are statements that will mislead you because they don't have to change. They don't have to see what you see, and they don't have to reach consensus. Pushing an agenda too hard doesn't win any converts. Of course, pushing dialogue too hard won't win any converts, either. It is a danger to so strongly believe in the potential of dialogue that you become a zealous evangelist overselling it to your workgroup.

THIRSTY?

Some people are so tired of the time wasted in team building and interpersonal skills training that they will have a natural resistance to the prospect of having a dialogue. The secret is to resist the urge to sell the concept and instead create enough curiosity and positive expectations that the group begins to genuinely want to dialogue.

You can't make 'em drink. But if they begin to think about how thirsty they are. . . . Dialogue is an oasis in the desert. Everyone will have a preconceived idea of what they think you mean when you say dialogue. Your first goal will be to ensure that everyone means the same thing. Allow yourself some one-on-one time to speak with the opinion leaders in your group. Talk about the process and build commitment by including them in your planning process.

SPEED KILLS

As badly as you may want to rush to dialogue, the danger of going too fast is that you may lose the opportunity altogether. Likewise, if you oversell it, then the onus will be on you to make this process work. And since you can't make it work (by yourself), that's not very smart. You need a critical mass of people who genuinely want dialogue to work. They need the space and the time to let it work. The right people need to be in the room. And they need enough training to know what they are supposed to be doing differently in order to create genuine dialogue. All of these steps take time and effort to arrange.

Yes, dialogue can occur without all of these elements. Yes, people can find themselves spontaneously moved to dialogue without any preparation. Yes, the process I'm about to describe seems like a bit of overkill when contrasted with the time pressures and urgent issues that must be addressed now. However, it is precisely because everything else is working against your ability to slow things down that you need to make such a production of it. Little details that seem irrelevant become important. Even how the chairs are arranged. Each decision that you make either takes you closer to dialogue or further away.

There are many decisions that a facilitator needs to make. In the corporate world, decisions need to be made about how much time you will spend in dialogue and who will participate. You need a strategy that sets the proper climate and creates positive expectations. Your first attempts at dialogue will mean selecting rules for the interaction. How the rules are selected is much more important than which rules are selected. You need to think all these things through before you begin.

This chapter gives an overview of all these issues and examines several perspectives you will want to consider when making the decisions that impact the group—predialogue. Once the process is underway, decisions continue to be made concerning the structure of the interactions, necessary interventions, the framing of those interventions, and the use of "process enhancers" to enrich the experience of dialogue. Chapter 6 will address these. First, let's consider the actions you can take prior to that time.

QUALITY CAN BE INCONVENIENT

How much time can you afford? Who really needs to be in the room? Should you invite the field staff? Should you meet off-site or on-site? Every situation will be different. There are a thousand variables to consider, and sometimes they will require counterintuitive moves. Decisions about who participates, the number and the length of dialogue sessions, and any applied limits on the content under review should always seek to serve the needs of the group. Except for the need for convenience. One of the most counterproductive "needs" driving many of our decisions when we design group process is the need for convenience. The tyranny of convenience has eroded the quality of many things (anyone forced to eat stir-fry made with frozen vegetables understands that).

Many groups meet without vital members or for less time because it would be "inconvenient" to include those extra members or take an extra hour. If you can't assemble the vital elements, it might be better to skip dialogue entirely. Making the whole day inconvenient might even be a valid strategy if you believe it will jolt the group out of established norms.

I'm not saying make it intentionally inconvenient. Just question your assumptions. Many people assume that a facilitator's "proper preparation" involves preprinted overheads rather than drawing imperfect visuals on a flip chart. They assume that to come prepared is good. And they miss the point that to come "unprepared" is to allow the group to influence what you draw and gives them the experience of watching it evolve. Or they assume that it is better to "get things going" than to wait until everyone has arrived. Not necessarily. There is much conventional wisdom about facilitation that does not transfer too well to dialogue.

BEING THERE

It is a good idea to be as inclusive as possible when deciding who will be involved. Dialogue is not about outcomes. The only benefits come from participation. Receiving a summary of the proceedings (even a video) is not the same as being there. The shared experience of dialogue is why you do it. Collective memories of the group experience build coherence. The group trains to think in sync. Whoever is missing misses the training.

There are different opinions about how many people you can include in a dialogue session. The physicist David Bohm, who is the granddaddy to our current fascination with dialogue, suggested twenty to forty people—with twenty as a serious lower limit. He felt smaller groups didn't have enough diversity of thought. In business, groups can be smaller. For instance, a dialogue session with the senior team might be eight to ten. If they are open-minded enough, it would be wonderful to add another ten people who represent a cross-section of the rest of the organization, but that doesn't happen often. I've participated in dialogue groups as large as fifty. Thirty is a very good number. The diversity enriches the process. I'd recommend adding people even if they are only loosely associated with the group until you've got at least twenty.

Many people are afraid of the idea of thirty smart, opinionated executives or employees let loose to say what they really think. As a facilitator, that single fear may be your greatest impediment as you try to create genuine dialogue. Starting small, so those who are fearful have a chance to experience going into and returning from chaos, is a good way to allay those fears.

There are times when you might deliberate over whether to invite individuals with a reputation for disrupting communication. It might be mean asking a particularly cynical individual to join the group or inviting two adversaries. If they are a source of conflict, then by all means they should be there. These are the ones you especially hope will emerge changed by the experience. A good rule of thumb is to include anyone who is considered part of the problem or could possibly be part of a solution. If you are hoping for individual ownership of future group decisions or actions, there is no substitute for participating in the thought process that sets the direction of those decisions or actions.

Frequently, resistance to the process begins before you even get in the room. Some people don't want to come. They give lots of good reasons. Underneath most of the reasons given are hidden reasons—hidden even to them. If people don't participate, it allows them to maintain their current point of view. If I don't talk to you, then I'm in no danger of realizing that you have a valid point of view. The assertion that "it won't do any good" is a defense against taking responsibility to ensure that it does do some good. Frequently, individuals believe that participating will trap them into some compromise they are not willing to make. If they aren't there, then they don't have to agree. So they abstain, hiding behind reasonable-sounding excuses.

What to do? You want them there. The danger here is that the group will build coherence or start moving in a new direction without them and the process might divide the system further. Then again, it might also build enough coherence with the ones who do participate that they create a polarizing effect that pulls the no-show into the fold over time. It's a tough call. Usually a one-on-one dialogue with these individuals will earn their participation. If not, you should review the costs of doing it without them. It may not be a good idea. Nor is it a good idea to give in to pressures to cut the amount of time needed. The risk of not having enough time is just as bad as not having the right people.

IT TAKES *HOW LONG?*

Dialogue sessions require a couple of hours, at least. The methodology outlined in this section requires even more time for the first run—a full day. Shifting norms takes time. Unless you have a lot of credibility with your group, there will be resistance to taking this much time for a process that has no predictable outcome and no agenda. Before we worry about how to get that sort of commitment, let's examine if you really do need that much time.

Dialogue requires that group members dramatically shift their communication and thought norms (unless your group participants already use what they know about dialogue, in which case you don't need this process). Old norms of rushing to consensus, fighting, flighting, or avoiding conflict must give way to slower thinking, facing conflicts, and listening intently to opinions that don't make sense. Shifting these kinds of norms is not possible in a fifteen-minute setup. Training your brain to think differently isn't either. Both take time. And they require a big chunk of time.

For the same reason that ten Fridays off won't give you the benefit of a two-week vacation, fifteen minutes of dialogue every other day doesn't deliver the full impact. There is a tension that seems to build during the setup (for which you may allocate up to four hours). Each mind-set you deliver stretches the group like a rubber band storing momentum. Even then, it isn't unusual for nothing to happen in the first hour after you begin the actual dialogue. Many groups don't begin to pop and tingle until well into the second hour. The frustration of waiting for "it" to happen is as much a part of the collective-thought training as the "Eureka!" effect that usually follows. People need to learn how to hang with the frustration of not getting anywhere. To think as a group, the biggest skill will come from learning how to stick with it until the magic happens.

Another reason you need so much time is to increase your chances that the group will have a positive first experience with dialogue. If the group participants don't achieve some sort of "aha" experience, they will be reluctant (justifiably) to try again. To give your group every chance of success, you need to have enough time. As long as I've had a full day to introduce dialogue to a group, the group experienced some sort of positive revelation that brought everyone together. They became believers through their experience. Trying to do it in less time has inevitably led to superficial discussions, an hour of boredom or, worse, reinforcement of negative opinions. A negative experience risks increasing cynicism about a process that makes such grand promises.

Make clear decisions about timing before you begin dialogue. Try to get commitment for a full day for the first run. If that is easy, then you can go for the additional commitment of at least four or five follow-on sessions of two to four hours each. I am usually satisfied with a commitment for the first full day. The experience of dialogue drives further commitment. If dialogue is providing benefit, the group will spontaneously choose to continue—and if it isn't, why should they?

Plans can be changed later by the group, but participants who are asked to commit to the process need a frame of reference. If you overestimate rather than underestimate the required time, you can always end early. Having enough time means you don't run the risk of ending a meeting in the middle of the chaos stage, which can do more harm than good.

Explain why the process needs time and ensure you have a quorum of agreement before you begin. There will always be a few holdouts. Don't worry about them too much. I've started a dialogue session when one of the members sat tapping away on his laptop, in open defiance of being asked to "waste" a full day. After the first hour he stopped tapping, and soon after that he put the laptop away and joined the dialogue. You don't need 100 percent buy-in. You only need enough to get things started and the process will do the rest. Just make sure your agreements on time are clear and allow enough time to let it happen.

WHAT ARE WE GOING TO DISCUSS?

Along with the time issues, people want to know what will be discussed. Of course, you don't know ahead of time what they are going to discuss, but if you say that, you risk sounding like an airhead. If pressed, I usually give an inclusive broad-topic answer to this question. You can say you'll be discussing strategic directions, cultural issues, or whatever is topical. To decide on a focused topic ahead of time stunts the group's potential inquiry. Dialogue is a process that examines not what you know, but what you don't know. You could send a memo that lists the topic as "What You Don't Understand and Are Afraid to Admit," but I doubt that will increase attendance. This is one of the times when trying to explain the technicalities about dialogue without the experience of doing it usually does more harm than good.

Experience is more powerful than language. Language without the experience invites preconception and bias. Art is like that. People can make judgments based on language that describes a piece of art and decide in a split second if they will like it or not—without ever seeing the art! If someone thinks they hate abstract art, the word *abstract* propels them to a conclusion they might not experience if they saw a particular piece of artwork in person. Until people commit to experience dialogue, categorizations or descriptions are risky.

So am I saying to lie so you can get people into a room and trick them into telling the truth? No. That is hardly walking the talk. I'm suggesting you oversimplify things until people can make their own decisions based on their own experience and more information. If they want to choose a topic, let them. People end up talking about whatever the group deems most important anyway.

To people who think they have tried dialogue (or "something just like it") and "it didn't work," you probably can't explain enough in a split second to warrant trying. These people aren't likely to be interested in how dialogue "is a process designed to peel back superficial issues and reveal underlying core assumptions." They have already labeled the entire process as unfocused and therefore a waste of time. In these situations, I think it is better to just pick a broad topic and give them the comfort of having a subject. Yes, pinning dialogue down to a specific topic subverts its ability to reveal the invisible or the undiscussable. But not having a topic may subvert your chances of trying it at all. It is a catch-22 to try to outline an agenda for discussing what people either don't know needs discussing or are afraid to discuss.

If you can, avoid limits on content. If they are necessary, make them as broad as possible. Once dialogue begins, the group will make its own real-time decisions on the topic, so don't spend too much time worrying about the official topic. This is a situation where an ability to tolerate ambiguity comes in handy.

Once the preliminary decisions of when, where, who, and an acceptable "what" have been made, you can plan what kind of setup you will use to prompt the shift into dialogue.

Chapter 6

It's All in the Setup

Half the failures of this world arise from pulling in one's horse as he is leaping.

JULIUS HARE AND AUGUSTUS HARE,
EIGHTEENTH-CENTURY ENGLISH CLERICS

E ven though we already know how to dialogue, most of us forget to use what we know. The time to help people remember what they know is before they begin. Once into dialogue, directive interruptions from you may take the group off track. Set it up right in the beginning and once they are into it, all you need do as a facilitator is make small reminders.

I recommend that you take the first half of a full day and devote it to dialogue to present models, facilitate experiences, and set the stage so that people expect a dramatically different communication experience. Group members need to do something to shift their norms. You can choose any sequence of models or exercises as long as they "set the stage." In my facilitation experience, I have not yet found anything that works faster to shift norms.

It seems as if the length of time is as important as the content presented. One hour moves the group fifteen degrees off old norms; two hours produce another fifteen-degree shift. It seems that after four hours you have moved them about as much as you can. A half-day of preparation seems to be the point of diminishing returns for the first day. How does it work? Either the models and exercises have a profound psychological effect in altering people's norms, or the investment of four hours causes the group to make damn sure its dialogue is worth the time it has spent setting it up. Probably both are true.

SETTING THE CLIMATE

It is possible that the climate of a group seeking the benefits of dialogue needs help. Except for farsighted organizations continually searching for a better way, most groups turn to dialogue to heal a rift, transcend unsolvable dilemmas, or shake loose an impasse. Often, by the time you introduce dialogue, people are low on trust and don't see much hope that anything will change. This sort of climate will decrease a group's ability to dialogue. In these situations, your ability to create a climate that invites dialogue will contribute to the group's success. Your initial goal as a facilitator should be directed toward four main objectives:

1 To create a safe place

2 To engender hope for the process of dialogue

3 To engage commitment

4 To build a foundation for self-monitoring

A SAFE PLACE FOR DANGEROUS TRUTHS

How do you make a place safe? Safe means different things to different people. Do you feel safe in a small town, surrounded by friends and family in a wood-frame house with the screen door unlocked and windows wide open? Or would you feel safer surrounded by expensive security alarms, gates, and impenetrable walls? Ideally, we would like to simulate the first example where a sense of safety results from the feeling that there is nothing to fear. In corporate life, that may not be possible. At times you must construct psychological protection for the group. For some people there are no safe places. To them, work is a jungle and nice guys finish last. For these people it doesn't matter what you do—they won't feel safe until they experience dialogue as a safe experience.

You do what you can. The tactics and strategies I recommend are subtle but cumulative. Each one may seem a trifling detail, yet together they can achieve the desired result. If you dedicate a full day to introduce dialogue, you have a half-day to create a climate that promises safety. The most important tool at your disposal is you. Climate will come from the little things that you do or don't do. If you feel safe, you communicate that to everyone. If you don't, you can't. A relaxed, confident, peaceful composure tells the group that you, at least, believe in this process and believe in them.

Take a read on the pulse of the group (Chapter 9 is devoted to that skill). Besides the value of understanding how safe people feel already, you can learn how they define "safe" and where the perceived dangers lurk. Often you only need to get the people to name their fears. Simply talking about a fear can often turn a big monster fear into a little mouse fear. For instance, one group of people was afraid that if they explored improving process, they might do such a good job they would get laid off. After they voiced that fear and put it on the table, it was still a big fear, but not so big they couldn't continue. There is strength in numbers. Naming a fear gives you an opportunity to make agreements tailored to the group's concerns; however, the biggest effect arises simply from naming the fear and discussing it openly.

The group will probably also wonder if you know what you are doing. Taking time to listen or demonstrating that you understand by naming their fears for them reduces their worries about your competence. People are always more confident in someone who values their opinion and understands their point of view. They will also wonder about your intentions. Tell them. If you don't tell them, they will make something up. Without good information to the contrary, people are usually wary. They may even decide you are setting them up to be exploited. Current work environments can be quite cynical. You need to demonstrate that your goal is to serve them as a group.

If your intentions are to covertly persuade or exploit in some way, this process will blow your cover. It is designed to serve the people who participate in it. The primary force of dialogue is to reveal what lies beneath the surface—especially hidden agendas. Model authenticity by explaining your agenda up front. Explain to the group in personal terms why you chose to facilitate this process. I always tell a few stories about my marketing career, when I developed a pet peeve against wasted effort and creativity. I explain that I do this work so that people can feel as if they can bring their whole being to work and can love what they do. I watch their eyes as they decide whether or not to believe me. If they do, we are well on our way to making this space safe for truth.

Any action that reveals your intent and how safe you feel impacts the group's conclusions about you. They will watch you like hawks. Modeling calmness and even a certain level of willing vulnerability will set the tone. Disarming self-disclosure, such as talking about your kids or telling a story of an inner conflict or insecurity, can encourage others to take risks, too. You have to take some risks to demonstrate that it is safe. Be appropriate—too much self-disclosure makes people uncomfortable. The goal of self-disclosure is to show that you respect and like these people and have every reason to think they will respect and like you.

If you are lucky, you will have the opportunity to be challenged by an aggressive or resistant participant. This is a wonderful chance to demonstrate openness, flexibility, and a willingness to invite inquiry. If you make it obvious that it is safe to question you, then the group gets the picture that it is safe to question other things.

Don't act like an expert. Taking on expert status indicates to people that you think they need "fixing," which is guaranteed to create defensiveness. A collaborative stance makes people feel safe. Corny as it sounds, before I walk into a room, I always say a little prayer to be of service. It changes my state. Instead of worrying about looking good or looking smart, I focus on providing service. I remember that I am surrounded by my equals. The prayer also decreases anxiety since it focuses my attention on them rather than me. Any anxiety brought into the room will decrease levels of perceived safety for the group.

Vocal speed and tone as well as body movements help create a safe climate. In Chapter 14 on storytelling, you will read a story about fast and slow voices. A fast voice and an urgent tone combined with nervous body movements put people on alert. Using a calm voice, a steady gaze, and a relaxed body will send strong nonverbal messages that this is a safe place. Use your body and voice as "exhibit A" to prove this is a safe place.

A predictable fear will center on potential retaliation from higher-status, higher-power participants. Always arrange the chairs for dialogue in a circle so that there is no higher- or lower-status seating (the preparation part can still be done classroom-style if necessary). You can also coach the highest-ranking members of the group to acknowledge and respect their fears and to make clear agreements with the group that promise safety. The group must believe the sincerity of the bosses. If they are not sincere, you've got no business trying dialogue. Most bosses (most human beings, period) are a confusing mix of good and bad intentions. If you've got a borderline case, deep down the boss usually wants to be a good guy. Giving people the opportunity to promise "no retaliation" helps them find their good intentions. Going public with the promise helps them stick with it. Yet, even when people feel safe, it is sometimes difficult to hope for too much.

DARE WE HOPE?

Anyone walking into the room has a set of expectations on the usefulness and practicality of this process. Even the chairs they choose are chosen according to some internal set of expectations, status rules, and personal objectives (i.e., gravitating toward the back of the room and near the door is especially telling). These expectations aren't on the surface. If you were to ask people what they expect they would say, "We don't know—you are the facilitator." Don't be fooled. It is impossible to participate in a social interaction without expectations. We always have expectations even if we don't know what they are. Relevant expectations will include whether they can trust you or not, whether this will be a waste of time or not, and how much they intend to participate or not. Their brains have located a category loosely labeled "the last time we did something like this," and they are responding to those old pictures as much as anything happening in the present.

Explanations of the process dialogue must be done in a way inspires the group to hope that this time will be different from the "last time." People need to expect that this time they will find the level of communication they have been looking for. To a certain extent, the first half-day is half sales presentation, half training session. Most groups walk in more or less cynical and pessimistic (or naïve). Something you say or do must break through their cynicism and give them some hope. They don't need to hope that the entire organization is going to change. They just need to hope that this afternoon will be different. That this "dialogue" crap could possibly, just maybe, be what they have been looking for: the chance to tell the truth without fear of repercussions and the opportunity to know that everyone else is telling the truth, too. Most people crave what dialogue has to offer. They have just given up hope.

Chapter 7, which explains the "recipe" for dialogue, gives you a menu of models that you can use to prompt a self-diagnostic process and develop expectations in a hopeful direction. Each of the models recommended in the sample recipe for dialogue (e.g., positive intent, content/process, go slow to go fast) is designed to shift prevalent thinking patterns over to the patterns necessary for dialogue. You may have models that are better than the ones presented in Chapter 7. It doesn't really matter which models you use.

The goal is to change the state of the group—to awaken hopes and call every ounce of attention people can muster to old thought and communication patterns. To inspire curiosity about how these habits have contributed to current problems and what alternatives they might discover. Every model you present, every story that you tell, should attach another rubber band between what people usually do and genuine dialogue. If you attach enough rubber bands, the group will be pulled toward dialogue. The most powerful rubber band will be the expectation that this process will not be "business as usual" but will be dramatically different.

If you want people to expect something dramatically different, you might want to act dramatically different. Get creative. If you have the personality to pull it off, bring a cardboard cutout of Einstein to stand next to you in the room, play *Star Wars* music, or bring love beads for everyone to wear. It doesn't have to be wacky; it just needs to be outside the group's norms. A facilitator friend of mine gave her group special hats and had them go inline skating before they began. Having fun is a great way to dislodge inhibitions. Protect your credibility—but do something that stretches people's expectations.

RAISE THE BAR

If the group knows you, you can stretch expectations even further. It could take the form of owning up to a mistake, sharing previously withheld information, or sharing any other truth that might raise eyebrows. One group I worked with was bitterly arguing the issue of sovereignty over a new and lucrative market. It was a case where the old guard rushed to the scene after a group of young upstarts had struck gold. Everyone wanted a piece of the action, and they were getting pretty hot under the collar about it. I was racking my brains for some facilitator trick to redirect the anger into inquiry, when one of the senior managers did it for me. He turned to a young woman so angry she was in tears and said, "I screwed up, and I'm sorry. I should have realized how inconsiderate it was." The entire state of the group shifted in seconds. There were a few moments of silence while everyone watched for her reaction. She responded, "It's okay. It was very inconsiderate. But I can see how it happened." From that moment on, the group changed. He had raised the bar by telling a dangerous truth.

If you are a high-ranking member of the group, find something that has been deemed undiscussable—a mistake that was swept under the rug, a decision clothed in secrecy, some dangerous truth—that you can openly discuss. Time it to create a dramatic impact and you will set the stage for a meaningful increase in the levels of honesty and openness. People will follow your lead and begin to test the waters for being truthful.

I'M IN

Simply expecting a statement to be truthful isn't quite enough to induce dialogue. The group needs to expect to discover new, significantly more productive ways to deal with the "truth." They need to expect that they will be richly rewarded for telling the truth rather than regretting it, which is usually what happened the last time they told the truth. The rewards you can promise are the abilities to think differently, feel differently, and behave differently—which are usually better in the end, but often difficult in the interim. At some point as they listen to you present the different stages of dialogue, including the escape strategies, they know this is going to be hard. This point is a small moment of truth: Will they commit even after they realize how difficult it will be?

At this point, you want people to hold in mind the last time the "truth set them free." The most powerful strategy is to link whatever models you use or stories you tell with participants' past positive experiences with dialogue. It might not have been a recent event, but everyone has experienced dialogue. Those "little d" dialogue experiences are the ingredients from which you build expectations for this "big D" dialogue. Give examples from your life and ask the group for examples. For instance, ask people in the group if they can "remember a time when conversation became deeper and moved to a true dialogue," or ask, "What is the difference between dialogue and a debate or a discussion?" These questions will normally generate memories that give the group a starting place from which to build a vision of dialogue and how it could be. The vision they create should be compelling enough to obtain the group's commitment to the process. If most of the group holds the same vision and is committed, it will work. Don't worry about the holdouts. Leave them alone. They will either come around or they won't. All you need is a critical mass of commitment and positive expectation.

One of the worries behind a group hesitation to commit may be a worry that the process will somehow change it against its best interests. It is funny how people forget that they are in charge of their own beliefs and thoughts. A facilitator can't change them and a process can't change them. They are the ones who will choose any changes in belief or behavior. This expectation is critical. The buck stops with them. They can prevent what they don't want and likewise are responsible to create what they do want.

You need to build the expectation that it will not be a waste of time as long as they are willing to take responsibility to ensure that it isn't. Their success will be directly linked to their level of effort. One of your toughest challenges will be to *not* take responsibility for their success. To walk the fine line of doing your job well while detaching yourself from their success or failure is a tough one. If you take too much responsibility, it sends the message that the group doesn't have to. Chapter 10 explores this concept more deeply.

I'LL DRIVE

It is the quintessential double-bind facilitator trick not only to get the monkey off your back and onto theirs, but also to have the finesse to get people to reach out and willingly remove it from your back and place it on their own. Responsibility is something we usually pass around like a hot potato until the facilitator steps in to hold it for the group. In dialogue, traditional concepts of responsibility and accountability don't apply. The process won't work unless everyone takes responsibility to do his part, which cannot happen if the facilitator is in the way. There is a nonlinear aspect to this process. My best advice is to create a vacuum so that people can take responsibility when they are ready and to make it attractive to do so.

You can be sure that they won't take responsibility unless it looks as if it is going to be worth the effort. Your goal in presenting the models is not purely informational. It should also be inspirational. The pictorial model of dialogue builds the expectation that they will "peel back the politeness and pretending"; it assures the group that "chaos" and "discarding and redefining" can be scary but most definitely will not be boring. You cannot promise a process that is always fun, but you can play up the fact that it will be interesting. Most groups expect discussions to be as boring as dirt. If you can use the models to build expectations of an interesting, even enlightening experience, you can awaken curiosity. The group will not only participate enthusiastically but will take that expectation and make it a self-fulfilling prophecy.

The models of the group and individual escape strategies (described in Chapter 4) are important at this stage. Present them so that the group can recognize past situations where these very issues sabotaged its ability to build a fruitful group communication. Ensure that the worst offenders recognize themselves so that they can resolve privately to self-correct. Your biggest challenge will be to ensure that no one gets embarrassed or defensive about lacking group communication skills. Presenting these models up front means they can save face, recognize their own limitations in the privacy of their own minds, and make the necessary internal adjustments to avoid whatever bad habits they have. Once you've got commitment, then you give the group participants an opportunity to anchor that commitment into clear agreements that will help them remember once they get in the middle of the process.

WHERE IS IT THAT WE ARE GOING?

Conceptual agreements don't translate to new behavior by themselves. This is the point where many attempts to dialogue fail. We agree in principle, but we don't link those idealistic principles to what that means specifically when someone wants to storm out of the room, mentally check out, or skewer someone else with a sarcastic sidebar. The behaviors of dialogue are easy to promise and hard to deliver. It is even harder when these are things we have promised (and been promised) before, without effect.

This next part of the process is designed to strap us in to our good intentions and make it difficult to forget to keep agreements. It works like this: Offer a too-long shopping list of guidelines from which you recommend the group select five to seven "rules." I use the word *rules* simply because it sounds more serious than the word *guidelines*. The choice of five to seven rules is arbitrary but designed to force the group members to make thoughtful choices and discuss their choices in terms of what they mean. The list I use is derived from everything I've read about dialogue in the last seven years, plus recommendations from dialogue groups.

When people ask you what a particular rule means, do everything you can to get them to define it for themselves. What do they want it to mean to them, in this situation? Initially, they may feel as if you are withholding information, but the meaning they express will mold their behavior ten times more than any meaning you express. Stretching the process of choosing their own rules over time is done purely to get the group members to think—to think about what they are willing and not willing to do when faced with dangerous truths. If you select for them or let the group pick without serious consideration, the rules will have little impact. Easier said than done because, by this time, most of the group will want to "just get on with it" and you will need to inspire one last burst of effort from the group.

SMORGASBORD OF RULES

Exhibit 6-1 offers a smorgasbord of rules from which to choose. Each of these rules is designed to shift the thinking and interaction norms of the group from traditional patterns to patterns that produce dialogue. They also help provide an illusion of structure for the process that will help minimize unnecessary frustration. There are no mandatory rules, only a collection of guidelines that in different situations seems to achieve the desired result of open inquiry, heightened tolerance and trust, and deep reflection into the assumptions, beliefs, and opinions that influence their world.

You may want to alter this list with rules more appropriate to the culture and background of your group. Different corporate or ethnic cultures warrant different choices. However, be careful about subtracting the recommended core rules (highlighted with an asterisk in Exhibit 6-1), especially the rules of "No Leader" and "No Task." The best way to engage members of the group in taking these rules seriously is to ask them to articulate what behaviors and patterns would occur differently if they chose them for their dialogue. The thought

Exhibit 6-1. Possible Rules for Dialogue

No Leader*	Listen and Speak Without Judgment*
No Agenda*	Acknowledge Each Speaker
No Decisions*	Respect Individual Differences*
No Task*	Suspend Roles and Status
Suspend Certainties*	Balance Inquiry and Advocacy
Listen to Your Listening	Avoid Cross-Talk
Slow Down the Inquiry*	Focus on Learning*
Be Aware of Thought	Seek the Next Level of Understanding
Maintain Peripheral Attention	Maintain a Spirit of Inquiry*
Suspend Assumptions	Devalue Consistency
Befriend Polarization*	Be Vulnerable
Observe the Observer	Embrace the Painful and the Pleasant
Speak Personally*	Speak When "Moved"
Avoid Generalizations	Release the Need for Specific Outcomes
Don't Fix or Convert Others	
Act as Colleagues	

* Recommended "core" rules of dialogue. This list is adapted from M. Scott Peck's *The Different Drum*, William Isaacs's work with the MIT-based Dialogue Project, materials from G. Gerard and L. Ellinor's *The Dialogue Group*, and many other sources.

process of translating the rules from concept to reality anchors good intentions to behavior. Exploring what might be different if they chose a particular rule is a self-awareness process. The mental and verbal process of explaining to themselves what "Listen and Speak Without judgment" means behavior-wise requires self-examination. As people articulate what a rule will mean (e.g., not cutting someone off, or talking about what they "see" rather than what "is"), they are internalizing the rule at an unconscious level. Even rules that are discussed and not chosen will alter the group's behavior.

Allow at least twenty minutes for the group to discuss and choose their rules. This process can be frustrating for everyone. One guy said he had never in all his life "spent so much time talking about talking without actually talking!" Considering that we spend so little time thinking about how we think and talking about how we talk, the frustration is understandable. However, if you generate as much attention as you can to these rules, they will more powerfully alter the thought and talk patterns created as you begin, finally, to dialogue.

THEIR PROCESS, NOT YOURS

Remember that the purpose of the rules is to encourage open reflection and inquiry into the group's beliefs and opinions, continually peeling these beliefs and opinions back to expose the underlying assumptions on which they are based and eventually revealing the meaning underneath. Any rule that enhances the safety of the environment, motivates the group toward exploration, or helps the group detach from traditional modes of thinking is appropriate. Too many rules clutter the field. Strive for the most simple and elegant combination. A choice of five to seven rules is recommended.

Once the rules have been selected and accepted by the group members, you need to explain to the group that your role is about to change. Explain that "No Leader" means that the group must lead itself to dialogue and that you will intervene only in matters that pertain to the process of dialogue, never interfering in the content of the discussion. Review the predictable avoidance strategies in order to sensitize the group to recognize these when they occur. Use flip chart paper as a reference for both the group and individual escape strategies to help participants monitor themselves through the process. Post the "rules" prominently for the same reason.

Draw on your experience with groups to determine the appropriate level of preparation. My process leans on the concepts of preempts and mind-sets described in Chapter 11, so you will find that I recommend more preparation than other theorists do. With this preparation, I have rarely found that I underestimated a group's ability and willingness to participate in dialogue. In general, groups live up to our expectations (high or low).

Once you have done all you can to set the stage for dialogue, it is time to take a different role as facilitator of the process. Up until now, your role has been similar to a trainer or a guide. Once the group begins to dialogue, you adopt a different set of behaviors.

Chapter 7

The Goal

Light is meaningful only in relation to darkness, and truth presupposes error. It is these mingled opposites which people our life, which make it pungent, intoxicating. We only exist in terms of this conflict, in the zone where black and white clash.

LOUIS ARAGON

Once the setup is complete, the active part of your job is over. A characteristic of this formal approach to dialogue is that you are directive before it starts and then essentially nondirective during the process. During the setup you actively present examples and models; you persuade, inspire, and do your best to disrupt old patterns of thinking and talking and suggest new ones. You provide "training." Although I heartily recommend you do it with a pull strategy rather than a push strategy, you still must lead. Once the process begins, you refrain from providing leadership. You stop doing and turn your attention to being. Remember, one of the core rules is "No Leader" and that means you, too. If you lead once dialogue begins, you sabotage the process. This isn't your show.

FAITH

This is the group's chance to practice and learn. They will make mistakes. Individuals will move in and out of true dialogue. Long silences will make you want to jump in and help. High tension and arguments might alert your "do something" alarm bells. Yet your goal is to do as little as possible. One of the most important skills of dialogue is for the group to learn how to self-correct. If you are doing it for them, they never get to learn that one. You will intervene at times, but oh-so-rarely.

The bottom line is that you have to trust the process and have faith in the people. Your faith will be tested. Your ego will want these people to dialogue as they never have before and afterward look to you in wonder at your skill in changing their lives. Your ego needs to take a hike. Egoless-ness is discussed in Chapter 13 in more detail, but suffice it to say that for those of us who tend to concentrate more on looking good and on doing rather than being, this dramatic shift in role will feel counterintuitive at times. (The ego sometimes masquerades as intuition.)

This chapter is designed to help frame what you see as the group moves to dialogue. Since dialogue may be different from anything you have facilitated before, you need a context. Old assumptions about the goals of facilitation might cause you to intervene when you shouldn't or in ways that do not support dialogue. Dialogue is not group therapy, conflict resolution, mediation, or consensus building. There will be some overlap, but the outcomes you sought and the tools you used for other sorts of facilitation tasks should all be filtered through a new lens.

In the next chapter, there are several tactics and intervention strategies available to you when you facilitate dialogue, but first let's spend time discussing what you are looking for in dialogue—the goal. You are looking for curiosity, tolerance, and open minds. But know that individuals fade in and out of those idealized thinking states. Your goal is to observe the group as a whole rather than focus on individuals. Ultimately, the skill of dialogue is a group skill. Tiny mistakes and fluctuations of individuals here and there are irrelevant when you observe the group as a whole. Interventions at the individual level may serve the individual but cost the group. Your job is to help the group develop a group skill. You need to focus on the whole, not the parts.

SOFT EYES

One of my mentors, a psychologist, was also an aikido master. He frequently used aikido terms to explain aspects of leadership and the art of consulting. One of those terms was "soft eyes." I try to have "soft eyes" when I facilitate.

Try this experiment. Look at an object near you in the room where you now sit. Focus on what you see. Feel the directness of your gaze? Now begin to widen your periphery vision until you have as wide a view as possible. Take in everything around you. That is what "soft eyes" feels like. As you move to the state where you are ready to facilitate dialogue, I recommend that you develop soft eyes. For most of us, it is unnatural and a bit of a strain initially. Learning to see everything as a whole takes practice.

As you observe the group, you want to look at the group as a whole. Many times there are individuals who are pairing—one guy surreptitiously checking his pager and another person whose eyes are bulging with an obviously undialogic anger. It doesn't matter. When you have soft eyes, you see the group as a whole; if the group is, for the most part, in dialogue, then it would only distract the group to point out individual aberrations.

THE BASIC GROUP SKILLS OF DIALOGUE

Dialogue is a team skill. Individual skills make up the foundation for the group skills, but ultimately dialogue is only possible when the group as a collective unit has developed the group skills of dialogue.

These are group thought and interaction skills. I don't include a discussion of these group skills in the setup because people have enough to remember already. These skills are best discussed after the group has tried dialogue. You can only accomplish so much up front. The depth of the group's understanding is so much deeper once the group members have tried dialogue. People find it too easy to idealistically embrace these concepts without understanding what they mean in action. Like a greenhorn who says he knows all about being a parent—it takes real-life experience before he can really discuss what that means. When you facilitate the third or fourth run of dialogue, you may want to include exercises or prediscussion of these group skills, but for now I describe them in the context of your observations as a facilitator.

These group skills are a mix of skills and values. Dialogue values learning over being right. It values mutual respect, exploration, and collaboration. It is an oversimplification to try to discuss them as skills. But this whole book is an oversimplification, so why stop now?

THE ABILITY TO SEE JUDGMENTS

The human mind is designed to interpret data and draw conclusions based on past experience. Every piece of incoming data is met with the question, "What does that mean to me?" Lightning-fast judgments are awarded (e.g., good/bad, relevant/irrelevant, smart/stupid); the mind chooses which fork in the road to take (the one most traveled) and takes it. You never even know that your mind made a choice. And you can be sure groups, in particular, rarely take the road less traveled and are usually quite unaware they even visited a mental fork in the road. To dialogue, a group must first develop an ability to "see" the forks in the road.

The reason we don't take the road (i.e., thought pattern) less traveled is that we don't see it there. One of my wilder friends in high school demonstrated this to me one afternoon when we were cutting school. She was driving my car, a very fast 1972 Dodge Charger, on back roads in the country. We were barreling down a road with a ninety-degree right turn at the end. To my horror, she seemed to speed up instead of slowing down to take the curve. The last thing I remember seeing was her evil grin before we hit the curve and I covered my face to protect myself from the inevitable crash. And then . . . nothing. I looked up to see that we were quite safely continuing along a much smaller dirt road that went straight instead of curving left. I hadn't seen it. It never occurred to me to look for it. Yet we were on it, and we didn't die. I thought we were history.

You could say that I lacked all the facts, but we are always missing all the facts. Unless you are omniscient (in which case I'm honored that you would take the time to read my book), you don't have all the facts on anything.

To function, your brain stops somewhere short of having all the facts and makes a judgment—a conclusion. And it then uses that conclusion exclusively. Arriving at work on time is good. Telling the whole truth to the boss is dumb. And so on. I'm not saying those judgments aren't functional. I'm just saying that there is a big difference between seeing them and not seeing them. When people in a group remove the autopilot and begin to see the thousands of judgments that they make about everything, it may feel overwhelming. Some will demonstrate a similar anxiety to the one I felt when I thought I was about to crash and burn on a ninety-degree turn. That panic will pass when people begin to see most roads accepted as truth are right next to another ignored alternate route that might lead to a shortcut.

Since the mind functions slower when it is forced to observe itself, this takes a lot of effort. The complexity of observed reality increases exponentially. Once the group begins to see judgments, the decision tree for a simple line of reasoning looks more like a crushed windshield than a logical path. As group members backtrack through the progression their thoughts have taken or are taking, they are flooded with unchosen alternatives. Not only is the rational brain flooded with unselected options for review, but the emotional brain is forced to take responsibility for having had the power of choosing all along. This is a skill of attention, detachment, and emotional maturity.

Every group operates on the basis on implicit judgments. Most of these judgments are the result of conclusions our culture has made about the way the world operates. Seeing judgments is like looking behind the curtain at the Wizard of Oz and seeing that he is . . . us! It is scary to realize how many judgments are arbitrarily made—how arbitrary our reality is. We like the security of knowing. In business we were trained to accept certain principles as dogma and it rarely occurs to us to see them as judgments. To look at them as arbitrary is to deconstruct your world. This isn't easy for a room of people who like to be in control.

When people begin to deconstruct their world, it sometimes looks like, well, a mess. They are disassembling their thought machinery to see how it works. And just like a disassembled motorcycle separated into pieces on the floor, it doesn't work too well. Most groups worry that they might never put things back together again.

As group members become consciously aware of their judgments, they willingly embrace going backward to have another look. The group begins to reward individuals for the courage to seek out judgments even though they expose a flawed judgment. The most telling evidence is that thought has slowed down so it can be observed. They may not be seeing the judgments you wish they would see, but it is enough if people have turned their attention to look for them.

They are backing off the certainty of conclusions and revisiting the "facts" (often another judgment). When the group members give permission to see judgments, they become open to seeing other points of view. It becomes a safe place for people to change their mind without repercussions. You will observe an increase in the ability of individuals to articulate their thought process out loud. Initial attempts at dialogue are often undermined because most people cannot describe their own thought process. As people begin to better "see" their thought process, they describe it better and communication improves dramatically.

The setup is designed to stimulate awareness of particular kinds of judgments. Each of the four individual thought barrier models is designed to heighten attention to the place where judgments tend to hide. Any common mental model will achieve the same objective. It doesn't matter which ones you use. Once attention is successfully drawn to the fact that humans seem to think in predictable patterns, the group members begin to notice the judgments (patterns) that keep them stuck.

Once they begin to notice one or two judgments, their ability to notice others accelerates. It is a snowball effect. They tune in. Just like once you begin to garden, you begin to notice plants, make distinctions about different sorts of dirt, learn about bugs—you see stuff you never noticed before. The same phenomenon occurs with judgments—one or two reveals an unexamined world of judgments.

When the group starts to see judgments, the next natural step is to question them.

HERETICAL THINKING

"Why?" "Who says?" "Are you sure?" "How do we know that?" "Maybe things have changed." The question "How do we know what we know?" must always be answered with less than complete certainty. I don't know about your group, but most groups I've worked with like to maintain the illusion that they know what is going on. The fact that none of us really understands it all is usually hidden beneath a bunch of bravado, intellectual debate on minor details, and all the defensive reasoning patterns we've discussed. When people begin to question their own basic assumptions, they willingly admit that "maybe we don't know everything we think we know." This is progress.

There are usually one or two people in a group who naturally question assumptions. More often than not they have been labeled as troublemakers. When the entire group begins to question assumptions, that's a good sign. It demonstrates a real shift toward embracing uncertainty, demonstrating trust, and engaging curiosity (i.e., learning). In dialogue, the assumptions that are questioned sometimes represent sacred dogma. The group starts thinking like a bunch of heretics.

Heretics, by definition, are the source of radically new concepts. When most of the population is steeped in the status quo and can't think outside the dots, the heretic questions dogma. Innovations in thought have taken decades (even centuries) to catch on with the larger group. In business, we are looking to speed up that process a fraction.

I was working with a team of project managers in the construction industry who were shifting to a team-based approach. I think it is safe to say that this whole team business has not lived up to our expectations. Not that it won't, eventually, but some of our first efforts have had dismal results. Like the team itself. The team members embraced the idealism of teamwork and had the best of intentions—until "cooperation" translated into one ambitious young guy disappearing into the swamps of Louisiana to save some obscure project. It meant the group's hotshot needed to slow down enough to include others and, well, you get the picture. For years the rewards in this organization went to individual achievers. The entire culture supported visibility and star quality. The guy down in the swamps assumed he would be invisible for two years and the hotshot didn't want to slow down for anyone. They weren't the only ones worried about injustice. A cascade of covert maneuverings had caused most of the group to become resentful and to take hidden actions to protect their jobs. This was a natural application for dialogue.

More than once, the group pointed to policies and decisions as "unfair." With a little prompting they began to question their assumptions on the definition of "fair." This is a common point of misunderstanding. Fair can mean whoever works hardest gets more, whoever produces the most (not necessarily working harder) gets more, or whoever has been here longest is most rewarded. Then again, some people feel that a team should share equally or that the person who brought the most to the pot in the beginning should get more. Several of the team members, each using a different definition, felt that they had been treated quite unfairly and felt justified in passing it on.

When they began to question their assumptions about the meaning of "fair," their feelings of injustice began to unravel. The effect spread to other assumptions including how this "team thing" was supposed to work. It was no small act of heresy to question the

wisdom of teamwork. They examined assumptions until they uncov-
ered several that were mutually exclusive. Among them was the new
team mantra, "All for one and one for all," which was in direct opposition to the more realistic Darwinian "survival of the fittest." It was
a dangerous truth to admit the culture and the new team policy were
in direct opposition. That took courage. Once they could question
that one, they asked themselves all sorts of questions. I wish I could
say they reached resolution on the team versus individual achieve-
ment issue, but there are no resolutions to this built-in business paradox. It is unresolvable—an ambiguity to be managed rather than
"solved."

They found their resolution from examining and disproving
the assumptions they had made about each other's intent. They discovered their judgments were off base. Sure, the hotshot was ambitious, but he wanted others to succeed as well. The guy in the swamp
was willing to be a team player as long as everyone recognized his sac-
rifice. They construct a new context where people weren't the problem
and turned their energy to managing the unresolvable conflict of individual versus collective effort. Potshots and covert games ceased for the
duration of the dialogue. All because they had the courage to question
what they thought they knew. Questioning assumptions about the
malicious intent, negligence, or self-serving behaviors of fellow group
members almost always reveals those assumptions as unsubstantiated
in part or whole. If the only benefit you derive from dialogue is a
renewed level of mutual respect, it is well worth the time.

It is natural to want to think you know what is going on. Yet
opinions, beliefs, and judgments are usually based on layers of
assumptions that are at best oversimplifications and at worst just
plain wrong. Questioning the underlying assumptions that form a
group's belief systems is critical to the process of dialogue. Individuals cannot identify assumptions as quickly as a group that works
together to discover the origins of their judgments. The skill involves
a collaborative "peeling back" of the layers of assumptions that create
a "position." It presents group members with the opportunity to
reassess their positions if they so desire. This skill depends on trust
among the members that it is the line of reasoning that is being
examined, not anyone's credibility or value as an expert.

Dialogue might even be seen as a support group for individuals willing to think heretical thoughts. When things get interest-

ing, you know the group has begun to develop another important skill—a genuine curiosity for contradictory views.

CURIOSITY TO HEAR OPPOSITE VIEWS

Several years ago I would have called this the skill of listening. But "listening" doesn't go far enough. Too many people fake listening. We nod our head, hold eye contact, and paraphrase just like we were taught in the training course on listening—but we aren't listening. Listening with a genuine desire to understand is different; it is more like curiosity.

Curiosity happens when the desire to learn outstrips the need for certainty. Curiosity provokes risk. It killed the cat, remember? Excitement and an anticipation of new knowledge become palpable. People in the group begin to venture outside the walls that normally protect them from hearing things that don't fit their worldview. For the brief period of dialogue, they feel a new curiosity about the words and beliefs of people who see things differently. They quiet the chatter in their own minds and are receptive to the meaning behind the words. Listening with curiosity helps the group naturally resist the escape routes operating to simplify its reality. It demonstrates a tolerance for uncertainty and a genuine desire to understand. It is a higher-level group skill.

It is more than hearing another's point of view—it is making room for that point of view. When a group develops the skill of curiosity, it develops other new habits that operate when someone is speaking. The group builds new norms where individuals ferret out facts and observations, particularly when they challenge their own position. The group begins to ask better questions, allows more time for answers, and spends more time in silence digesting what was said. The group begins to correct members who rush past listening. Time is forgotten. The questions being asked interest everyone. They are fascinated by the exchange. Adversaries become allies with a new mutual goal—the goal to learn. For the period of dialogue, mutual curiosity brings adversaries together in a common quest.

You can see people become aware that they are separate from their thinking. They examine their thoughts, judgments, and assumptions as tools that either serve or impair them. They begin to test them against their intentions. A group of doctors about to split their practice revisited their original intention in coming together: to help people. With that alliance, they turned their curiosity to the judgments that had brought them to the edge of a split. They found that tiny variations in judgments about compensation made years ago had grown into fissures so wide the partners were cut off from understanding each other. Once they followed their reasoning back to the original split, they found a third option they had never considered. Fueled with a curiosity to hear opposite views, most groups can create new thought patterns that drive a new reality for the group.

A group that has developed the skill of curiosity, values this time to wonder and examine as an opportunity to increase its understanding, even if the group members like what they understand. Ultimately, the skill of curiosity is fundamental to any group's (or individual's) ability to learn and adapt to an ambiguous, constantly changing world.

PERSONAL RESPONSIBILITY

If curiosity killed the cat, then what exactly was the cause of death? We have this cultural archetype that protects dangerous truths from examination—a big "Don't go there" sign with lots of dead cats piled up at the threshold and no clear reason why. What is this deep fear of digging too deep? It might be because inevitably, if we dig deep enough, we always find that new learning demands new action. A deep examination of any problem ultimately reveals core assumptions that are to some extent a function of choices we, ourselves, have made. Diving once more into this messy breach, dear friends, is to admit that we share responsibility for the mess.

All of us are traveling down roads that—had we stopped to think—we would have abandoned long ago. Yet, to stop and think, to curiously wonder, feels risky. Dialogue presents the group with an opportunity to stop and think. It begins when the group starts to see judgments as choices, to question the assumptions behind those choices, to develop a genuine curiosity to understand all the alternatives, and then (if the group members don't wig out) acknowledge that they can change it all. The ultimate result of dialogue is that people in the group begin to see reality as a function of their choices rather than purely as an externally imposed set of criteria. They recognize their level of participation in creating what is good about their situation as well as what is not so good.

When a group identifies too closely with its thinking, questioning that thinking is risky. To allow that there are equally valid alternatives forces a group to acknowledge that it has collectively chosen its current reality—problems and all. That is a big responsibility. When the group stops hiding from this responsibility and steps up to the challenge, dialogue is working its magic. The group has developed the skills and found enough emotional maturity to really dialogue. For the emotionally immature, it is easier to pretend to be powerless. To share power with a group opens the floodgates for hopes and fears about what that means. To acknowledge interdependence usually means a more personal redefinition of, well, everything. The independent cowboys suddenly see the value of less proactive members and the followers in the group begin to acknowledge their opportunities to lead.

This is the point where "why are we here" and "why are we doing this" conversations begin to emerge. If there are no good answers to these questions, then you have just identified your major source of problems. Humans don't stick with meaningless tasks once they have identified them as meaningless. They don't "take ownership." They don't "give their all." They don't "get onboard." If dialogue reveals a common sense of futility, don't worry—the futility must be acknowledged before dialogue can fill that yawning gap with new meaning.

I facilitated dialogue for an academic department that faced the dangerous truth that most of the staff members did not see benefit in collaboration of any kind. The department head's stated goal in bringing the group to dialogue gives a clearer picture: He wanted to shift the culture from a "predatorial to performance-based" focus. (Walking into Jurassic Park University, where they eat facilitators for breakfast, is testament to my belief in the power of dialogue!) Once freed from the obligation to give politically correct answers about "teamwork" and allowed to express assumptions about the meaninglessness of that term, the group spontaneously began to give it a new meaning. This was not a fluke. I see this all the time in dialogue.

Meaninglessness is a vacuum that human beings must fill. If we fill it as individuals, we have a fractured, incoherent combination of many meanings. If we fill it together, we blend our meanings into a cohesive set of understandings that transcends individual differences. It was when they began to focus on student needs that this group of academics began to come together. Their state changed. They began to see each other as colleagues as well as competitors. While they didn't leave arm in arm singing a silly tune, they left with a renewed mutual respect that translated into more sharing of information, less back-stabbing, and more personal responsibility for creating a healthy working environment.

Dialogue simultaneously reveals and modifies meaning, intentions, and deeper goals. It binds the group as a whole to take more responsibility to better address the underlying reasons behind its work. This is where passion lives. After dialogue, people are frequently reinspired to work together and create new realities. They see the potential for new realities and they are working together to build a better one.

They take responsibility for their collective past and their collective future.

Chapter 8

Structure for an Unstructured Process

Artistic growth is, more than it is anything else, a refining of the sense of truthfulness. The stupid believe that to be truthful is easy; only the artist, the great artist, knows how difficult it is.

WILLA CATHER

Facilitating dialogue is an art. An artist friend is teaching me about art. For instance, a good artist will usually have good "studio skills." That means that she has mastered the basics of mixing colors, understands textures, and knows how to get a paintbrush to do what she wants it to do. After that, she can be much more creative because she has more options. If you can't paint a straight line, your options are limited (at least in my experience). And yet once an artist has mastered all the "rules," she is free to break them.

This chapter is designed to cover a few "studio skills" useful in the art of facilitating dialogue with a large group. There are a few rules that can be very useful, but that you are free to break. If you go in with nothing but good intentions, the dialogue may never take shape. If you "go by the book," the dialogue has no room to develop. The balance is in between, in providing a structure for an unstructured process.

Most work groups you encounter will demand some structure. You need to give them enough to make them comfortable, yet not too much and not so rigid as to dampen the dialogue. Experience in delivering hard structure for a group will help, but you need to create structure that goes beyond the literal interpretation and adapts itself to the different stages and needs of the group. Whatever structure you choose, whatever rules you select, they must always bend to the will of the group members as they enter dialogue.

THE BASICS

Generally, dialogue groups sit in a circle. This physical shift can stimulate mental shifts around status and hierarchy. Participants must commit to a minimum of two hours for the process (in addition to any training, review beforehand, or reflection afterward). Most facilitators also insist that the group commit to several sessions. Off-site is better than on-site if you have a group that finds it hard to stay away from phones and problem solving. If you have been sitting classroom style, it is best to take the chairs and form a circle away from tables, desks, paper, and pens. This also signals to the group that you are no longer a part of their circle. When you shift control back to them, you remove yourself from visual focus. Find an unobtrusive spot from which to observe. Avoid receiving eye contact to encourage them to address each other instead of you.

Even though your goal is to never intervene, in the beginning you will be their coach. That means carefully chosen interventions that keep the power in the group. Here are six types of interventions you can use to keep the group moving in the direction of dialogue without taking center stage:

- Rounds

- Psychological silence

- Intervention of awareness

- Intervention to facilitate new skills

- Silence

- Stories

ROUNDS

After setting the climate and reaching agreement on the rules, the process will begin all by itself and progress naturally. Most groups struggle with the question, "Are we doing this right?" In the beginning, your answer should always be "yes." It is more important to get them to experience their competence than to give correction. If they need a jump-start, you can use "rounds" to shift the dynamics of the conversation. If you are worried that they might jump right into a free-for-all argument, a mind-numbing recitation of popular opinion, or a superficial pretense, a set of rounds can focus their attention elsewhere.

I explain rounds to a group in technical terms to avoid the technique being labeled as touchy-feely. Rounds is a process that gives everyone a chance to speak and, more important, several chances to practice listening. It eliminates cross-talk and gives the members of the group a "read" on where they are at. To do rounds, the group goes around the room once, allowing each person to say whatever he or she wishes without interruption. It also operates to allow all group members to listen to themselves as well as listen to others.

You can ask all members of the group to contribute a brief comment or observation that reflects their present state of mind. This operates to orient the group members to the present moment. They get "quiet" mentally and ready for dialogue. Or you may want to make rounds more specific. A facilitator friend of mine asked the people in a group to begin by sharing the one experience that had been most formative in their approach to getting things done at work. This allowed the group to begin the process of self-disclosure. It stimulated curiosity and began to peel back assumptions about why people were doing what they were doing. She realized that there were several misunderstandings and used rounds to target the assumptions that had been undermining trust for that group.

Another time, I asked every member of a group (senior staff members of a large church) to share why they were there and what they thought they contributed to the team. My goal was to prompt the group members to anchor themselves in their common goals and begin to question the assumptions of self-effacement and self-denial that seemed to be causing resentment and bad feelings. They all found it difficult to focus on their personal contribution. Each had been trained to acknowledge others, but not themselves. The process shifted their norms so that they began to see judgments they would not have noticed otherwise. Once that happened, they were ready to discuss how overwork had been creating resentment and bad feelings.

When I teamed up with another facilitator to take a doctor's practice to dialogue, she opened the day with a set of rounds on why each person had become a doctor in the first place. It shifted the state of the group. As they listened and remembered the good intentions that sustained them through medical school and residency horrors, they rediscovered a sense of mutual respect that conflicts had eroded over time. As each person began to describe the burning passion to be of service and help people, the rest of the people in the group witnessed the "good" in their colleague. And when it came their turn, everyone else, at least for a minute, returned to their core intentions. It loosened the grip on divisive positions about money.

Be creative. You can use rounds to set the stage or, later in the process, to redirect people when they seem to be disappearing down one of the escape routes. Use rounds to let the group members describe an event that galvanized their beliefs or values about a certain subject. Ask them to describe what they think is at the heart of the matter. Target any underlying meaning that might forge a common bond between group members.

Don't forget to be clear on time limits. If you forget to set the limit to one or two sentences, you will find yourself trapped as one group member rambles on indefinitely. To interrupt runs the risk of offending the group and modeling the behavior of cutting people off. You can avoid that if you stress time constraints up front.

The process of rounds can operate as an equalizer, a depth finder, a redirector, or a connector.

PSYCHOLOGICAL SILENCE

Except for rounds your goal is to do nothing—to so completely hand over the reins that the group members have to take them up. In a way, it is an intervention. Your objective is for the group to achieve free-flowing interaction, to operate within the spirit of dialogue (the rules are secondary), and to move through the stages of dialogue without you. As long as their interaction continues on target, your job is to remain silent and visually unobtrusive. This isn't easy! The skill of being unobtrusive is just as important as a speaking intervention. At this level of subtlety, even to stand and walk to the other side of the room is an intervention. Any facilitator attempting to create dialogue must master the skill of psychological silence. (Chapter 13 on egoless-ness will help.)

There are three situations where facilitator interventions may be appropriate in dialogue. All interventions will ideally become unnecessary as the group develops. To get the ball rolling, it is useful to intervene with rounds or something that models the process of dialogue. Second, you will need to assert yourself when group members are avoiding the process of dialogue by using any of the escape routes. Also, you may choose to enhance the process with an intervention that will inspire or guide reflection.

But most of the time, you don't want to do anything. It takes effort to observe without intrusion. In the beginning, you will probably have to monitor your facial expressions and body language. You need to override amused smiles, raised eyebrows, or nervous twitches. Maintaining your psychological silence will discourage the group members' wanting to escape into dependency when they begin asking, "Are we doing this right?" or "What do you think?" Try not to receive eye contact from group members. If a member of the group insists on addressing you, carefully redirect him to the other member(s) of the group him should be talking to. After being so directive in the beginning, you need to be particularly silent in the first fifteen or twenty minutes to retrain the group to adjust to your new nondirective role.

Once they have stopped looking to you to tell them what to do, you have more latitude to make minor interventions without disturbing their process. It is rarely appropriate to intervene until well into the first hour. At that point, if the group is in danger of disappearing into one of the escape routes, it may be appropriate to make an intervention of awareness. Since you have already discussed most avoidance patterns and defensive routines, awareness is usually enough to bring the group back to dialogue.

INTERVENTION OF AWARENESS

Escape strategies such as flight, fight, pairing, and dependency (described in Chapter 4) allow a group to avoid deep reflection and resist new thinking. When group members engage in these avoidance strategies or abandon the agreed-on rules of interaction, they move away from dialogue. Eventually, the group will engage in self-correction, but in the beginning, your intervention may be necessary. Just because you observe an avoidance strategy doesn't mean you need to intervene. Wait until the group has had every opportunity to self-correct and is threatening to derail the process of dialogue before you call the group's attention to the situation.

An intervention of awareness is not an accusation, a critique, or a correction. It is, metaphorically, shining a light onto an interaction that enables the group to see it more clearly. For instance, if a group is escaping the process of dialogue by scapegoating a group member, an intervention of awareness might be to say, "I notice that there is a lot of negative stuff being directed at Frank. Sometimes group members need a way to vent frustrations and they will choose an individual to receive those frustrations." Don't get into a deep analysis. The intervention is restricted to simply creating an awareness of the individual or group behavior.

If you have taped the escape strategy "icon" drawings on the wall (see Chapter 4), you can simply walk over and point to the one causing the problem. For instance, one group began to discuss breaking off into small groups to study a situation. When they began to look at me, I walked over to the flip chart paper and pointed to the flight icon and turned away. They did the rest. I didn't need to say anything.

Interventions of awareness are delicate and require the facilitator to make a subjective judgment on when and how to intervene. Concentrate on group needs rather than individual needs. It is rare that you would intervene on an individual's behavior; that would occur only when it seriously threatens the dialogue. For more experienced facilitators, passing up the opportunity to help an individual develop his skills is tough. Yet the focus on the individual can sabotage the "groupness" necessary for dialogue. It helps to remember that keeping the group in a collective dialogue ultimately serves individuals better than a facilitator intervention focused on an individual.

There are rare exceptions. If an individual's behavior is strongly pulling the group away from dialogue, you need to intervene. For instance, it is a good idea to coach the "boss" or informal leader beforehand to sensitize her to the fact that her behavior sets the tone for the group. Even when this person embraces the "No Leader" rule, her power influences the group. If she is digging her heels deeply into rigid thinking, the group is likely to follow suit. In this situation, you serve the group by intervening on an individual defense pattern. Depending on the culture, you might want to point to an icon or ask a question. Always ensure that the leader has given you permission to give feedback. If she hasn't, you risk alienating her.

Most interventions of awareness, however, will be directed at the group rather than an individual. If dialogue is working right, the dialogue itself will intervene on the individual. You won't need to.

Using awareness rather than critique places power with the group rather than with you, the facilitator. You are helping the group members learn how to facilitate themselves by training their awareness to monitor counterproductive habits and thought patterns. There will be times when awareness isn't enough. Sometimes you need to move from awareness to demonstration. Still miles away from critique, you simply walk them through a better alternative.

INTERVENTION TO FACILITATE NEW SKILLS

Until the skills of seeing judgments, heretical thinking, curiosity, and personal responsibility are learned (see Chapter 7), it may be necessary to walk the group through, using an intervention. At some point, the opportunity will present itself. Some members of the group will be so closely wedded to a particular point of view they can't see any other alternatives. This is an opportunity to use questions to walk them through an experience of reflection. Telling is never as good as showing. Through your questions and words, you can inspire an examination of the underlying assumptions behind a belief or opinion without judging those assumptions. You model for them how to use questions to prompt the same sort of nonjudgmental reflection in others.

There are no firm rules to follow, but the guidelines given in Chapter 12 on the Socratic method will help. Your questions should walk their minds through self-observation, beginning with a self-awareness of the "now" and moving back into the thoughts and beliefs that created the current situation. The flow of an intervention is unpredictable. You have to ask the questions you feel will further group inquiry. You might:

- *Direct attention to an awareness of what is happening "right now."* Questions to ask include: Where is the group right now? What is happening? What do you observe about your interactions?

- *Ask a question that takes the group one step behind surface meaning.* Questions to ask include: What judgments can you see? What judgments are hidden? What is being labeled as right/wrong or good/bad? What would happen if you questioned those labels?

■ *Refer the group to personal experience as a test for these judgments.* Draw attention to people's power in choosing meaning. Questions to ask include: What do these labels mean in practice? Do they fit what you have observed in real life? Have you observed situations where they did not fit?

■ *Slow down the group's thinking and search backward rather than forward.* Questions to ask include: What assumptions lie beneath these judgments? Are there other assumptions behind those? How long ago was that assumption put into place? Was there an event that solidified that assumption? What has changed since then?

■ *Call attention to the emotional reactions that are contributing to perceptions.* Questions to ask include: What emotions are attached to this assumption? How does the emotion impact the conclusions you have made? What emotion would you feel if you redefined this judgment?

Walking group members through a thought process gives them experience in the style of open reflection and inquiry embodied in dialogue. Chapter 15 on modeling goes into further depth about opportunities to model interactions and new thought patterns. There are no strict guidelines. Strict guidelines miss the point. Your goal is to enhance the process. At times silence will enhance more than words.

SILENCE

If emotions begin to escalate or an escape strategy is taking hold, then three minutes of silence is enough to break the momentum taking the group away from dialogue. Used sparingly, silence can be quite effective to encourage individual introspection. This process intervention is particularly useful in prompting a shift from the state of chaos to the state of discarding and redefining (be careful though—it could pop the group back into politeness and pretending). When chaos edges close to fighting, you can ask the group members to take three minutes of silence and use the time to "empty themselves of preconceptions," or to "think about what fears might be driving closely held beliefs," or whatever question or comment you feel will support the process.

Even if a group is well into the fight escape strategy, silence can shift the dynamics. You may want to simply suggest a few minutes of silence to reflect, or you can ask questions to further shift their thinking. Ask one or two questions at most. If you want to prompt reflection during the silence, you might ask them to consider the assumptions that are fueling the conflict, or you can try to develop the group's agility in seeing other positions by asking, "How would the person next to you describe what they see?" Or, "Consider the person most opposite to your point of view. How might that person describe her intentions to a compassionate listener?" Most of the time, this is enough to get people to step back and observe thought and emotion. On rare occasions you may want to tell a story to propel a group's journey into dialogue.

STORIES

Telling a story is one of the most powerful ways to make a point without being directive. When you tell a story, you allow the listeners to create images and thoughts in their own minds that simulate the reflective process. One time when a group was getting caught up in an old argument where both sides were sure they were right, one of the participants suggested it was "just like the burning building." That sort of comment usually stimulates enough curiosity to get everyone's attention. She began to explain:

> Well, say we had all been in this building that burnt down. You guys were in the back and we were in the front of the building. When the firemen came, they had to spend most of their time saving people from the front because their equipment was in the front and they couldn't get to the back. In the front, we saw how bravely they worked to save us. But you in the back only saw one or two firemen trying to help without doing much good. We were all in the same burning building, but we had different experiences and ended up with different opinions about how helpful the firemen were. Those of us in the front

would argue until we were blue in the face that the firemen did everything they could, and you guys would think they hardly helped at all. But we would both be right.

This story shifted the group members' perception of the disagreement, and they began to examine the idea that they were both right. Told well, a story can shift the climate of the group. As a facilitator, you will probably use lots of stories in the climate-setting stage, but you might want to consider using a story as an intervention as well. I've used this story many times and it works much, much better than a more explicit intervention.

Chapter 14 on storytelling offers advice on when, where, and how to use stories.

BRINGING IT TO CLOSURE

You just seem to know when dialogue is over. The people in the group know, too. Something has usually shifted for them and there is a sense of satisfaction with a "job well done." When you begin to get that sense, it is time to bring the dialogue to closure.

After two hours or so, the group is probably exhausted with the rigors of genuine dialogue. It is time to put the day-to-day norms back in place, to put their guards back up a bit, and to shift back into action mode. They need a little transition time and some sort of process to help with the transition. A set of "closing rounds" is the best way I know to wrap things up. Everyone gets a chance to say a few last words—whatever they feel will bring some closure to the experience. Sometimes I cheat a bit. I pick a starting point that will allow the most positive people to go last. Because the last words spoken tend to hang in the air, you would much prefer those words to be positive rather than negative. Every group has a pessimist. If they go first in rounds, it gives the optimists an opportunity to reframe their words for the group.

This last set of rounds can be particularly helpful in allowing group members to express their feelings to the group. Many people will have done most of their work inside their heads, so this will be a valuable opportunity to try to articulate the changes that occurred in their point of view. You may want to encourage all of the group members to restate the new thinking that occurred during the dialogue process, in order to solidify tenuous alignments.

At times you may be forced to end a session during one of the less cohesive stages of dialogue. In this situation, you have to make a judgment whether it is better to simply end the session or if it is better to facilitate a working consensus until the next dialogue session. There are times when alignment comes in stages. Use your judgment, and, if necessary, step into a more directive role and help the group participants find some agreements that protect their ability to work together.

Remind everyone that dialogue is not required for all interactions and that the agreements they made were for their dialogue sessions only. If they want to make new agreements on how they interact outside the formal process, that's great. Facilitate these agreements immediately, and it will speed the integration of dialogue skills into their informal group communications. At the same time that you help them anticipate the consequences of reentering old situations with new beliefs and attitudes, you can discuss strategies for retaining new group learning and blending their new communication norms into the "outside world."

Research shows that new beliefs are always inconsistently applied in the beginning. Help them anticipate how they will handle this situation. For instance, if the group has increased levels of trust, remind people to expect that behavior will be inconsistent initially and not to write the whole thing off just because someone backslides. Ask the group for ideas. Get everyone involved in planning ways to capitalize on the increased understanding that evolved from the dialogue.

THE BALANCE

The secret lies in the balance between structure and freedom. Dialogue could be destroyed by too much structure, yet a nonlinear, stream-of-consciousness description of how to do it will lose most of the high-performance managers in a workgroup and all of the engineers. We have to meet people where they are. To ask a group to dive into dangerous truths is asking a great deal. This unstructured structure gives some guidance but not too much, some constraints but not too many. The secret is to be mindful of every choice you make as a facilitator. The goal of your words, silence, action, and inaction is to create an environment ripe for dialogue. It is a delicate balance.

Many people who first investigate the idea of facilitating dialogue decide that it is too risky to try without further preparation. I encourage that level of caution. Dangerous truths can disrupt the status quo to the point where people can get hurt. Not all organizations will welcome the opportunity to face their conflicts, no matter how much creativity you might release.

Still, some facilitators are definitely better than others in helping the toughest group reach dialogue safely. What is it that makes these facilitators so good? The next section is devoted to examining seven facilitator skills that seem to make the difference.

PART 3

Building Blocks: Seven Basic Facilitator Skills

Chapter 9

Taking the Pulse of the Group

The great enemy of the truth is very often not the lie—deliberate, contrived, and dishonest—but the myth—persistent, persuasive, and unrealistic.

JOHN F. KENNEDY

One of the differences between training and facilitation is that training assumes a transfer of skill and knowledge and facilitation assumes an awakening of skill and knowledge. To facilitate dialogue is to facilitate the awakening of a group, so group members may discard counterproductive habits that hamper their innate capacity to learn, develop, and co-create. How many different methods exist to wake someone up? How do you wake up your spouse? Your kids? Your parents? It depends, right? My dog is the sweetest animal in the world, but if he is dead asleep and you accidentally brush your foot anywhere near that long greyhound monkey-tail of his, he turns into Cujo for about three seconds. Just long enough to scare the bejesus out of whoever was unfortunate enough to decide they wanted to pet "the sweet doggy."

If you think of your job as awakening a group, then how you go about it will depend on what is going on within the group at the time (i.e., how asleep are they?). The trick is to develop your skills in reading the vital signs of the group. Understanding the group's current frame of mind helps you modify your approach. Just as you would use different wake-up tactics in different situations—a gentle nudge for an elder, all the way to a cop's whistle for the kids—you adapt. If you want a group to wake up and smell the coffee, it helps to know if they like coffee.

117

Before you do anything, you need information about why these people are here, what they expect from you, and where their cynicism lives. Until you know these things, every move you make is a shot in the dark. You risk stepping into a hidden minefield. Understanding the mental terrain in advance gives you the ability to significantly accelerate a group's path to dialogue.

BACKGROUND MATERIAL WILL MAKE YOU GO BLIND

Invariably, when I am asked to facilitate a group to dialogue, the individual responsible for my involvement will want to send me five pounds of background material. This treatise usually includes notes from every meeting over the last three years, an organization chart du jour, several in-depth reports, feasibility studies, and other internal documents that, frankly, only distract me from what I want to know. Most of these documents have a heavy spin toward the writer's vested interests. They make everyone look terribly rational and rarely contain any dangerous truths. Even the bipartisan efforts focus on content rather than process. They don't tell me what is really going on. The information I need is not about content, but about the group's habits and norms. I need to know not "what" has been going on, but "how" it has been going on.

Your desire to do a good job may activate outdated "success" routines in your mind. For instance, in order to feel prepared, you may feel compelled to study as you would to properly prepare for semester exams. It is natural to want to be on top of things. In fact, the group will make judgments on your credibility based on your grasp of the "facts." If you don't know the name of the product they launched last year, it will cost you credibility points. So you need to know the basics, but loading yourself down with too much data is dangerous.

Reading too much background material can predispose you to develop opinions on what decisions you believe are best for this group. If you have an opinion on which way they should go and what they should do next, it will be difficult for you to maintain the objective, nonjudgmental position necessary to facilitate dialogue. Besides, this content-focused data takes up valuable space in your brain where you should be filing information about the "process" habits of this group. You need to discover the habits, patterns, and myths that lock this group into predictable thought loops. Of course, before they tell you anything, they will want to know a bit about you, first.

WHO ARE *YOU?*

To succeed in discovering the hidden habits of the group, you need credibility. From the first mention of you and this process, everyone in the group will begin developing an opinion about both. They will believe either that you have something to offer or that you are going to waste their time. In most organizations, it is safe to assume that a significant proportion of people believe you will waste their time. Until those people change their minds, you can't do your job.

They need to trust you before they will tell you about their history or let you anywhere near their dangerous truths. Trust is a topic big enough to warrant another book. However, I believe you already know enough about trust. You only need to use what you know. To be trusted, you must visibly demonstrate your trustworthiness. Sure, there are lots of tricks and techniques to build rapport and trust. But you can't rush trust. In fact, rushing trust often has the opposite effect. We live in a post-Dilbert world. Dogbert is the enemy. Consultants are labeled as witch doctors. That "touchy-feely crap" is eyed with suspicion. One business magazine even has a regular section to debunk consultants. In this environment, there is more to be gained by not rushing it and not using slick trust-building techniques. You need only return to the basics.

To trust you, people need to first know who you are. Tell them. If people don't know you, they can't trust you. Share more about who you are than what you have done. Trust requires familiarity, and familiarity is built by sharing more than the superficial details. Share something about your personal values when you introduce yourself to a group. For instance, I always make it clear to a group that I would like to operate not as an expert but only as a mirror, so they may see themselves better. I explain that some of the sequencing has been designed to have a psychological effect and could be interpreted as manipulative, but that I will make these tactics as transparent as possible to them and will always defer to their judgment. To look someone in the eye and mean what you say builds more trust than all of the NLP, rapport building, and rope-a-dope tactics put together.

In the spirit of dialogue, allow me to highlight an assumption. I have a strong bias against the expert model of facilitation/consulting. I believe that, for the purposes of facilitating dialogue, taking the role of the expert is disrespectful to the group and, worse, sabotages the group members' ability to tap into their own wisdom. If you act like the expert, your group is much more likely to escape into either dependence or fighting. It will encourage participants to lean on your facilitation so much that they don't develop their own skills, or it encourages them to react against you—possibly using you as a lightning rod for their frustrations. A little humility goes a long way.

Yet, your role demands that you offer something to the group. Otherwise, why are you there? The goal is to balance an awareness of your expertise on process with deference to the group's expertise on who it is and what it needs. Both are equally valuable. The difficulty is that gathering data and taking the pulse of the group can pull you toward the expert role. As long as you are aware of that, you stand a better chance of resisting the urge to act like an expert. With that caution, let's look at what data you need and how you gather it.

PROCESS, NOT CONTENT

If you aren't going to study the pile of background material (although I do suggest you skim it), then how do you find out what is going on? Where is the evidence for process? What is it that you need to know?

You want to know the current norms and habits used to avoid conflict and the communication habits that operate to prevent dialogue. Contrary to a traditional gap analysis, you are more interested in what needs to be removed than what needs to be added. Any group of human beings intuitively knows how to dialogue—the problem comes when other habits get in the way. What are those other habits? Like the sculptor who chips away everything that doesn't look like his goal, you are looking for communication habits that do not look like dialogue so that the group can chip them away.

Before you begin dialogue, take the opportunity to have a few one-on-one conversations. You may even want to set up formal interviews. Initially, private conversations will be the best time to probe for counterproductive patterns. You can ask questions such as, "How is negative feedback handled in this group? When someone needs to give bad news about inferior work or outside events, how is it usually delivered and received?" Ask for a few examples and the patterns will become clear. While there are many variations, most organizations have a few basic themes. Some common themes include groups that pretend there is nothing wrong, play the blame game, discredit the source, blow up and storm out, shoot the messenger, or break into factions. Themes usually follow one of the group avoidance strategies (flight, fight, pairing, or dependency).

Ask about conflict. If you discover that resources are clearly allocated in senior meetings only to be reallocated by middle management based on the "possession-is-nine-tenths-of-the-law," rule then that may give you a clue about the senior group's tendency to use politeness and pretending for superficial solutions. Or do they have a habit of brawling? There are certain macho industries, such as the construction industry, where norms redefine a genuine question as a sign of weakness. When you know that sort of thing before you go in, you can either adapt your style or call this assumption into question. If you find out that a group uses code speak to avoid open conflict, you can take another tack—maybe use a few code-speak words yourself.

What is the level of trust in the group? You can ask this question either individually or anonymously as a group. Sometimes I ask group members to anonymously rate their level of trust (from 1 to 100) on an index card and pass the cards to the front. I shuffle them to protect anonymity and read the numbers out loud. This is a real-time self-awareness exercise. When the numbers run around 30 percent to 70 percent (as is the case most of the time), it stimulates the group's desire for dialogue and prompts attention to trust-building factors. In addition, it gives you an indication on how much time you need to spend up front to build enough temporary trust to achieve dialogue.

This is a rich exercise. For instance, if everyone rates the trust level in the 90 percent range, then you may have a group in denial (I wish that weren't so, but it has been true in my experience). If almost everyone rates the trust level at 90 or above and one person rates it 15, you can be pretty sure that you have at least one person in the group actively circulating a resume. If you pay attention, soon enough you will know who that person is. Once you know, your facilitation style can help prevent scapegoating and protect what little diversity is visible in the group.

You may also want to use this exercise to "read" the level of coherence within the group. Once people in a group understand the concept of coherence, they can use it as a self-diagnostic tool. How aligned, how closely connected are they? Are they fractured or tightly unified? They can rate coherence, like trust, on a scale of 1 to 100 on pieces of paper anonymously passed to you. By the way, these numbers don't mean anything. They aren't statistically significant and they aren't theoretically valid. Using numbers simply gives you and the group a language to talk about the invisible. When a group hears that the average rating of coherence is less than 50 percent, group members begin to wonder what that means. Wondering takes them a step closer to dialogue.

These conversations do more than gather data. They begin a powerful process of self-awareness. Answering these questions turns people's attention to reflect on their own beliefs and habits around conflict, negative feedback, trust, and coherence. This attention alone will operate to alter old patterns. The data is almost a bonus you can use to tailor your setup design to target the habits of the group. Even though most of the data is gathered before the process, you want to keep the lines open during the process as well.

HELL-L-L-O-O-O?

If you aren't connecting with the group, for heaven's sake, stop and find out why. They will usually tell you. When the people in the group, for some reason, have decided that this process is dangerous, stupid, wasteful, or whatever, they can't hear half of what you are saying. It doesn't matter what you say—they translate it through a filter of judgment. You can't facilitate a group that isn't listening to you. If you sense a disconnection, stop talking and start asking questions.

This may sound obvious, but I can't tell you how many facilitators I see launch right into their spiel without first understanding a group's attitudes and perceptions. Maybe they get nervous or are so attached to their agenda that they think it won't matter—but it does matter. The very act of taking the time to check in with the group builds trust, models inquiry, and lets you know where the minefields are.

I remember one group that hated the word *dialogue*. Of course, I didn't know that when I began. No one told me. But I could sense that we weren't connecting. When I checked in, I found out that a year ago these same people had spent two unpleasant days with a consultant who used the word in a way that left them with strong negative connotations. If I hadn't taken the time to ask, I wouldn't have found out, early on, that I needed to either find another word for this process or diffuse the old negative perceptions. I took the pulse of the group and found their blood pressure was skyrocketing.

Armed with that knowledge, I abandoned my agenda and asked them to tell me everything they hated about those two days. (Note that I did not try to convince them that "this time is different." I began asking questions.) Their answer naturally formed itself into a list of "don't wants." So I skipped ahead and began a process that I call the "wants/don't wants process." (See the Appendix.) When the group members had vented all their frustrations, I began the "wants" part of the process. I asked them, "What would you have wanted to happen instead?" and then had them make a list. Once they developed the list of what they did want, I could point to their list and say, "Can we develop a new definition of dialogue that means doing this (pointing to the wants) and not doing that (pointing to the don't wants)? Would you invest time in doing that?" We reconnected and took off from there.

If I had plowed through without taking the pulse of the group, I would not have gotten very far. If I had taken the pulse and ignored what I discovered, it would have been worse. Taking the pulse of the group isn't so much a skill of being a good discoverer as it is a skill of reacting appropriately to what you discover.

FLEXIBILITY

The purpose of taking the pulse of the group is to change what you are doing or how you are doing it so that it works better for the group. You need to meet the group members "where they are," even if that means scrubbing the whole day. I try to always remember that every group has the option of choosing *not* to dialogue. Either they will exercise that option openly, or they will passively resist by shutting down or pretending to dialogue. If they don't want to dialogue, they won't. Remembering this fact prevents me from turning this process into just another cattle chute that squeezes people into faking it so they can make their escape.

This may be one of those weird paradoxes of facilitation, but it seems that opening the door to leave makes the group want to stay.

I've never had to abort the process. I have, however, had to delay it considerably while we dealt with negative perceptions, fears of retribution, and sources of apathy. I didn't always want to delay. Sometimes we had lunch waiting (by the way, try to arrange a cold lunch for the first day of dialogue). Sometimes it would mean dropping big chunks of content from the setup. It may have even meant I wouldn't get to tell some of my best stories. Yet the goal was for the group members to reach genuine dialogue, not for me to do it the way I wanted to do it.

More than once the dialogue has turned into a dialogue about dialogue. That's fine. For the first run, any subject that allows group members to practice seeing judgments, questioning assumptions, developing curiosity, and taking responsibility for their choices works. A group that spends two hours exploring which truths are dangerous in its culture is one step closer to addressing those truths.

Your flexibility will not be limited to responding to the barriers preventing dialogue. Yes, it is important to watch for the barriers and respond to them, but there is something more important to watch out for. You want to be ready to change on a dime once you discover the most valuable piece of information about the group—what is important enough to warrant the time and effort required for dialogue.

FIND THEIR DESIRE

Too many facilitators assume that their job is to reach a particular outcome. That is a trainer's job, not a facilitator's job. A facilitator cannot reach an outcome—only the group can do that. You are a coach. Since you can't inject a group with motivation, you have to find the group's intrinsic motivation. For any group, there is something compelling enough to warrant the investment of time and effort. Your job is to help the group discover that compelling shared passion. If the group doesn't articulate some pretty compelling "wants" during the wants/don't wants process, you may want to massage the discussion until group participants discover a compelling reason to continue.

For some groups, it is simply a desire to stop pretending everything is just fine. Every group has a passion that connects the people in the group. You need to help them find it. A group of volunteers lost in petty disagreements, and then rapidly retreated into apathy, found new energy when they began to dialogue about why they volunteered in the first place. You may discover an old injustice that seems irrelevant to the present situation but holds lots of energy and has been the source of many misunderstandings. Start there. When people start leaning forward and paying attention, read that response and explore it. The group needs a compelling reason for dialogue. The reason may not look like a business topic, but if it has an emotional charge, it will almost always yield a dialogue that produces valuable results.

Resist the urge to give a reason. They must discover their own reasons for themselves. Remember you are taking the pulse of the group, not giving it mouth-to-mouth. They are alive in there—somewhere deep down, maybe—but there is aliveness. Once they touch it, dialogue is an almost natural response. Any group will be drawn to touch and feel this aliveness by exploring it together. To know and be known is a powerful urge. When the barriers are cleared, groups with a common interest inevitably want to dialogue. We all seek community.

If you are willing to get psychological about it, we simultaneously need dialogue and are afraid of it. Taking the pulse of the group gives you clues about what will help group members to overcome their fears and tap into their hopes. Uncovering the collective hopes and fears of a group requires that you keep a respectful distance. Otherwise, you run the risk of confusing your hopes and fears with theirs. The best skill to help you avoid this pitfall is to learn to take responsibility to not take responsibility.

Chapter 10

Taking Responsibility to Not Take Responsibility

Delight at having understood a very abstract and obscure system leads most people to believe in the truth of what it demonstrates.

G. C. LICHTENBERG

As a facilitator of dialogue, your responsibility is to get group members to take responsibility for themselves and their choices about how they talk to each other. It is not your direct responsibility to get them to tell the truth. Nor is it your direct responsibility to get them to see their judgments or to examine their assumptions. Those choices are theirs to make, not yours. It is not even your responsibility to get them to make new choices. Your only responsibility as their facilitator is to create an opportunity for them to be aware of the choices they are choosing. If you think this is mumbo-jumbo, psychobabble, I entreat you to hang with it for a minute. Splitting hairs on this particular issue is worth the effort. It is probably the most important and hardest-to-achieve skill (definitely hardest to explain) that I have ever learned in my years as a facilitator. Maybe because it is hardest to swallow. It goes against everything our culture ever taught us about accountability and responsibility.

RETOOLING BASIC EXPECTATIONS

Workgroups in our Western culture seem to walk into a facilitated group meeting with certain expectations. Most groups expect the manager or consultant in the front of the room to lead some undetermined process that has been designed to make them more productive so the organization will make more money. There are certain fundamental assumptions associated with that scenario. The "leader" is going to "do" something "to" the group that is designed to stimulate a desired response. The process is assumed to be for the organization's good first and for the individual's good second, if at all. And more often than not, the assumption of most participants is that no matter what happens, nothing significant is going to change for the better, anyway.

Even those who still hope for a good outcome ("I just love this team-building stuff") are waiting for you to "do" something "to" them. They sit and wait for you to do your thing. At the end of the day they will grade you on some hidden checklist or hard copy "happy sheet" as to how well you did your job and whether or not you got them anywhere. If you focus your efforts on acing an evaluation form or hidden checklist, you will miss your opportunity to facilitate dialogue.

Dialogue doesn't work that way. The traditional role where you as the facilitator are responsible for "doing" something "to" the group sabotages the process. In fact, all of those assumptions are counterproductive to the process of dialogue, but the most dangerous one is that most of the responsibility lies with the facilitator. You need to radically shift expectations about who is responsible for this process early in the day. For this to work, group members have to take responsibility. For a successful process the monkey needs to be transferred from your back onto theirs. This is not shirking responsibility. Anyone who has ever tried it knows that it takes more work to get people to do something than just doing it yourself. You want them to collaborate in doing it together rather than waiting for you to do "it" to them. But how?

CREATING A VACUUM OF RESPONSIBILITY (OR SUCKING THEM IN)

Two objects cannot occupy the same space at the same time. If you are sitting in the chair of responsibility, then no one else can sit there. For me, getting group members to take responsibility for their process starts there. That chair must be empty. If I sit there—if I take responsibility for them—then the implicit message is that they don't have to. So up front, I always say, "I will not take responsibility for your success or failure to reach dialogue. I am willing to leave here having accomplished nothing." This always creates furrowed eyebrows, sideways glances, and suspicious looks.

It is an overstatement. The truth is that I embrace a deep sense of responsibility for their success, but I have learned that I have to downplay my feelings of responsibility to give them room to take the reins. I don't ever release the reins completely, but I try to move my focus back and concentrate purely on my responsibility to create opportunities for them to take responsibility. At critical junctures, I leave the ship seemingly captainless so they will feel an urgency to take the helm. Stepping away from the controls may be the most risky part of facilitating dialogue. But it is unavoidable.

If you as a facilitator take 100 percent responsibility, then you run the risk of trying to do it for them. You can't, of course, but that won't stop a facilitator with an overactive sense of responsibility from trying. There is a question of respect here, too. Many of us have experienced a group (or two) that acted like a bunch of children instead of a group of adults. I hear about it all the time. "They act like eight-year-olds." After a while we tend to coordinate our actions to fit those experiences. It never occurs to us that those experiences might have been generated because we were acting like a parent! In other words, we might have been the cause of their childish responses. Instead, we tend to operate from the basic assumption that a tight agenda and clear structure are the best way to prevent a group process from "getting out of hand."

Dialogue will not emerge from a tight agenda and a clear structure. There isn't enough room. It is like trying to build a ship within an office building. You can't, without knocking down the structural walls. Our traditional dependence using structure and agenda to "control" the group process encourages us to think it is our responsibility to bring structure and agenda to a group in order to facilitate the outcome. Dialogue turns that upside down. Your responsibility is to remove walls, agendas, and thought structures/patterns. The best you can do is to prepare the group to accept this increased uncertainty and then abdicate responsibility yourself so that the members of the group may collectively take up the mantle.

What do you think will happen when you don't take responsibility for their outcome? When you don't act like a parent? When you don't give clear structure and an agenda? Despite your impulse to answer that the result will probably resemble your worst nightmare, my experience is that any group (with the proper preparation) usually steps up to the plate and is well equipped to do so. But you will never know that for sure until you try it. Group members can't take responsibility if you don't give them room and time. It may take awhile, but if you have laid the groundwork, the very act of removing yourself from the position of responsibility creates a vacuum that sucks them right in to that space.

The downside is that you invariably have to swallow your anxieties about everything going to hell in a hand basket.

HELPING THINGS "GET OUT OF HAND"

Facilitators newly introduced to this style of process are always worried that things will "get out of hand." I want to ask: Get out of whose hands? Your hands? The group's process shouldn't be in your hands. It should be in the group's hands. Besides, creativity is all about letting things get out of hand. It is our desire to keep things under control (reductionistic thought) that sabotages our ability to think big picture, to think creatively, and to allow new paradigms to emerge.

Dialogue is a mad scientist's thought experiment. It is a cocktail mix of minds, beliefs, and opinions given the opportunity to react together and produce a completely unpredictable result. Creativity and unpredictability are a package deal. Learning and uncertainty are also a package deal. As a facilitator, your ability to stimulate dialogue and your willingness to let things get out of hand—another package deal.

For it to work, you have to be willing to let it fail. This is a genuine paradox. This single issue frequently prevents even the most skilled facilitators from introducing dialogue to a group. Yet, you have undoubtedly experienced in your own life the common wisdom that truly great leaps in development and learning almost always require a leap of faith. To achieve exceptional results, we have to risk exceptional failure. As a facilitator, I experience this as a test of faith. My gut tightens up every time I finish the setup and the rules process and hand the reins over to the group. Inevitably, things feel out of hand because they are—out of my hands, anyway. The good news is that every time I facilitate dialogue, I learn to trust "their" hands more and more.

DON'T BECOME A LOAD-BEARING WALL

Much of our training in facilitation and managing process concentrates on tools to mold and guide a group's thought process. These are good tools to have. Traditional group process has its place, certainly. It helps us think "in step." For instance, most volunteer committee meetings run much, much better with a decent facilitator and an agenda. Total quality management (TQM) quality tools that help us think together, like the Pareto process or fishbone diagram, are wonderful tools that we as facilitators can use to link minds in a collective inquiry process. There are great decision-making tools that optimize the rational analysis of several viewpoints and produce a decision most people can live with. All of these tools are designed to enable a facilitator to perform a vital function for the group.

However, the goal of facilitating dialogue is to transfer the skills of collective reasoning into the minds and habits of the group. The more you help, the more dependent the group becomes on your help. You run the risk of becoming a load-bearing wall as the group develops new habits of dialogue. As the group takes its initially wobbly steps without you, your brain may scream for you to step in and "do something." If you do, it cheats the people in the group of their opportunity to learn how, without you. Maintaining such an extremely nondirective position is an exercise in self-discipline (and trust). It helps to know your weaknesses in terms of wanting to jump in.

BEING A GOOD LIFEGUARD

Once the group begins to dialogue, taking responsibility to not take responsibility means minimizing your interventions. Interventions sometimes come from an overactive sense of responsibility to help the group "get there" or to save it from imagined dangers.

Facilitating is similar to being a lifeguard. I remember when I was a kid and learning new strokes in swimming class, I particularly wanted to learn how to do the butterfly stroke. It looked so graceful and dolphin-like. I wanted to swim like that. I wasn't very good at it, though. The trick seemed to be to splash my arms down hard enough to get my head above water and breathe before my foot stroke took me under again. One day I was diligently practicing my butterfly stroke, splashing and gasping, and the poor lifeguard took one glance and was convinced I was drowning. He threw his hamburger to the side and, with a pickle still hanging from his mouth, jumped in to save me. Embarrassed does not begin to describe my feelings. The more I struggled, the tighter his arm held me as he dragged me to the side of the pool. I never tried the butterfly stroke again in public and still don't know how to do it. Some facilitators act like that lifeguard when they facilitate. They've got a hair-trigger impulse to intervene.

If you are a smoother, if you don't like conflict, then your challenge will be to resist the urge to jump in and rescue the group. Make no bones about it; sometimes dialogue can be painful. Sometimes conflicts that have festered for years come out into the open and people reveal some pretty hurtful assumptions. When this happens, the air fairly crackles with emotional intensity. An overactive sense of responsibility will zero in on some "victim" in this drama that you need to jump in and protect. If you do that, you mess up their dialogue and their chance to learn.

If you jump in at the point when group members have an opportunity to redesign their beliefs (replace old hurtful assumptions with more realistic, more tolerant assumptions), at best you factor yourself into the redesign; at worst you prevent it. A redesign of beliefs created without your Good Samaritan efforts will be more stable and will more powerfully affect future behavior. The secret is to trust people to take care of themselves. If you take care of them as if they couldn't or wouldn't do it for themselves, it is disrespectful. To act as if they can't "handle it" is to make them small. It is a subtle reframe, but it is an important one: To not protect a group members from the pain of dialogue is to take responsibility to help them grow and develop.

People struggle with this one. I struggle with this one. In the beginning, it is usually better to intervene less rather than more. If you stay quiet, you will get an opportunity to see for yourself how magnificently people rise to the occasion.

Now, if you like the stimulation of conflict, your problem won't be stopping yourself from saving people from conflict but limiting how often you stir things up. We assertive types want the conflict on the surface as soon as possible. It helps to remember that any group's decision to reveal what it keeps hidden or not is the members call. Pushing only increases resistance or their sense of dependence on you. If you have done a good job on the setup, then you have provided ample opportunity for group members to peel back politeness and pretending and reveal their underlying assumptions. They will do this in their own time. This might mean next week when you are not around. The process of dialogue often yields results long after the formal process. As the facilitator, you don't always get to be there for the good parts.

It requires discipline to allow things to unfold in their own time. More than likely you will have inside information, or you know of a major dangerous truth that they are avoiding. If you step in too early with a question that is some version of "Does anyone else see that the emperor is as naked as a jaybird?" then you might blow it.

A good lifeguard doesn't keep someone from learning how to swim or push people into the deep end. You want to push a bit, but you can't rush it. Despite our desire to accelerate a group's sense of personal responsibility, it all starts with letting the group take responsibility for its own timing.

THE CULTURE OF DEPENDENCE

One of the biggest challenges in the next wave of our social development will be a shift from a culture of dependence to a culture of interdependence. The culture of dependence permeates our organizations to the point where people assume this is just the "way things are." Culture is like that. It seems inevitable. The very fact that you are reading this book means that you are seeking ways to change the culture of your organization, but I encourage you to examine first how that culture has affected you. I don't believe we can teach anything we haven't learned for ourselves. Before you attempt to facilitate dialogue, it might be a good idea to find a like-minded soul willing to dialogue with you on how this culture of dependence may have affected your own assumptions. For instance, what assumptions do you hold about change? What can change and what can't?

If you are convinced that people don't want to take responsibility, or that senior management won't let them, you are caught up in the very culture of dependence you want to change. Both of those

assumptions are based on the paradigm of a centrally controlled patri-
archal or a hierarchical system. Both assumptions will corrupt your
ability to facilitate dialogue. It is currently true that most existing
organizations are designed on this basis. But to jump to the conclusion that they will always be organized on this basis is a leap up the
ladder of assumptions.

Dialogue is a process designed to produce a culture of interdependence. It will tend to disrupt the culture of dependence and it
definitely subverts hierarchy. Which is why, I assume, you are interested in it. For all of our talk about how we want everyone to take
responsibility, we rarely talk about what the costs might be or what
that means to those who were previously in charge. Most facilitators
are burdened with unexamined assumptions firmly anchored in the
culture of dependence. In the old kinds of group process, the facilitator was in charge. With dialogue, not only are you not in charge, but
you must consciously commit to stay that way.

When assumptions about who is in charge remain unexam-
ined, there are two levels of risk. If you deep down believe that people
can't or won't change things, then you will not demonstrate enough
confidence to engage the group. When you don't think things will
get better, it shows. If you don't think a group wants to take responsibility, it shows—you will encourage too much dependence on you
and your leadership. There are no leaders in dialogue. This means you.
To break out of the culture of dependence is the greatest challenge we
face in facilitating dialogue. Even when we embrace new assumptions, our systems are littered with accountability methods that support the culture of dependence.

ACCOUNTABILITY OF ANOTHER KIND

When first faced with this concept, many traditional facilitators
think, "My organization/clients will never go for this. They expect me
to be accountable—getting them there is my job," or "They will
throw me out of the room if I waltz in telling them I'm not responsible." Maybe so, but if you haven't tested that assumption, you can't be
sure. The secret is in how you say it.

No piece of this process can make sense without looking at
the whole. To assess the principle of "taking responsibility to not take
responsibility" outside of the extensive setup, the molding of expec-

tations, guiding the group to pick its own rules—that is, to consider it separately—is meaningless. You probably would get thrown out of the room if you simply told the group that you weren't taking responsibility for their success.

Yet, considered in the context of the whole process, this particular skill requires a higher level of accountability than any checklist can measure. To take responsibility to create an environment of willing uncertainty is much harder than creating an environment of certainty. In our current culture, you don't usually get as many pats on the head for creating uncertainty. Even when organizations say they want it, success is hard to measure.

The standard post-process "happy sheets" aren't suited to measure the success of a process like dialogue. Frequently, people don't feel happy after dialogue. They may not have enjoyed the process. You and I know from experience that learning ain't always a bowl of cherries. I sometimes wish our evaluation forms could rate things such as, "Did you discover that you were wrong about something or someone?" Or better yet, "Are you leaving confused?" For some people, being confused is definitely a step in the right direction!

Current systems of accountability frequently undermine our ability to stimulate genuine learning or creative thinking. You probably already know that. I'm not going to gripe about it here. I'd rather talk about solutions. Whatever environment you enter will have certain basic assumptions about accountability. I would suggest that you have a one-on-one dialogue with the highest-level person you can access and discuss an alternative measure of accountability. It helps to have the support of someone important when you do this work.

People who don't understand the process might look at the end of the first day and think it was a big failure. They may have wanted resolution and instead got a better view of an unresolvable conflict. People who understand dialogue have no problem with the fact that dialogue can be disturbing, disruptive, and even painful. They realize that it requires an accountability of another kind—an accountability that recognizes when a step back is really a step forward.

One of your best strategies for protecting your position on not taking responsibility will be your ability to deliver successful mind-sets and preempts.

Chapter 11

Mind-Sets and Preempts

He who wishes to teach us a truth should not tell it to us, but simply suggest it with a brief gesture, a gesture which starts an ideal trajectory in the air along which we glide until we find ourselves at the feet of the new truth.

José Ortega y Gasset

The use of mind-set and preempt is the cornerstone of the dialogue process presented in this book. The entire setup is full of mind-sets and preempts. I use them in all of my work in one form or another. You can use preempts and mind-sets to facilitate dialogue, to facilitate training, to facilitate your spouse in taking out the garbage without being asked, or anywhere you need to improve communication. It is the tactic of encouraging behavior away from (preempt) or toward (mind-set) a particular direction "before the fact." To give you enough background so that you can play with these ideas on your own, let me share some of the contributing pieces that have influenced my use of preempts and mind-sets.

THEORY OF DISSIPATIVE STRUCTURES

I was introduced to the Theory of Dissipative Structures back in 1987 in Australia. My introduction to the theory occurred during an informal dialogue with a friend, aided by notebook paper and a pen. I've since learned that this theory was developed by Ilya Prigogine, who has written extensively on the subject (most of which I don't understand). Yet his theory (or my understanding of it) has informed much of my work. You can see it clearly in the five-stage model of dialogue described in Chapter 3.

Basically, the theory says that a stable system (i.e., a belief system) will continue to loop through a predictable pattern until disturbed by some external force. Once disturbed, it becomes unstable and thus adaptable. In the case of a belief system, this destabilizing force might be disconfirming data, contradictory experience, a meaningful conversation, or some other disturbance. When any of these forces disturbs the system, it will dissipate into a state of instability (chaos), seek to reorganize itself (discarding and redefining) into a higher-order system (resolution), and finally develop into a new equilibrium (closure). That means our thought patterns continue along predictable patterns until something shakes things up enough so that our minds must create new patterns to incorporate whatever disconfirming data it was that shook our system up.

For instance, a product development team believes that it is smart to withhold information from marketing—for team members, this is a stable belief system. They believe that if they tell marketing anything, marketing will turn it all backwards, prematurely tell customers, and make a big fat mess of customer expectations. Constant requests to share information go in one ear and out the other, until the manager of product development hears directly from a customer that the company lost a sale because the customer received conflicting information from the two departments. If the manager is open to that new piece of information (i.e., if he doesn't fly into his "marketing is full of idiots" tirade), it disconfirms his "treat 'em like mushrooms" belief system. At that point the manager may then develop a new belief system that makes distinctions about sharing at least some kinds of information with the marketing department—maybe not all information, but more than before. The product development manager reorganizes his belief system into a more sophisticated system that incorporates a new if-then routine. The new belief system develops in response to the information that demonstrated the old belief system wasn't working (i.e., the lost sale).

When you use this model of learning, it becomes very clear that the trick is to safely facilitate a disturbance of current beliefs and norms. Belief systems are difficult to destabilize. Adult learning is more often a function of "unlearning" (i.e., destabilizing old thought patterns) than learning. Yet, the mind automatically acts to protect equilibrium by deflecting disconfirming data or any other disturbance. We like being right so much that we will ignore, discount, or attack any information or experience that threatens our current world-view. People have a powerful arsenal dedicated to defending current beliefs. To get past this arsenal you need to lay the groundwork—to build a path through the resistance. Mind-sets and preempts help you prepare the ground so that belief systems are more receptive to productive disturbance.

Since our belief systems evolve only as a result of incoming feedback, why not accelerate our own development? The entire process of dialogue is just that. People get together in a room and use the input from diverse perspectives to create a bit of useful instability in their minds so they can evolve their belief systems a notch higher up the levels of understanding. As a facilitator of dialogue, your job is to help the group stay open to these productive disturbances and, second, to stay mindful as it construct its new beliefs. To help a group stay open, I recommend that you use a series of mind-sets and preempts as a before-the-fact tactic to distract participants' ego defense systems from mindlessly protecting existing beliefs as iron-clad reality. You help them stay open by reminding them of how they tend to close things down.

GIVING EGO A JOB

The ego likes to be right. Dialogue is a process where participants discover that they are wrong as often, if not more often, than they are right. To accelerate the process (indeed, to allow it to occur), it is best to give participants' egos something else to do. Preempts can engage the ego in demonstrating its "power" by resisting resistance—in the form of the group and individual defensive strategies presented in the setup. When you present a list of behaviors that sabotage dialogue, it provides a menu for the goal-oriented ego. The ego now has a job: to focus on resisting the urge to pair, fight, or engage in reductionistic thinking. Some will even compete to be the most open-minded of the group. If you can't change human nature, why not work with it?

As you set the stage for the process, present the escape strategies in a way that alerts the awareness of each group member and engages their desire to avoid these pitfalls. Any group already knows, intellectually, that fighting is a waste of time. Your goal is not to point this fact out, but for the group members to resolve, as you draw the picture on the board, that "that's not going to be me!" Any group of adults in a work environment knows what they shouldn't do—the trick is to help them to remember to use what they know once their emotions get involved. You don't need to convince anyone that fighting is counterproductive; they already know. Why do they still fight? They fight because fighting is a habit. Many of our actions do not match our professed beliefs (how's the diet going?). We can believe that acting a certain way is good and yet never display these beliefs in action. The preempt is designed to tap into dormant beliefs in a way that gives them enough power to mold behavior and resist bad habits long enough to dialogue.

This concept may activate a few old assumptions. Do you believe that people really want to communicate? Do they want to face their dangerous truths? If you don't think they do, then none of this makes much sense. But if you believe that people have a deep need to face their fears and address their dangerous truths, preempts are like giving a group a cheat sheet so it can get there. Preempts mine deep, find the good intentions of a group, and pump enough attention through them to give them strength.

WITHOUT POINTING FINGERS

The material on the four group and four individual escape strategies (see Chapter 4) redefines success for the group. Ideally, presenting the models reattaches a group's natural desire to achieve away from a more traditional focus on outcome and toward a focus on developing more dialogic patterns. Current patterns and norms exert such a strong pull it takes strong preemptive messages to prevent the old counterproductive patterns. The secret is to deliver the preempt without pointing fingers at anyone.

For instance, the model you present on content/process leads the minds of all participants to focus on how they say what they say as much as what they say. Any direct comment toward one participant may put her on the defensive and let everyone else off the hook. However, a good discussion on tone that includes everyone will sink in. That message may preempt one person two hours later from using a sarcastic tone, and let another guy notice the anger in his tone in the next five minutes. When the preempt is delivered indirectly, participants are more likely to hear their tone more clearly than they might have without the discussion.

A well-told story can preempt many negative habits. If a participant thinks he recognizes himself in a story, he will be on the alert. For instance, I frequently tell a story about a charismatic manager who inadvertently dominated a group into agreeing to take an action that the group knew would fail. His charisma overpowered their willingness to disagree because they so wanted him to be right. That story delivers a message. The story is designed to help the group's leader or any of the more charismatic individuals in a group to think twice before using charisma to push their conclusions. A skillfully delivered mind-set elegantly preempts counterproductive behavior by addressing the whole system. I don't take the most charismatic guy aside, but I tell the story to the whole group. Social behaviors frequently look as if they are coming from one place, but they are part of a system. Preempts address the whole system.

Part of the magic here is that even though you don't know ahead of time which behaviors plague the group, you can bet they fall into the eight broad categories. This knowledge lets the people in the group recognize themselves according to their experiences. They know which behaviors need preempting, and they are much better placed to control these behaviors anyway. This is another instance where the traditional facilitator role is shared with the group—where you are teaching them how to facilitate themselves.

LET THEM MAKE THE CONNECTION

If you come off as critical, you lose the group. You want to deliver an informative session on the predictable defense strategies, closed-loop thought patterns, and mindless avoidance techniques—not a finger-pointing session. Ultimately the goal is to inspire creative thought, not to shut people down. It is a delicate balancing act. Criticism shuts people down. It is a matter of tone, body language, and intent. As a facilitator, your job is to conduct a tour through the gallery of behaviors and thought patterns that sabotage dialogue. Your hope is that on that tour, people will recognize themselves and their habits. They need to make their own connections. They are the only ones in charge of their thoughts and behaviors. They are the only ones who can alter their old patterns.

Resist the urge to reduce the concept of preempts down to a simple process of reverse psychology—"I bet you can't spend two hours without pairing!" The "Oh, yeah? Watch this!" response doesn't have enough energy in most adults to achieve dialogue. They aren't children (not that reverse psychology works that great on kids). Instead of a silly trick, a well-delivered preempt is designed to heighten awareness and to tap into existing good intentions. Most people seem to have an innate sense of their weaknesses in communication. Presenting a menu of eight (plus any you choose to add) predictable ways that dialogue is sabotaged usually means every person recognizes two or three maneuvers they know they practice.

You will find that during the process of selecting rules of dialogue, people choose rules perfectly suited to preempt their own most problematic communication weaknesses. You could never choose as well, no matter how much time you observed the group. Preempts support group members in facilitating themselves.

Whereas preempts help to channel the energy of a group away from escape routes and old habits, mind-sets help the group channel their energy toward the process of dialogue.

"THIS WAY ⇨ TO DIALOGUE" SIGNS

If a preempt is a DON'T GO THIS WAY sign placed at each escape route running away from genuine dialogue, then a mind-set is a GO THIS WAY sign. The five stages of dialogue make up one big mind-set designed to prepare group members to expect a certain set of events so strongly that they cause them to happen. If your first response is to brand this as manipulative, you are right. I can only say that when I use mind-sets, I generally tell the group when and how I am using them. For instance, as I talk about the stages, I explain that expecting each stage means we have a better chance of getting there. For me, the distinction between a collaborative manipulation and a clandestine manipulation makes all the difference, ethically.

A mind-set works on several levels. On the surface, it operates as a self-fulfilling prophecy, but there are other levels of impact. One of the problems we have in facilitating dialogue is that it can be an arduous journey. It is unfamiliar and can feel uncomfortable at times. Just as you wouldn't dream of taking the ladies' garden club on a hike through Nepal without a few pointers, you will want to give any group unfamiliar with the process of dialogue a few pointers.

Expecting hardship allows us to prepare mentally and thus better handle the less pleasant aspects.

One of the most important mind-sets delivered will be nested in the way you talk about the stage of discarding and redefining. This is not a fun stage. I've heard it referred to as the "groan zone." In most models of development (e.g., adult, child, emotional), there is always a stage in between what you used to "know" and whatever new knowledge you are about to gain. The in-between point is where "you don't know nothin'." In dialogue it is marked by long silences, feelings of confusion, and people talking slowly and even contradicting themselves. Without a proper mind-set, our cultural standards will cause us to label this part of the process as some sort of breakdown. Once labeled as a breakdown, the group may circumvent this necessary stage of dialogue and sabotage the process. However, when people in a group have been briefed on what to expect and what to look for, they are much more tolerant of this stage and better prepared to weather the discomfort of uncertainty. After a while they may even relish this stage.

Some groups respond to the mind-set about how valuable chaos can be by increasing their tolerance and allowing more chaos than usual. This can be useful for a group that hides in the politeness and pretending stage most of the time. Mind-set is a primary means of indirect influence available to you as a facilitator. Mind-setting is the skill of thinking ahead and saying the things that need to be said before the problems begin.

CHOOSING MIND-SETS

The mind-sets already embedded in this process include the positive intent model, content/process, the five stages, all of the metaphors, and the "go slow to go fast" model. Each of these represents a GO THIS WAY sign. As you come up with your own mind-sets to add to this list or change the list to suit your group, focus on how to best lead this group to dialogue. Your experience with the group may lead you to mind-set them around particular issues you foresee as opportunities. If the group is risk-averse, you may want to include several extra mind-sets about risk, creativity, rewards of risk, and how to reframe failures. There are an infinite number of mind-sets that can help pave the way for a group to dialogue.

You may also want to prepare the ground for your own style of facilitation. It is a good idea to think ahead and choose a few mindsets that will help build acceptance for your personality and your style of facilitation. If your style is counterculture, you may wish to avoid easily predicted reactions. An aggressive culture may label your tolerant-listener style as wimpy. A speedy culture may label a slower, more mindful style as pedantic. If you think ahead, you can counter expected negative reactions to your personal style with a good mindset.

A well-placed comment on how "mindfulness can look slow" and a story about a slow-looking but mindful decision that saved a group from a million-dollar failure can get the group members to value your "slowness" before they get a chance to label it as pedantic. Or, if you are rather direct, you may want to describe a time when people were put off at first and then appreciative of your directness since it helped them face issues they were avoiding. After a mind-set, you can even ask them which way they would prefer you act. In the previous example you might ask if they want you to be direct or indirect. If you delivered a good mind-set, most of the time they will ask you to be direct. At that point you have their permission, indeed their request, to be exactly as you are, without excuses. Later, when you are being very direct, they implicitly remember that they asked you to be that way.

No one is perfect, and you can avoid too much focus on your own imperfections as a facilitator with a few good mind-sets. If you have a soft voice, you may mention how people tell you that your soft voice helps to create an atmosphere of reflection, and so on. The goal is to shift their focus away from distractions and toward dialogue.

NOW OR NEVER

The time to deliver a mind-set is before the fact, when everyone is still speaking in the hypothetical. This is the time to stake out the signs of what to look for and what to avoid. Once you get into the middle of the process, it is usually too late to discuss these issues in any constructive way. Early on you can address them without coming off as giving advice or being overly directive. Once someone has stepped into quicksand, it is a little late to tell the group where it is. Of course, simply staking out the quicksand through a preempt doesn't mean someone won't step in it! But mind-sets and preempts set things up so that you can use the more collaborative Socratic method (detailed in Chapter 12) to help the group make corrections. When you have discussed these things up front, the group is much more receptive to your reminders.

The Socratic Method

Creativity begins with an awakening perplexity—not just the unencumbering of the conceit of knowledge but a productive state: the first stirring of creative thought.

Hugh Benson, *Essays on the Philosophy of Socrates*

We are a rebellious lot. The vast majority of us don't take kindly to anyone telling us what they think we should change. This approach is more likely to generate a belligerent, "Oh yeah, who made you king for a day?" rather than the desired, "Thank you, wise one, tell me more." It is human nature. We value our own discoveries more than the discoveries of others. When group members persist in escaping the hard work of dialogue, directly pointing it out cheats them of the opportunity to see it for themselves—not to mention that it sets you up as a lightning rod for their frustrations. The Socratic method is an important tool for you as a facilitator to stimulate introspection and self-monitoring without giving "the answer" or generating defensive or dependent reactions. It is a powerful tool to prompt self-discovery.

The goal of dialogue is collective learning. Learning requires that we explore our ignorance and find our mistaken beliefs. Since most people have not traditionally been rewarded for saying "I don't know" or "I was wrong," you'll need to give them some help on this one.

SOCRATES—MORE THAN ONE VOICE

Socrates never wrote anything (that we know of). Apparently he thought writing was too limited whereas real conversations better stimulated true learning. The fact is, Socrates invented dialogue. At least, he was the first one on record who used the dialogue method. He consciously avoided teaching what he felt people should discover for themselves. Socrates knew that we value what we discover more highly than what is handed to us on a platter. He also knew that distasteful bits of self-awareness necessary for our development are more effective coming from the inside out.

Most of what is written about Socrates (thanks to Plato) was delivered in a dialogue format. To Socrates, learning required more than one voice, each voice coming from an individual's experience. Socrates felt learning required the interaction of human minds. The individual voices clash, bang, and eventually come to a new harmony that represents generative learning. In a way, your goal will be to generate the unholy cacophony of many wrong notes as the group seeks to find a common voice. You need to keep them singing and keep them searching even when it sounds like hell.

DON'T GIVE THEM FISH—HELP THEM LEARN HOW TO FISH

The Socratic method is the art of asking questions that inspire learning. With the Socratic method you do not teach a solution but instead help the individual or group reach a solution. One of the goals of the dialogue process is for the group to develop the skill of thinking collectively. Many people are out of practice in thinking, much less thinking collectively. Through no fault of their own they were trained in a school system and then a hierarchical organization to do as they were told and to not think. Few were trained to take responsibility for their own learning. The Socratic method is a way to retrain a group to think—more specifically, it is a way for the group to retrain itself.

Thinking is hard work. When the going gets tough, people would rather you give them the answer. The group will ask you, "Are we doing it right? Tell us how to dialogue." You will frequently need to resist the urge to give your group the answer. Besides the fact that your answer will inevitably be inferior to theirs (once they begin to think as a collective), giving them the answer cheats them.

Your job is not to give the group some fish but to teach it how to fish. As a dialogue facilitator, you coax the group members to face the facts when they would rather escape into group or defensive patterns. You point out the times when they are not listening, when they are jumping to conclusions, when they are being too persuasive. In other words, you help them to see their faults. But if you do this like a teacher with a ruler, even though you may fix a problem, you have not helped the group members avoid the same problem in the future. To draw a conclusion for them may solve their current dilemma, but it does not help them solve future dilemmas. You want to coach them through the discovery process rather than do it for them.

A MIDWIFE ASSISTS

Socrates considered himself a kind of midwife. (His mother was a midwife.) He believed that people already know everything they need to know; they just need a little assistance drawing it forth. He took the metaphor even further by talking about the pain and suffering of labor. That fits with my experience. Every true dialogue includes some pain. The group is giving birth to new ideas and beliefs. You have to be okay with the pain. You don't yank the baby out too soon. Rushing kills the magic. And too much interference makes things worse. You don't force. You don't do it for them. You assist.

Traditional training treats a person like an empty receptacle to be filled from the outside with better ideas, but Socrates shows us how to tap into the creative intelligence of others. This requires us, as facilitators, to act on the belief that with the right kind of assistance people in a group will produce their own ideas and can see for themselves whether they are true or false. With that belief, assistance means asking the right kind of questions. Socrates maintained that wisdom is inside all of us and all we need to do is ask the right questions to reveal what we already know. (Once you start using the Socratic method, you will be amazed at how much smarter people become.)

EXPERIENCE IS THE BEST TEACHER

Socrates insisted that each voice speaks from experience. Much of the B.S. in group discussions develops from hypothetical examples that allow individuals or groups to distance themselves from the situation at hand. A compensation team can discuss the philosophical definition of "fair" and waste hours, flame tempers, and get nowhere until they address what would be most fair for these people, here and now.

The discipline of the Socratic method is to keep the people in the group examining themselves, their particular beliefs and assumptions, their behavior. A foray into generalized statements such as "Many people don't like the new system" can be refocused with a comment such as, "Let's look specifically at who doesn't like it and try to understand why."

Socrates was quoted as saying, "Unless you have the courage to speak freely, then the inquiry cannot proceed." Courage to speak of dangerous truths comes when the subject is about you and your life—when you have enough at stake to speak the truth. In a philosophical debate, the participants do not have enough at stake to bear the discomfort of a real dialogue—they will wander, spar, and dawdle. The Socratic method is your tool to keep people interested. It helps the group pursue intellectual advancements that have a practical application. It makes learning real.

In a group of doctors, several bitterly complained about "some people who weren't pulling their weight." The group was obviously looping back through the same conversation it always had when this issue arose. The points seemed minor, but several members displayed strong emotion. They were stuck in their complaining and were not learning anything. So I inquired, "Everyone seems to know who these people are. I wonder if you would be willing to use their names." You can imagine the silence. Eyes darted to check the climate, and the conversation picked up where it had left off as if I had never spoken. However—and this is often how it goes—two minutes later one guy burst forth, "This is stupid; we all know who we are talking about. Frank, Jeff, we are carrying around this assumption that you guys are slacking off and that has been making life hard for the rest of us." It was tense for a while, but once they addressed the specific people, they learned that not all was what it seemed. Frank and Jeff had their reasons. Once the hypothetical turned real, the doctors in this group learned new data that reframed what they were seeing. It began to make sense. Finally, they could stop looping through the same tired old argument. Whereas the abstract allowed continued conflict, moving to the specific gave the group enough grounding to explore reality and choose a new, mutual point of view.

Speaking from experience makes it personal. When the subject gets personal, boredom disappears and energy flows into the learning process. The doctors mentioned before went from blank stares, low slumps, and wandering minds to leaning forward, focused attention, and interest. Even more important is that this level of personal learning allows the learners to take credit for what is learned and "own" the learning as their discovery. Ultimately, it ensures that people walk the talk of their dialogue.

HIDING FROM REALITY

Speaking from experience not only keeps the dialogue relevant, it keeps people honest—or helps them discover what honest looks like. The goal of a Socratic question is to help people say what they really think as evidenced by their behavior. None of us completely walk our talk. But when the B.S. is high and the difference between what people say and what they do is at issue, then your Socratic questions will help the group explore this conflict. Most groups can't solve problems because each individual's spin on how he or she would like to be seen cumulatively increases the distance of their words from reality. People's desire to look good eventually takes them to the point where the entire group is working on some doctored hologram instead of the real issue.

Socrates always brought a discussion back to reality. It has been said that in a Socratic dialogue it is impossible to defend a position that is at odds with one's own behavior (i.e., impossible to B.S. your way through). This is one of the important secrets to facilitating true dialogue—asking questions that inspire the group members to compare what they say they do with what they do.

Employees in one group I facilitated had decided their boss was dishonest. You can imagine how this affected group productivity. They all felt completely justified in being dishonest right back to this woman. When asked, "Can we reassemble the chain of events that brought the group to that conclusion?" there were several instances of extenuating circumstances that reduced the brightness of the group's lily-white hats and diluted the manager's status as the villain. When a group is plagued with black-and-white thinking, there is nothing like a little dose of reality to soften up the hard-liners.

Kenneth Seeskin, in his book *Dialogue and Discovery: A Study in Socratic Method* (State University of New York Press, 1987), points out that when someone avoids the Socratic method, "the irony is that they are running away from the discovery of what they themselves really think." Irony maybe, but this is scary stuff for most people.

Introspection can be a painful process because it usually involves an awareness of our contributing culpability. Successful dialogue almost always expands each participant's sense of personal responsibility for a situation. Whereas they were once able to blame the others, we discover our interdependence and shared responsibility. This is not a fun trip. It is exciting once you get there, but the road is arduous. Most groups balk at the prospect.

Fortunately, we are attracted as well as repelled by the prospect of self-knowledge. The Socratic method teases the balance in favor of attraction over repulsion by tapping into curiosity. Self-examination can bring about the same level of exhilaration discovered by the students in the movie *Dead Poets Society*. Some people even describe dialogue as a spiritual journey. (Since Socrates said his purpose was to help a man find his soul, he would probably like that description.) Your goal is to ask questions that awaken the group's desire to brave the risks of being wrong or looking inconsistent in favor of the thrill of learning (or of discovering their collective soul).

THE WRONG QUESTIONS

Most questions aren't really questions. "Let me ask you a question" is the same as saying, "Let me take you by the hand and lead your blind ass to the truth." Most questions are really statements, accusations, or advice reshaped in an attempt to appear politically correct. These nonquestions fall smack-dab under the category of B.S.

"What did you expect?" is usually code speak for "I don't think you had a clue how it would turn out." Likewise, "How can you say that?" delivered with a touch of attitude is really an accusation that "I have just become aware of the extent to which I underestimated your stupidity." The comment "Have you tried X?" usually means "Any idiot can see you should do X."

These are not questions—much less Socratic questions. The goal of these nonquestions is not exploration. Their goal is to manipulate, convince, or bring the other guy around to your particular way of seeing things. A Socratic question has no hidden agenda. Any attachment you have to a particular outcome will corrupt your ability to ask good questions.

AWAKENING PERPLEXITY

Socratic questions invite exploration. Real questions don't come out of a box with their own matching answers. The tough part as a facilitator is that you need to be curious, too. If you as a facilitator think you know "the answer," your mind is closed and it will prevent you from asking good questions. Your goal is to awaken perplexity in the face of comforting certainty, not to introduce a new certainty to replace the current one. This is where many attempts at dialogue falter—everyone wants to convince everyone else. Your responsibility to model real questions becomes doubly important.

Curiosity and wonder are at the opposite ends of the spectrum from certainty and security. Both poles have a mighty strong pull. Sometimes it takes a damn good question to encourage a group to leave the protection of certainty in search of the unknown.

ASKING GOOD QUESTIONS

At the core, Socratic questioning is designed to help people identify their relevant assumptions and beliefs and to test them against current reality. Most people have no idea what they really believe. You may think you are a trusting person when a careful examination of your behavior reveals otherwise. Beliefs (the real ones) are hidden away in the recesses of our mind and protected by our ego. The ego realizes that changing a belief could start an avalanche of uncertainty, and one thing our egos hate is uncertainty.

Dialogue is a deconstruction and rebuilding of the group's belief systems. The fact that the group commits enough time for dialogue means the group is prepared to close shop for renovations. Good questions are a tour through the current belief structure, revealing the structural weaknesses of the current belief system. Good questions move the furniture back, pry open the drywall, and put a flashlight into the darkness. They also test the implications of new alternatives for structural integrity.

Use questions that help the individual or group articulate fundamental assumptions, such as, "Do you operate from the belief that everyone has a hidden agenda?" Or help them question the implications of their assumptions: "If you think people can't change, what behaviors does that create?" Questions can also shift perceptions to a bigger picture: "What do you think the competition hopes you will do?" Ask questions that provoke introspection. But ask the questions from a place of genuine inquiry—never believe that you already know the answer. You are simply a prompt to help the group (whose participants know more than you do about their situation) look deeper. Remember the midwife metaphor and use restraint.

FINDING THE SPIRIT OF INQUIRY

As a facilitator, your comfort level with self-examination will guide the group. Most facilitators secretly desire to be the one with the answers. Yet the Socratic method requires the questioner to continually model her own self-examination and exploration. This is hard when dialogue turns to moral issues.

Dialogue inevitably reveals underlying morals or principles. It brings people face-to-face with the necessary provisionality of their principles. Once the group is in true dialogue, no one can propose that one definition or a magical sentence will clear everything up. Abstract principles such as "We value teamwork" need to reinterpreted on a regular basis. With an infinite number of definitions, the best any group can do is choose an appropriate definition for right now.

Dialogue creates a recalibration of the group to fit the latest changes in events and environment. Whereas "sit and wait" may have been negligent one year ago, it could turn out to be wise for now. Evangelism for the continuous quality process may have been appropriate six months ago but has now reached a level of diminishing returns. To vigorously protect the R&D budget against cuts may have saved the company at one time, but it is now encouraging too much fat in the department. Your questions should invite the group to such a level of reexamination.

There is a significant benefit in admitting your ignorance— it means that you continue to search (i.e., to learn). In Plato's demonstration of the Socratic method, he elected to blatantly show the failures of each line of inquiry in full view of the reader. Here is a philosopher who straightforwardly admits he doesn't know. He values an honest failure to define something as far better than a false belief that one has it down pat. If we ever feel as if we have the Socratic method "down pat," we've got a problem (that includes me). Successful use of the Socratic method also requires that we have a profound belief in the group's ability to get there by itself.

BELIEVE THEY CAN DO IT

As a facilitator, you need to believe in the group's ability and basic good intentions. An important foundation for Socrates was that he believed no one does evil knowingly; people only do wrong acts out of faulty assumptions and beliefs. To oversimplify: A wrong action comes from wrong beliefs. The sales manager who is exploiting his employees is under the mistaken belief this action is for the good of the organization or will be for his own personal good in some way. Most people are coming to the realization that ethics not only contribute to a smooth society but to personal happiness as well. What a person thinks he wants often does not turn out to be even close to what he really wants (with new knowledge or further analysis).

Socrates would not try to point out to the sales manager his "wrong-ness." He would not see him as wrong. He would see a good person plagued with a wrong belief. To help, he would seek to prompt a journey of self-examination that ultimately proved cheating does not, in the bigger picture, make you happy, so why keep doing it?

If, as a facilitator, you fall into the trap of labeling people as wrong, you will never awaken their desire to see things differently. If you become the arbiter of ethics, you violate the spirit of inquiry. Your questions no longer communicate a level of respect. Only if you hold your judgment can you find the belief that interprets a person's action as "right" and guides the individual through a reevaluation of this belief.

When we look at thinking as a social activity, we can see that the enemies of social harmony (arrogance, conceit, and hostility) also threaten dialogue. Plato said that only when people ask and answer questions in a spirit of benevolence could a philosophical discovery be made.

AWAKEN THE DESIRE

Your goal is to ensure that group members believe that they are on the verge of a great discovery. Stoke their desires. Sometimes questions need to be interspersed with reassurance that the group is making progress. People in one group became depressed as they faced uncertainty in their ability to meet goals. Their fears and the effort to deny those fears were draining vital energy from the group's creativity, but no one wanted to be the one to admit it. When someone finally said, "I don't think we are going to get there," the resulting silence indicated that she spoke for the entire group. It made them sick to their stomachs to admit it. Of course, "it" was only a belief that seriously needed revisiting, but at that moment it became a dangerous truth to them. This happens often in dialogue.

The truth may set us free, but it frequently feels as if it might destroy us first. Why else would we avoid it? Part of the Socratic method is providing reassurance when courage is needed. The group was reassured with a simple comment, "This may be scary, but at least you are making the effort to face these issues now rather than letting yourselves fail." At that, they rejuvenated and found the energy to delve even deeper. Ultimately, they discovered corrections that prevented their failure.

This method is psychological rather than logical. Questions should help the group members embrace the idea that they don't know as much as reveal what they don't know. This is difficult. You have to believe the group has the innate ability and desire to reason. Many facilitators allow their frustration with difficult groups to turn into a belief that the group doesn't want to face problems. Once you believe the group doesn't want to learn, you cannot be an effective facilitator. When you train yourself to assume that the reasoning ability is there, then the only problem you need to address is a lack of awareness. Particularly when a group is mired in resistance, a few Socratic questions heighten awareness and can refocus attention on learning how to overcome resistance.

LET THEM DISCOVER THEIR BARRIERS

Deep down, people are not satisfied with what they think. Probe the beliefs of any group deeply enough and you will find doubt, confusion, and sometimes shame. The Socratic method is designed to take the group to the place where individuals become conscious of not meeting their own internal standards. No wonder they resist!

The resulting emotions create defensive reactions that could include sarcasm, personal attacks, apathy, and projection. No matter what you see, it is important that they recognize their own resistance. This involves the skill of staying silent. If you are babbling on, or telling people what their problem is, then you may as well dig their heels in for them. Artful facilitation means they do the self-analysis, not you.

The goal is for the group to take a close look and to see if it like what it sees. It is when they feel unsatisfied with what they see that they create an opportunity to learn. This is also the place they least wish to visit. Two hours into a dialogue with a group struggling with an abusive manager, one guy almost directly addressed the problem. He almost discussed the "undiscussable" and revealed a dangerous truth. There was a brief minute of panicked silence before the group rushed away to an inconsequential detail. After five minutes, I asked them, "Did anyone else feel like the group just opened a door into the real problem and then slammed it shut again?" There were looks of recognition across the room and someone found the courage to admit, "We are afraid to talk about it." The group then examined the source of this fear. The root cause was that the group had set a precedence of retribution that prevented open discussion. The one who spoke the truth was usually abandoned and left to fend for himself. For this group of people, examining this pattern and forging new agreements yielded a dramatic improvement in communication that eventually allowed the group to address the abusive manager.

When I asked my question, they could just as likely have looked at me with blank stares and denied it. At that point, my job would have been to stay silent and respect their decision. Any facilitator who tries to force a group to see its barriers only creates more barriers. Don't forget that before you began the dialogue, you introduced the eight common ways groups resist, so you are set up to successfully use the Socratic method.

Before the fact, group members always agree that they don't want to escape into fight or flight, so when they start doing it, you can ask questions that they, in effect, asked you to ask. Notice how the Socratic method keeps the power in the hands of the group rather than the facilitator. This is the balance of facilitation.

AVOIDING THE HEMLOCK RESPONSE

We all know the reward Socrates got for helping people learn—he was forced to drink the poison hemlock! If you want to avoid the

1990s version of hemlock, you will learn to pace your questions. People avoid dangerous truths for a reason. Part of them believes their own B.S. That part of them needs to believe it in order to maintain what may be a fragile ego or a comforting picture of the world where other people are the problem. If you, too quickly or too forcefully, invade their closely held beliefs with disturbing questions, you might stimulate a seek-and-destroy program that could get you ousted from the group.

The next chapter is about ego, which will help with tone, but for now take heed that pacing is a critical issue. Know when to back off. If you are the type of person who hates conflict, you probably won't go too far. But if you "enjoy a hearty discussion," watch out! You will need to learn how to back off when someone isn't quite ready to "go there." Trust the process enough to know that maybe, in time, they will make progress. You may not get the gratification of witnessing it, but that's not the point.

When Socrates was on trial, he likened the situation to a doctor being tried by a jury of children on charges brought by a cook. Since the doctor fed them bad-tasting medicine and the cook baked them lots of sweets and goodies, the children went with the cook. We all know consultants and facilitators who keep things smooth and light. It is a tough call when medicine is needed, but there is no need to be a martyr. The exhilaration of real dialogue is such a high that, over time, group members will embrace the Socratic method for themselves. If you get yourself killed before they figure this out, you haven't done anyone any good.

Chapter 13

Egoless-ness

The first element of greatness is fundamental humbleness (this should not be confused with servility); the second is freedom from self; the third is intrepid courage, which, taken in its widest interpretation, generally goes with truth; and the fourth—the power to love—although I have put it last, is the rarest.

MARGOT ASQUITH

Why do you want to facilitate dialogue? Take a few minutes to think about it. What draws you to facilitation and to dialogue? Why are you reading this book? For all of our good intentions to "make things better," there is a part of us that wants to be the hero who takes a group to the promised land. It could be a mild evangelism for preaching the gospel of collective wisdom all the way to a semi-delusional desire to save the world (guilty). Either way, that part of us wants to make a difference, to be a catalyst for change. Herein lies one of the subtle paradoxes of facilitating dialogue. To want to be a catalyst puts too much focus on self at the same time that it fuels our efforts.

Overfocus on self, even with the highest ideals and the best of intentions, is an expression of ego. We have all seen a facilitator with an overactive ego—lots of "I" stories, condescending explanations, smug expressions, right/wrong messages, and parent-like directives. These ego-driven behaviors alienate rather than connect. We know that. What we don't always know is that our own ego-based behaviors can be just as alienating to others yet remain totally invisible to us. Only those who keep vigil against ego evade the alienating effects of overfocus on self.

Ego isn't inherently bad. Focus on self fuels the level of effort required to facilitate a group. The drive required to study the art and

159

skill of facilitation often originates with an achievement-oriented ego need. But ego can only take us so far. Great strengths are often the source of weaknesses. Perseverance turns into bullheadedness. Gentleness translates into passivity. Ego turns into being overly directive, narrow-minded, or, Lord help us, self-righteous.

If we pay attention, we can use this strength when it helps and drop it when it doesn't. Ego gives you the confidence to take on the massive task of helping a group face dangerous truths and dialogue with courage. You need a healthy ego to even try to facilitate dialogue. But if you aren't careful, ego can also sabotage your best efforts. One of the basic skills that will help you avoid this is to understand how your ego works and when and how it will try to step in and take charge when you are in front of the room. Ultimately, I believe that great facilitators of dialogue reach a state of egoless-ness where choices are free from ego needs and focused on group needs. They become selfless, unself-conscious in its most literal meaning.

HOW TO BECOME UNNECESSARY

As a facilitator of dialogue, your goal is to make yourself unnecessary. If you enjoy being the center of attention, the two are in conflict. It is seductive to believe that you have answers those in the group don't have. More important than giving answers is modeling your trust in the group members' ability to find their own answers.

Ego trips for the well-trained facilitator are hard to spot. We are so good at helping. Often you could help a tough discussion move more smoothly—except smoothness is not the goal for this process. Frequently, you will find that you could say something that would clarify an issue much more easily than the way the group seems to be going—but easy isn't the goal. The group needs the struggle to reach a deeper understanding. "Helping" doesn't help in these situations. Every time you step into the spotlight, you interrupt the group process. Sometimes it does serve the group to intervene, but sometimes it is your ego masquerading as concern.

To facilitate a group to dialogue without you will require that you answer a few questions for yourself. First, is there any reason why you need the group to depend on you? External consultants are in a double bind of needing to keep a client and wanting to do such a good job that the client doesn't need them anymore. If you focus on billable hours, then you have a goal mutually exclusive to your goal of becoming unnecessary. It's a tough call. I don't have any answers and I'm not going to preach, but I think it is worth mentioning that a desire to be called back and the goal of becoming unnecessary dictate different behaviors.

THE SEDUCTION OF BEING IN FRONT OF THE ROOM

Ahhh! Your chance to make a difference: the opportunity to discover again that you are important, have something to offer, and can make things better. It's the challenge of leading a group of people through complexity, helping them rediscover their own wisdom, and watching the walls that divide fall away. It is so seductive to think that you can do that level of work—that you can cause a connection to happen. Be careful that you do not cross the tiny line from "We did it" into "I did it." When you are thinking "I did it" or "I'm doing it," you are in dangerous territory. Excuse me, we are in dangerous territory.

The art of facilitating dialogue differs from traditional facilitation on the major issue of "no leader." No leader means you don't lead. After the setup, your role is reduced to highlighting points for the group's awareness, modeling reflection, asking Socratic questions (that you don't know the answers to), and generally getting out of the group's way. My experience is that I must constantly battle the temptation to step in and rescue, to say something that will "move" the group members or get them to "go deeper." When I win the battle against my ego, I don't do any of those things and I sit silently. Nine times out of ten, I am bowled over by the depth, creativity, and wisdom of the group. The good news is that the more you witness the power of dialogue, the easier it gets to tell your ego to shut up and watch.

IN THE PRESENCE OF YOUR EQUALS

In dialogue there is more to be gained by helping group members tap into what they already know than by teaching them what you know. Sure, you have to use what you know to do that, but there is a subtle shift in emphasis when you constantly remind yourself that this is a smart group of people. Every group is smart. I've facilitated groups of homeless people and learned from them. I am still following a line of inquiry opened up for me by an illiterate man who had spent sixteen years in federal prisons. No matter who we facilitate, we are in the presence of our equals.

It is unlikely you can facilitate a group successfully without confidence that the participants have what it takes to engage in a successful dialogue. You need a deep respect for people in a group and for their willingness and ability to get there. If you don't believe in them, they know it. Worse, if you don't believe in them, they probably won't either. This is not something you can fake. To demonstrate genuine affection for and confidence in a group, you need to feel it on the inside.

Which brings me to a pet peeve of mine.

"Fakey" facilitators drive me nuts. We all have our little "issues" and this is mine. Those holier-than-thou, excessively spiritual, overwhelmingly deep guru-wannabes make me want to throw up. You can spot one a mile away. The worst ones have that "fake smile." Since emotion unconsciously registers on the face based on some sort of primitive coding system, facial expressions are hard to hide. If you look, it is easy to distinguish a real smile from a put-on smile. A real smile is genuine and speaks from the eyes a message of respect and affection. A fake smile is corrupted with other emotional cues. For instance, there is a specific face for disgust. The lips rise up and the nose wrinkles a bit, like a response to a bad smell. I've got an experiment for you. Find a mirror and make a face of disgust—lips and nose scrunched up—then smile on top of that. *That* is the smile you never want to have when you are facilitating dialogue. It is a fake, patronizing, "Here let me help you poor unfortunates" sort of smile.

There are other fake smiles, too. Your beliefs about a group show through no matter how well you think you hide them. If you feel the slightest scorn for a group, you would do better replacing a day of prep time with a day spent discovering something good about the people you are about to facilitate. Any level of disdain you might have for a group will corrupt your ability to communicate confidence in the group's abilities. If you think they are a bunch of greedy, self-centered opportunists, it shows. If you think they are a bunch of apathetic lay-abouts, it shows.

When you believe in a group, people will take their cue from you. Demonstrating that you think you are in the presence of your equals means listening when they speak, holding eye contact, treating questions as genuine inquiries (even if they have trip-up characteristics), and never, ever talking down to a group (or using that fake smile). The real test of your positive regard comes after the setup when your job during most of their dialogue session will be to stay silent.

BODY LANGUAGE

It is impossible to be completely silent as long as you are in the room. Your body speaks and, if your thoughts are egocentric, then your body language will send the same message. Awareness can control the messages that get out. You can be silent and still send an "I know something you don't know" body message. Smugness is not silence. Tilts of the head, raised eyebrows, and widened eyes can be louder than words. Holding your tongue isn't enough. You need to monitor your thoughts for ego messages such as "They don't get it" or "I'm going to have to step in" or "That's stupid." If these thoughts are in your brain, they are probably coming out in your body language. Your brow may be furrowed, lips pursed, or eyes widened.

Consider what your body is saying about your confidence in the group. Signs of disappointment or criticism distract a group. You can actually use your body as a facilitation tool.

After standing quietly for a long time, every move you make has the potential to become an intervention—standing up, leaning back, leaning forward, even looking out the window. Consider every move you make a message that either supports dialogue or undermines it. In this way, you can make subtle interventions. If a group is getting way off track, you might choose to casually walk over to the "escape routes" flip chart and lean against the wall to send a message. Most of the time that action will be enough of an intervention for a group to shift awareness to watch for escape-route behaviors. When a group's confidence falters, people will watch your reaction to answer their question, "Are we doing this right?" As long as ego is in check, your body language can deliver the message that you trust their opinion more than yours.

Monitoring body language takes discipline. When the group members stay in politeness and pretending for over an hour, your ego may scream, "This isn't working—save them." Yet if you can manage to keep the screaming in your head and out of your body language, you will usually find that the group self-corrects. Staying silent until the last possible moment gives you the opportunity to learn something new, such as how well the group can fix the situation without you. And in the situations where you eventually decide to intervene, you often find your ultimate intervention is different from (and better than) your first impulse. In facilitating dialogue, you can't always trust your first impulses. Frequently impulses come from the ego rather than genuine intuition.

DON'T HOLD THAT THOUGHT

At times, flashes of brilliance invade your mind and move you to speak. Even if you do not interrupt the group immediately, you hold the thought, waiting for your opportunity to share this brilliance. Leaning forward, you wait for your chance.

Trouble is, the entire time you are waiting for the right moment, you have abandoned the job of facilitating the group's next flash of brilliance. If your thought is truly brilliant, it will come again. When you let go of your brilliant flashes, you get to see that the group often finds it on its own or, more often, comes up with something much better. Ego usually craves the opportunity to make a significant contribution (i.e., to look smart, valuable, or important). Which is why ego keeps pushing you to speak. But a group in genuine dialogue is always smarter than a lone facilitator brain. If you can keep ego from trying to prove how smart, valuable, and important you are, the people in the group get to discover how smart, valuable, and important they are.

COCKINESS: AN EARLY WARNING SYSTEM

There is a difference between feeling confident and feeling cocky. Traditional training often stimulates a cocky, "I'm doing great" feeling. Since training and motivational speaking depend on the charisma and motivating power of a facilitator, cockiness may even help. In those situations, one person motivates the others and "moves" them to achieve. However, facilitating dialogue and cockiness don't mix. The desire to shine like a star or to be the guru corrupts your ability.

Cockiness is driven by a need for certainty—to know for sure that this process works and that you are good at it. Nothing is 100 percent sure. To be cocky—or completely sure of yourself—is to run the risk of being disrespectful or inflexible. You risk forgetting that you don't know what you don't know. We are all susceptible to the ego's need to construct a clear image of "I can do this." If the image gets too clear, we run the risk of coming off as cocky. A cocky facilitator ultimately invites the group to use the escape strategies of dependence (for those who like you) or fight (for those who don't).

Confident, yes. Cocky, no. Confidence allows uncertainty to mix with good feelings of positive expectations of self and others. It is a "we" feeling, not an "I" feeling. If you find yourself feeling cocky, treat it as an early warning system and mix in a little humility as soon as you can. If you don't, someone or some event will do it for you.

THE FEAR OF LOOKING UNINVOLVED, UNINTERESTED, OR UNIMPORTANT

As you practice these concepts, you inevitably come to an important question. If you don't blow your own horn, who will? This question is rooted deeply in the value system of our individualistic culture. The assumption behind this question is that someone needs to be blowing your horn. It assumes a performer and an audience. This assumption of separateness is the same barrier that often prevents groups from genuine dialogue. In dialogue, there are no distinctions between performer and audience. The terms have no meaning. We are both.

Dialogue is a collective practice. There are no individual stars. Everyone is a star. At different times some may shine brighter, but none eclipse the group. The rewards are distinctly different from what our egos have been trained to want. Ego promotes actions that seek "star quality" rewards. Yet star quality is out of balance for achieving sustainable action. It is one-way rather than two-way. Instead of seeking the less stable one-way admiration, dialogue teaches us to seek the more stable, more fulfilling, and more productive mutual admiration.

In practice, this means not "giving answers," even when you have the opportunity to look really smart. At times, you'll have to maintain psychological silence when it feels as if you are becoming invisible. This goes against what we learned about how to succeed in an organization. The fact is, we need to unlearn much of what we have been taught about success before we can successfully facilitate dialogue. Your group will face many of the same feelings you face as a facilitator. As they slow things down and question their thoughts, they have the same fears of losing self-importance. How you deal with your fears will give the group members confidence to face their own.

COMMON EGO TRIP-UPS

Following is a list of common ego trip-ups that were identified by participants in one of my workshops on how to facilitate dialogue. Scan the list and see if you recognize any behavior that is high-risk for you. These replies were given in answer to the question, "What does your ego make you want to do instead of facilitate dialogue?"

> "Help them out."

> "Keep it from failing."

> "Encourage him/her/them."

> "Conclude that 'this is an exception' and I should step in."

> "Stay involved—don't look useless."

> "Make them do dialogue according to my beliefs about how it should be done."

> "Give positive feedback—reinforce, encourage, acknowledge."

> "Say something that makes me a hero or a wise one."

> "Defend the process."

> "Reduce my level of discomfort with the process by making it easier, clearer."

> "Give them the answers—the rules about life."

> "Moderate the emotional temperature in the room."

> "Steer the process to harmony."

> "Look for a brilliant intervention."

> "Make my presence known in the room."

> "Be fearful of participants' wounds and take the role of protector."

"Choose some other, less risky process."

"Guide the group to a business-related outcome."

Notice that none of the behaviors are blatant ego trips. At this level, the ego is subtler. Take a few minutes to answer for yourself the question, "What does your ego make you want to do instead of facilitate dialogue?"

Chapter 14

Storytelling

We're not going to turn people around with statistics. Jay (a story-teller) can get right into your nerve endings.

DICK WHEELER, RETIRED EDUCATOR AND KAYAKER WHO TRAVELED MORE THAN 1,300 MILES OF OPEN SEA IN THE NAME OF AN EXTINCT BIRD

Invariably, when I explain dialogue to a group, I end up talking about my dog Larry. Larry is a rescued greyhound. He obviously didn't win too many races because Larry was retired at three years old. Retired greyhounds make wonderful pets, but there are certain life skills you need to share with them that they don't learn in a kennel. They need to learn that nice dogs don't go on the oriental carpet and a few basic road rules. They know about leashes, but a walk in the neighborhood may present a few surprises. Larry, for instance, has not yet figured out (and shows no signs of figuring out) that if he walks on one side of a telephone pole and I walk on the other forward progress grinds to a halt. He feels the backward pull of his leash and looks up at me with wonder on his little dog face, without a clue as to why we stopped moving.

No matter that I'm the adult and he is the dog; he isn't going to back off until I back off. We could continue going nowhere indefinitely. But if I back off, he will follow my lead. It is just that I have to go first.

When I tell this story, people begin to get the picture. They see that the story I'm telling isn't really about Larry and me hung up on a telephone pole. It is really about backing off what you think you know, giving others room to do the same, and discovering that you can see plenty of alternatives when your ego isn't so attached to your way. It is about backing off to move forward and going slow to go fast.

People seem to enjoy this story. They don't always like the point of the story, but when a point is delivered within a story, people can listen better than when they hear it as a bullet point. Stories have a magical capacity to sneak past resistance and deliver a message that could not be heard in another format.

WHEN NOTHING ELSE CAN BREAK THROUGH

Story, metaphor, and humor are important tools to any communicator, and particularly important to you as a facilitator. The academics call it giving examples. Religious teachers call it teaching through parable. Trainers call it illustrating a point. Whatever you call it, a well-told story has the power to permeate the mind, body, and emotion of a listener. It can sneak past resistance, engage the right brain's powers of imagination, and anchor an abstract point to any of a thousand connections including past experiences as well as visual, auditory, and even, through imagination, kinesthetic and olfactory sensory reference points. A story gives life to dry content. You can even say that storytelling is "process" applied to content. It is the "how" that can deliver a "what" when all other roads are blocked.

When I first returned to the United States in 1991 to attend graduate school, a dear friend invited me to the National Storytelling Festival in Jonesborough, Tennessee. I was studying group process, group dynamics, adult education, and social psychology. The science of behavior and behavior change can get a bit dry, so it was nice to sit in a tent in the cool October air with hundreds of other like-minded people and listen to stories. It wasn't until afterward that I realized I had been doing field research.

One storyteller told about his experiences in the civil rights movement. His story changed my perceptions forever. I was moved. History lessons and newspaper accounts had never made the events real to me. His story made it real. His words took us back to the sixties when he, a young black man, bravely traveled into the maw of Mississippi for a civil rights march. He told us of his fear and the comfort he took in the friendships of others as they sat around a flickering campfire and sang songs to comfort their anxieties. He even got us to sing a soft round of "Swing Low, Sweet Chariot." We were surely in the sort of trance that hypnotists use.

As I looked around, I realized that his story had engaged something deep and common to everyone there. For a few moments we shared a common state. We were more connected than when we had walked in. We had all known similar fears. We had all wondered at one time or another if doing what we thought was right was worth the risk. Strangers' eyes met for a second longer to acknowledge the connection. Even the old guy in the overalls who had made a racist comment before the storyteller began was caught up in the spell. He didn't sing very loud, but he sang along with everyone else. The story had touched a part of us that was the same. And his story had changed people in a way that a lecture on the civil rights movement would have never achieved. I discovered the power of story.

A COMMON EXPERIENCE

Story, metaphor, humor, poetry, music, and art are all vehicles of communication that have the power to tap into our sameness and overcome apparent differences. The process of dialogue is designed to link participants in a collaborative thinking process. To link together, a group needs to tune into a common wavelength somewhere along the way. Often this will happen through a story.

One of the early stories I came across through reading about dialogue told of the MIT group's experiments with dialogue between management and union leaders in the steel industry. In the beginning, they could barely stand to sit in the same room. There were hard feelings and no trust, until the men happened upon a conversation where some of them began to tell stories of their children, and through those stories they discovered what they had in common. They realized that each of them wanted to be a good father. They loved their children and wanted them to do well. And they wanted to do a good job and provide a good example for their kids so their children would be proud of them. This apparently irrelevant conversation changed the tone and pitch of their communication. They still disagreed on many things, but they had found common ground that frankly was more important than their disagreements. I often tell this story to tap into a group's sense of sameness and connection. It inspires a reflective state to take the time to consider an "adversary" as a fellow human being with the same hopes and fears we all share.

A story has the power to reveal our commonality at an experiential level. When you tell or listen to a story, you re-create the experience in your imagination. For instance, when you read the story about Larry, you probably conjured up a picture of Larry and me hooked around the telephone pole. It was your picture, not mine. The thoughts you had about the story were yours, not mine. You created your own experience. Storytelling is the best way I know to simulate experience. When you tell a story that speaks to what is common to the participants in the group, they share an experience. That collective experience begins to build cohesion and forge new paths of communication between group members.

If a group is divided into factions, you can talk until you are blue in the face about the "big picture." But tell a story or get one of them to tell a story, and you might just give the group an opportunity to reconnect its split perceptions. Storytelling provides the opportunity to recombine thoughts with feelings—connections we lose in our habit of breaking things down into analyzable pieces. Storytelling blends emotional content, meaning, and relationship back into the "facts." It can also provide a safe way to speak of a dangerous truth.

DANGEROUS TRUTHS

There is a Jewish story about Truth, who, when naked, was turned away at every door. When Parable dressed Truth in story, Truth was allowed in and invited to sit at the table and dine. Dangerous truths often need clothes. Storytelling can allow people to tell each other "truths" that would be otherwise turned away.

If you set the stage for storytelling, people are more likely to tell their own stories. When people start telling their own stories, they naturally incorporate many of the "rules" of dialogue. They speak personally, they focus on process as much as content, and they back off outcome in favor of observation. For all of these reasons (and for reasons that I don't understand), telling a story is a safe way to address a dangerous truth.

Think about the woman mentioned in Chapter 8 who told the story of two groups being on two sides of a burning building. The groups had two contradictory experiences of how hard the firemen worked to save the people (the firemen couldn't reach the back of the building so they poured valiant efforts into saving the front). Her message was that the people in her group were not being respectful of each other and were being a bit small-minded to think they had all the facts. Yet, if she had said this outright, they might have turned on her. How dare she say those things! She chose a story instead. She had much more room to tell the truth through a story than she might ever have had addressing the dangerous truth directly.

Many rifts can only be healed when people feel they have had the opportunity to tell their side of the story. The very act of telling a story can diminish the storyteller's perceptions of how dangerous a truth really is—or even how true it is. Frequently I see a disagreement disappear of its own accord when people get a chance to tell their story. The understanding that comes from hearing another's point of view, through story and without accusations, can render apparent disagreements impotent. People begin to see both sides.

Not only do people need to tell their story, but it is often in the retelling that they see their story differently. As they speak, they listen through the ears of the others present, which has the effect of subtly changing the facts and amending their memories. The speaker begins to blend in other points of view as he or she adjusts the story to the listeners. Being listened to encourages a speaker to listen to herself. Just as the physicist David Bohm asserted that a "thought observed is transformed," a story heard is transformed. I have experienced this myself. I can be as mad as hell and then a good listener asks me to tell what happened, and that moment gives me an opportunity to see things I didn't see before. Going back to the chain of events pulls me down my ladder of assumptions and allows me to deconstruct what I thought I saw in favor of what I might have missed.

But I get ahead of myself. Chronologically in the facilitation process, the first stories told will probably be stories that you tell to deliver your message about what dialogue is, how it works, and what the group needs to be doing differently to get there. Your stories will be designed to stimulate introspection and to build expectations for the process.

STORIES THAT STIMULATE INTROSPECTION

In your various roles as a consultant, manager, trainer, and facilitator, you continually maneuver between being directive and nondirective and back again. I have found that when working with groups that need to develop better interpersonal skills, resolve internal conflicts, or develop more trust, the directive approach is rarely successful. Flashing "ten communication skills" on a screen, learning them by heart, and post-testing the group's retention of the information are more likely to stimulate an e-mail to Scott Adams for a new Dilbert cartoon than change the group's behavior. In these situations, the direct approach doesn't get it. People need to come to their own conclusions that they want to adopt new behaviors. A well-told story can prompt the introspection process that will create these conclusions.

The Larry story is an example. Storytelling is more of a pull strategy than a push strategy. Even the lead-in phrase, "I want to tell you a little story," takes the group into a different state. They sit back and become much more receptive than if you were to say, "I'm going to tell you how you are likely to screw this up," or "I am going to teach you how to monitor your negative behavior patterns." If you can find a story that prompts the listeners to reflect on their own situation and habits, it is just as effective as running a complete needs assessment on each individual and then tailoring your approach to twenty different learning needs all at once. Except they do their own needs assessment and training in their head. The use of storytelling is the concept of distributed power applied to training. Your story will have twenty different interpretations and will prompt twenty different paths of introspection perfectly tailored by the mind of each listener.

The first stories you tell will be designed to get people to think about their current habits of communication—to reflect and consider if your story about the guy who always digs his heels in might apply to "me." Other stories will help you help the group members develop a picture of how dialogue might be different from and better than their "old" way of communicating. Stories help you promote introspection, deliver touchy mind-sets, and make your models come alive.

For the rest of this chapter, I will share some of the things I've learned about storytelling that have improved my ability to use stories as a facilitator. Most of what I have learned has come from a dear friend, Doug Lipman, who is a professional storyteller and a coach of other professional storytellers. Doug runs workshops and writes books and can be reached by e-mail at doug@storypower.com.

I've attempted to tailor the following summary on the skills of storytelling to our needs as facilitators.

DEVELOPMENTAL STAGES

Have you ever noticed that bullet points don't have any sense of timing? They don't develop. They have no history, no reason why, no personality. They are boring, really. Presentation software has helped a bit. Instead of the overhead where we slide a piece of paper slowly down the screen revealing each point, we can use the "reveal" function and build our bullet points one at a time. But they are still pretty one-dimensional. Storytelling gives you an opportunity to change that. A story develops. It travels from point A to B to C to D, and on to J or K. Your listeners travel with you and develop their own interpretation within the context of time. Time is a necessary ingredient for the process of learning. Stories are a way to stretch your bullet points out over time (even as short as a minute or two) so that learning has an opportunity to occur. When a story is presented with a beginning, a middle, and an end, a listener can travel to his own conclusion and integrate the meaning of a concept into his world.

Another thing about bullet points or conceptual models on a screen is that they are, of necessity, presented in a linear fashion. Consider the positive intent model. Everyone will conceptually agree that often people intend a positive outcome but create negative outcomes. A group might even agree to "assume positive intent" as a rule. But it doesn't mean anything in a linear format. You only get the cognitive piece. For a group to integrate the positive intent model into its behavior, people need to add nonlinear aspects such as emotion, the complexities of misunderstanding, and reinterpreted experiences. A story about a manager who wanted to create independence and instead created feelings of isolation can weave in these nonlinear elements and add enough time to reconstitute a dry bullet point into something relevant.

When I was working in the advertising industry at J. Walter Thompson, this knowledge was brought home to me. It was there that I was introduced to the concept of the key response. The key response takes into account that you cannot imprint a belief into people's minds, but you can provide an experience that encourages them to create that belief in their own minds. The goal is to find an experience that creates the key response you want. One of the frustrating things about advertising is that people always want to tell a consumer how great the product is. They don't get it—telling someone to like the product doesn't work.

Our instructor used this example: If a skinny guy with glasses were to walk in the room right now and say "I'm funny," you would probably look at him and think, "Sure, buddy." He could be Woody Allen, but if you had never heard of him before, never experienced him, you could not take in his words. However, if he came in and told a few funny stories and made you laugh, you would conclude for yourself that he was funny. Your experience, within as little as a few minutes of time, and the effect of your own laughter would be much more powerful than his bullet point "I am funny." The experience travels from A to B to C instead of jumping to C, and because of that, C makes more sense. A story unfolds similar to the way that real experiences unfold—and we all know that experience is the best teacher. The clarity you inject into a story as it unfolds strengthens the experiential impact of your story.

One of the secrets to storytelling is to understand the difference between language and oral language. Once you recognize the difference, you can use your whole body to paint a vibrant picture with clear images that delivers a strong experiential effect.

ORAL LANGUAGE

You are already a storyteller. To become a more powerful storyteller, you need only turn your attention to it. Stories are delivered through oral language. With written words you are limited to what I can convey in ink on paper, but if we were together in the same room, your experience of my stories and me would be very different. For one thing, you could look at my eyes and see how they light up when I talk about dialogue and my experiences with other groups. You would hear the rise and fall in my tone of voice: softer when I describe the men talking of their children and their desire to be good daddies, louder when I talk about chaos and the defense strategy of fighting— even sarcastic as I refer to our common preference to see ourselves as the "reasonable" ones in any group discussion.

When I write, I try to find the perfect words, but when I tell a story, I don't worry so much about each single word. It is my intent that counts. You have surely heard the common wisdom that says verbal content is only 15 percent of your oral message. I experience that to be true. To tell a story well, I have to be present. I have to speak from the heart with sincerity. Any trace of smugness or insincerity on my part and I may as well not have told the story. In fact, I just provided my listener with an experience of my own incongruence, rather than an experience of my story. If you have told a story so often that it is just a recitation of words, stop telling it. Your intent speaks louder than your words. If a story has lost its meaning for you, it is unlikely that it will stimulate meaning for others.

When a story means something to you, your intent is powerful. You can embody the central message of your story, and you can use your words, body, and tone of voice as instruments to emit a clear signal that resonates with your listeners. When running workshops on my last book on territorial games, I use a story of two managers— one who was territorial and the other who valued collaboration over protecting personal turf. As the story unfolds, the territorial manager grabbing for power ends up with less and less power than the collegial manager. It is a true story. But when I tell that story, I don't pretend that I have completely resolved that issue for myself. There are many situations when being territorial (about your own intellectual property, for instance) makes sense. However, I tell the story from a place of being a fellow witness to something I don't quite understand either. The message permeates much better than if I told the story as if I understood everything—as if the lesson were easy to understand and clearly applied. When I tell that story, my intent is to stimulate reflection, and I have to visit my own confusion about the subject for the story to have effect. When using oral language, your unspoken thoughts and feelings inform the story as much as your spoken words. Even the pictures in your head inform the story.

THE MAGIC OF "IRRELEVANT DETAIL"

A story comes alive when you add details. When I talk about my dog Larry, I often add details that have nothing to do with the story but help describe a vibrant word picture that I have in my head. The clearer the picture is in my head, the richer the descriptions. I picture Larry in my head—black and sleek, with a white blaze on his chest, looking very dignified (considering his racing name was Curly Larry

Mo)—and I can see our walking path clearly. The magic of describing even a few of those "irrelevant details" is that my listeners begin to see them, too. The bizarre part is that they don't see what I see. They see their own picture, which is much more relevant to them. Their picture is tailor-made to connect to their reality better than my picture. City people may see sidewalks and shops, other pedestrians trying to walk around us. The suburb people may see wide green lawns and sidewalks leading to the park.

It is a paradox that my clarity increases your clarity and both will look completely different. Imagery seems to hook the right brain into participating by adding imagination to thoughts. Let's try an experiment. When I work on getting a group to build a common understanding of the unique state of dialogue, I often refer to the situation of a family gathered after a funeral. People seem to agree that this situation shifts the perceptions of a group so that people's habitual modes of communication are dropped in favor of more reflective types of interactions. This shift is similar to the shift of norms we hope to achieve through dialogue.

So what just happened? Did you "get" what I was talking about? Can you easily remember a funeral where that happened? Okay, consider a more detailed example: I'm from Louisiana, and my family likes to argue. Sunday dinner at my grandmother's house always preceded a good-natured knock-down drag-out debate on either politics or religion. When my cousins were down from Arkansas, there were about ten adults around the table. In the great Southern tradition, these debates were a ritual of drama where the women asserted their opinions on the Bible and the Republicans in a way denied them outside of the family. Grandmother was always right because it was her house and she could quote more Bible verses than anyone else. I watched and learned the power dynamics as everyone restated the same contrary opinions every Sunday. It was a structured dance of power, and family members played their prescribed roles.

But it was different when my Aunt Myrtle died. We all packed into our cars, casserole dishes wrapped in tea towels on the floor of the backseat, and traveled up to El Dorado, Arkansas, for the funeral. My Uncle Bill and my cousins met us at the door, red-eyed, and we went into the living room to sit before going to the funeral home. No one had any fight left in them. The same people were there, but the dynamics were different. In the situation of Aunt Myrtle's premature death, the adults were reflective. Any one of them could have had an overreaction to anesthesia on the operating table.

Their conversation turned to things that connected rather than divided. They told stories about Aunt Myrtle's wonderful cooking, recipes she used to make, and how she was always thoughtful and kind. In that living room, being "right" didn't matter anymore. They were concerned with more important things. I remember seeing through my child's eyes my Aunt Raelene—who disagreed, on principle, with anything Aunt Pearl said—taking her hand and squeezing it. Aunt Pearl smiled back. I realized that death can create a sacred safe space where differences don't matter and we turn to more important things. Our goal with dialogue is to create a similar safe space where arguing seems silly and understanding becomes the important thing.

How was that different? Now can you remember a funeral where you experienced a shift in the communication norms? It is probably easier than before. If you and I were in the same room, it would be easier still. This is the magic of irrelevant detail. If you want a story to come alive, add details by building a clear image in your own head. But for heaven's sake, try not to overdo it.

THE GREATEST SIN: A BORING STORY

Some people tell a story not for the listeners but because they want to be center stage. They want to feel the connection of storytelling so badly that they try too hard. Your stories should be for them, not for you. Storytelling is not a performance but a natural communication process. Most of your stories should last no more than a minute or two. Leave the epics for the performers. As a facilitator, your use of story should be tightly tied to your goals of helping the group reach dialogue. Every now and then you might tell a story to entertain, but most of the time your story should be tied to the goals of the group. As you try out new stories, always check to find out what people heard in the story. Stories develop as a collaborative process between you and your listeners. I've even found that a story takes on a richer direction than I ever intended when I let my listeners influence it through their interpretations.

You might also want to be wary of the "storytelling voice." Professional storytellers disdain the storytelling voice—a louder, more dramatic voice usually accompanied by grand gestures and exaggerated pauses. It is a big turnoff to listen to this voice. It makes people cringe. Use a natural voice that comes straight from the heart and you can't go wrong.

THE POWER OF STORIES

You can use stories to engage both the left and right sides of the brain, create a mood, and deliver guidance without being overly directive. Stories can be used to give a mind-set, to inspire group reflection and introspection, to build your credibility, and to engage distracted group members. Stories can also tap into common ground and build connections. One of the great things about telling stories is that you model storytelling for the group. You can use your own stories to model self-disclosure, reflection, or any of the principles of dialogue. When you start telling stories, the participants do, too. Modeling is one of the most important skills you can use as a facilitator.

Chapter 15

Modeling

He preaches well that lives well.

MIGUEL DE CERVANTES, IN *DON QUIXOTE*

W hat is the best way to teach a skill? If you were learning how to ski, would you rather read a book on skiing or have your own live ski instructor demonstrate for you and then let you try it out yourself? Probably the latter. Dialogue is the same. You have to demonstrate, demonstrate, demonstrate and practice, practice, practice. All skills are best taught with demonstration and practice. Thinking skills and interpersonal skills are no different. Group members will learn by watching you and by watching each other. An intellectual grasp of the concepts of dialogue is very different from having the skills to dialogue. If the group is going to learn how to dialogue, you have to do more than talk about it—you are going to have to show them.

WALK YOUR TALK

Your actions always speak louder than your words. If you say one thing and demonstrate another, your actions will influence the group more than your words. If you can't demonstrate the assumption of positive intent, embracing diversity and respect for all opinions, then you won't have much success in facilitating a group to dialogue. You are asking people to take a big risk here, to speak of dangerous truths, to question what they think they know, and to embrace uncertainty. This is a big deal. If you want them to jump off this cliff, you should be willing to go first. I admit that there are some people who are so charismatic and eloquent in their rhetoric that they can persuade a group to embrace principles that they themselves do not embrace. But this book is not about that. Even if I could do that, I'm not interested. Why would you want to teach something you don't value enough to do yourself?

I began my work in dialogue because I wanted to learn how to influence a group. I discovered that it demanded a willingness to be influenced myself. It requires a different state of mind, body, and soul. I have to achieve that state before I can expect the group to achieve that state. I move from the state of "me" to "us." This is no small task. It has taken me years to achieve the mental and emotional agility necessary to change my state. There is a lot of personal work involved. You may find it easier than I did to move into a state of "us." But you will probably face your own struggle with some other aspect of dialogue. I don't know anyone who has learned to facilitate dialogue without facing some personal dilemma.

Learning to facilitate dialogue is as much a personal journey as a group process. You may find that you need to behave in ways that run contrary to your habits. You may find that facilitating dialogue requires behaviors that run counter to behaviors that have previously been richly rewarded and reinforced in corporate culture. In the beginning, it can be exhausting to remain hypervigilant of the ways you don't want to be and the ways you do want to be as a facilitator. The good news is that, after a while, the pull to dialogue exceeds the pull away from dialogue, and you can relax. Breaking the grip of your orbit through old closed-loop belief systems is the hard part. Once you are free, facilitating dialogue (heck, life) gets much easier.

FACILITATE YOURSELF

It is another paradox that you may end up spending as much or more time facilitating your own behavior as you do facilitating the behavior of the group. Returning to one of the first metaphors in this book, you can show people how to dance much easier than tell them how to dance. Even more important, if you were teaching dance, you would want the beauty and appeal of your dance to inspire them to say, "I want to dance just like that." Like dance, dialogue is best taught by someone with a passion for it.

Your passion will be evident in your actions. There will be times when you are confused and uncertain. The way in which you embrace that uncertainty will demonstrate to the group that uncertainty is to be welcomed. Despite your obligations to stay on time, you will be presented with participants who have something they want to say. The time you take to understand their point will demonstrate for the group your willingness to go slow to go fast. When frustration finds you, your tone of voice and your willingness to share the assumptions behind your frustration will teach group members how to suspend their assumptions when they are frustrated. When you demonstrate a vivacious curiosity for new information—even when it contradicts your own assumptions—you show the group members what curiosity looks like so they can recognize it in themselves. Anchoring your perceptual filter to seek positive intent from all participants will teach them that they, too, can find positive intent in even the most incendiary statements.

Facilitating dialogue is not a walk in the park. It is more like a trek through the Himalayan mountains. And even crazier than wanting to trek through the Himalayans, you want to be a guide. To be a guide you need to know ten times as much as the participants and know that you will only ever use a fraction of what you know each time you guide a group. The desire to facilitate dialogue is a desire that is hard to explain. But, if you are still reading this book, I don't need to explain it.

I should instead give you some tips on where this modeling technique gets really tricky.

BUT DIDN'T YOU JUST SAY . . . ?

From the moment you begin, there will be opportunities to demonstrate the skills of dialogue. The best opportunity will arise when someone in the group tries to trip you up. This usually happens. Expect it. There is one in every group who waits and watches for the point at which you contradict yourself. You can't discuss dialogue without a few apparent contradictions. It is too complex. That is why one of the proposed rules (see Chapter 6) is to "devalue consistency." There are pieces of dialogue (and reality) that defy the Newtonian imperative for consistency.

If you get defensive, you've blown an opportunity to model "assuming positive intent" for the group. However, if you anchor your thoughts and actions to a belief that the questioner sincerely wants to learn how to dialogue, and that this is the best way people know to learn, then you can embrace the question. When you embrace the question as an opportunity, your actions will model for the group members how they can handle trip-up questions. You stay centered and calm. You listen to what the person has to say. Treat the person raising the questions with respect and the entire group gets to see what that looks like. Even if they were consciously trying to trip you up, you still can locate their positive intent.

The Socratic method is useful here. Find out how your apparent contradiction might confuse people about their own behavior. Or better yet, become a co-inquirer and see what you both can learn from examining the contradiction. Move the dynamics away from a hypothetical contest of intellects and bring it back to the now—this group, this dialogue session, "our" behavior.

A common contradiction comes when, after introducing the concept of "go slow to go fast," a participant wants to deliver a soliloquy. You need to move on, but someone nails you with: "But you said sometimes we have to go slow . . ." How you model resolution of two mutually exclusive goals is very important. Either you can come across as dictating that the group must move on ("We are going to have to move on here") or you can openly discuss your dilemma and include the group in the decision. For example, "I want to share my concern about time here. You may or may not choose to continue this discussion, but I'd like to give you some new information about timing. It is 10:30 right now, and if we are going to break for lunch at 12:00, what would you like to do?" Most of the time people say to move on. If they don't, they usually have a good reason that you should know about. Regardless, you have modeled a collaborative rather than leader/follower relationship.

When you make a mistake or the group notices an inconsistency between two things you said, or between what you said and what you are doing, it is also a wonderful opportunity to demonstrate "identifying assumptions." Don't be afraid to verbally retrace your thinking and publicly find the source of your inconsistency.

LET ME "SEE"

There will be times when someone in the group asks you a question that reveals a bona fide inconsistency in your thinking. I've been asked, "How you can say that our goal is to dialogue when we are not supposed to have an outcome? Aren't task and goal two ways to say the same thing?" Well, yes, they are. Too slick of an answer here would indicate that I think I understand this one. That would be insincere, and I don't want to model insincerity for the group. (People get enough of that already.) I want to model sincerity and show a willingness to climb down my ladder of assumptions and examine my own thinking. So instead of a glib response, I will take some time and verbally articulate my thoughts on the apparent contradiction.

One of the most difficult skills in dialogue is the ability to articulate your thoughts and assumptions. It is sort of a public introspection process. Since extroverts tend to do it sloppily and introverts hate doing it at all, most groups need help in this situation. The critical distinction lies in an ability to retrace your thoughts without justifying each step along the way. Don't justify; just articulate. "Well, when I use the word *task*, my assumption is that we use that word in terms of a work task. And if the group focuses on work tasks, then you will have a tendency to not want to unravel your thinking because it slows you down. In dialogue, the goal—there I used it again—is to unravel our thinking. I guess I started using the word *goal* when I talk about process as a distinction between a process task and a content task. I wonder if we risk anything by allowing ourselves a process 'task.' I'm not sure how we could approach dialogue without any sort of goal. There may be another way. I don't know."

At that point the participant will usually have something interesting to say and we get a chance to model a bit of dialogue before the formal dialogue process. If I wasn't looking for opportunities to model dialogue, I might have answered, "There is a distinction between process and content. What I meant was that we do want a process outcome—a goal—and we do not want to have a content outcome—a task. Okay?" This answer is slick, insincere, and dismissive, and it does not in any way model the skills of dialogue. Every question you get is an opportunity to model dialogue. You won't choose to model every single time because it takes too long, but try to find at least a few critical junctures that will impact the group's perceptions. One place you want to look is the point at which you uncover an either/or issue.

FROM EITHER/OR TO BOTH/AND

There are many gray areas where our traditional methods of analysis have led us to treat reality as if it traveled on a linear continuum. For instance, we are led to believe that we must find a point along the continuum between employee satisfaction and customer satisfaction. When the two are in conflict, we have to choose one or the other as more important. In real life, both employee and customer satisfaction are important. But not on that linear balance beam. Dialogue is not about either/or. Dialogue is about holding the space for both/and. Both are true. It takes mental agility to hold that it is not *x* or *y,* but *x* and *y.*

To facilitate dialogue, this mental skill of both/and needs to be incorporated into your belief system. When people see things as either/or, there's a mental chess match where each person uses logical analysis and debate tactics to maneuver an "opponent" into a checkmate ("Gotcha") position—but that is not dialogue. However, it has been such a mainstay of our interactions in business that we automatically draw our word sword the minute they draw theirs. As a facilitator, your goal is to resist the urge to engage in verbal swordplay, but to instead whip out a mirror or a magnifying glass and examine what is right about both points of view.

For instance, the group members may point out that you recommended that they "devalue consistency," and then you recommended that they choose rules, so the group asks, "Aren't rules all about consistency?" This question could easily prompt a frustrated sigh and a dismissive answer. Or you might stop, think, and say something such as, "You know, you are right. I've wondered about that one, too." To address the question in the spirit of dialogue rather than from a reductionist framework, you might elaborate, "If we are consistently inconsistent, does that mean we are consistent or inconsistent? (A sense of humor never hurts.) It isn't an either/or. I think the answer lies in both/and. My favorite bumper sticker reads, 'If you haven't changed your mind lately, are you sure you still have one?' Learning seems to require inconsistency. We have to let go of the old—being inconsistent with what we used to believe—to take on the new." Modeling that you aren't afraid to reveal your own confusion helps people see that they have a choice when they get caught, too. You have successfully modeled a new response style for them. As you show them how, then they will begin to pull out their mirrors and magnifying glasses instead of automatically going for their word swords when challenged.

The opportunity to model dialogue skills is so important you may even prompt discussion about an apparent contradiction. Your flexibility and willingness to discuss things that other facilitators usually avoid lights the way to dialogue. Not to mention that it builds your credibility as someone who is finally going to be different from all the rest of the facilitators they have seen.

WHEN YOU SCREW UP

You will screw up at some point. You might be tired, the woman trying to trip you up might remind you of your mother, or your own insecurity about looking smart will rear its ugly head and take you off track. Or you made a bad call somewhere. All is not lost.

Some of my greatest learnings have come from screwing up. Most of Chapter 12 on the Socratic method, was a result of one participant's barrage of questions about "exactly" what I meant by Socratic questions. He pummeled me with questions: When was it that Socrates was alive? What was the political context of his time? Could I just summarize his philosophy, please? I was dying. I thought I knew about the Socratic method, but I didn't know anything about Socrates. He had zeroed in on a genuine weakness. In my mind, my credibility teetered precariously in the balance. I fell back on old habits, asking a question for each of his. What "exactly" was it that was unclear for him? Could he help me understand how these questions were related to his participation in dialogue? The room was growing tense, and I suggested that because of time constraints, we needed to move on, so I asked, "Would it be okay for us to discuss this later?" What was he going to say? He said, "Fine." But he didn't feel fine about it. Neither did I. I didn't know what I was talking about—he could see that—and I didn't admit that I didn't know. It was not good modeling.

Five minutes later he still sat with his arms crossed and was still unhappy with my response. I stopped what we were doing and said, "You know, I want to go back to David's questions. I was avoiding admitting that I don't know the answer to most of what he was asking me. I can only share what I know, and that is getting smaller and smaller in my own mind. But I promise that I'm going to go do some more homework so that the next time someone asks, I will have the answers. David, I'm sorry I can't answer your questions, and I apologize for putting you off." He said, "It's okay. It's just that I like the idea of Socratic questions and I'm really curious." The tension drained out of the room and we moved on.

The point is, well, there are several points actually. One, when you screw up, it is never too late to fix it. Two, you look smarter when you admit your ignorance than when you try to hide it. And three, every screwup is an opportunity to learn. If it hadn't been for David, I would never have spent so much time researching Socrates and trying to understand his life. Through that research I learned ten times more about the Socratic method and deepened my ability to use it. Dialogue means being more tolerant of all uncertainty, especially your own. Only in uncertainty can we find the gift of learning. Modeling a welcoming attitude toward your own uncertainty will help you take group members to their own fertile uncertainty.

Chapter 16

Dialogue in the Real World

Why is it that reality, when set down untransposed in a book, sounds false?

SIMONE WEIL

This book isn't real life. In the real world, the question "How do I facilitate dialogue?" has to be answered with, "It depends." You have to adapt any "recipe" to fit your situation—you work with what you've got. Your experience with dialogue will teach you much more than reading about my experience. To increase your chances for a successful experience, you'll want input from several points of view. This chapter is designed to broaden your perspective as you begin to experiment with dialogue.

Any concept, such as dialogue, that promises so much invites naysayers. This chapter covers some of the contrary perspectives you may hear about dialogue in the real world. You may even get a chance to explore a few of your own contrary perspectives. Remember that if you strongly disagree with a particular concept, you need to look closely at the assumptions behind your disagreement. A thorough examination may hold the key to a new opportunity for you to experiment and learn. Innovation is born from questioning "common wisdom."

The facilitator model presented in this book is a tightly woven gestalt developed over eight years of practice. Like dialogue, it is difficult to chunk into modules. Delete a piece and the invisible threads connecting it to the others may cause the whole to wobble. Then again, delete another piece and it might become faster and more powerful. Along with questions, input from others will help you make good decisions that guide your experiments away from the wobble and toward the powerful. There are many paths to dialogue. As this chapter explores dialogue in the real world, you will find the words and thoughts of other people traveling alternative paths to dialogue with advice on how they get there. As you seek your own path, it helps to hear from fellow travelers. We start with the most common roadblocks you'll face and then move on to discuss a few forks in the road offering equally viable alternatives.

YOU CAN'T HAVE A CONVERSATION WITH THAT MANY PEOPLE

People often hold the assumption that you just can't hold a conversation that includes up to forty people at the same time. They reject the idea out of hand on the grounds that "it is just too hard." Some will say, "You're inviting unproductive chaos," or "It will deteriorate into a free-for-all." Somewhere along the way, they had an experience of a painfully unproductive large group and they don't want to go there again. That is understandable. However, it limits their ability to learn how mind-sets, preempts, training in self-facilitation, and ground rules can dramatically change the result of large group interactions. If you challenge the "common wisdom" that large groups are too unwieldy for productive conversation, you get to discover that the creativity of one large group can far exceed the capabilities of that group when it is subdivided into smaller groups.

Many managers/facilitators automatically break a large group into "easier to handle" small groups that then report back. When you do this, it fractures a group's thinking into pieces. When the smaller groups report back, they have each traveled a thought process that did not include the whole group. Reporting a list of conclusions is not the same as participating in the thinking that created those conclusions. Sometimes it doesn't matter. However, if you need buy-in on big decisions, it is best to let everyone experience firsthand the complexity, the alternatives explored and rejected, and the thinking that went into choosing a direction. Dialogue with a larger group as a whole is the best way to avoid time lost revisiting decisions later when implementation is critical and time is at a premium.

Large groups also offer exponential increases in creativity. The same reason that large groups verge on the edge of chaos—diversity of opinion, experience, and perspective—gives a large group a bigger palette from which to paint a brighter picture. If a group can reach the state of dialogue, it exceeds traditionally expected limitations that sabotage a group's ability to think, and the group has the capacity to tap into the creativity of twenty or thirty brains all at once. This is the birthplace of breakthrough thinking that can translate into seamless implementation. It requires an investment of time certainly, but it is worth it.

WE DON'T HAVE A WHOLE DAY

How many times have I heard that? "Can't we do something in just a couple of hours?" Sure, but it might not be dialogue. There are all kinds of dialogues: from a heart-to-heart over a cup of coffee all the way to the large group process described here. Nancy Dixon (author of *Perspectives on Dialogue*) points out, "People already know how to dialogue. And if they know how—but they don't do it—then it must be that they learn that they are not supposed to." Why do you need a day to teach people how to do what they already know how to do? Maybe the training is more to help the group members unlearn the "they are not supposed to" part. That kind of training takes time.

Learning for adults is rarely limited to teaching a cognitive skill. It more often requires an element of emotional skill. Just like going on a diet, the difference between knowing that I shouldn't eat this cake and not eating this cake is vast. Telling people in a group to have a dialogue and giving them a list of rules is equivalent to giving a fat person a diet book and telling him to read it and lose weight. The preparation time invested by practicing the principles of dialogue and engaging in self-awareness exercises will be proportionately reflected in how far the group members shift from old communication norms and the depth to which they dive into the hidden meanings within their relationships. To shorten the process is to risk airing dangerous truths before the group is ready to constructively handle those truths. For most work situations, I won't introduce the process of dialogue in anything less than one whole day.

However, you may be forced to chunk the preparation training into shorter sessions. You could try four preparation sessions of an hour each, followed by a review and a two-hour dialogue session. As long as you have at least two hours for the actual dialogue, you can be creative with other time frames. Just don't fall into the trap of trying to do something that can't be done. If you are going to invite people to face their dangerous truths, you need to ensure they have enough time to see them in the context of the group's strength and collaborative power.

YOU MUST HAVE AN AGENDA TO ACCOMPLISH ANYTHING

We are so well trained! Particularly those of us who went to business school. We know that groups without an agenda will dissolve into wandering and waffling. Right? So how do you explain a group of thirty-five people, including extreme union representatives, members of management, a couple of class clowns, and not a few apathetic eye rollers, who, at the end of the day, said dialogue (no agenda) was the most productive thing they had done in years? At the risk of sounding a bit "out there," sometimes the only way to reach an outcome is to stop trying so hard. For this group, there were no topics that did not polarize the group into well-practiced adversarial positions. It was only through a "no agenda" rule that they had permission to explore new territory and find common ground.

Of course, the skeptics in the group began the dialogue with a sarcastic conversation about a recent baseball game—"You said no agenda!" But that lasted only five minutes before the group spontaneously shifted to something of interest to everyone. It happened to be a recent complaint handled through the union where a manager believed he had not had a chance to make reparation before the complaint escalated to his boss. Outcome-wise, the group was supposed to be doing action plans. A traditional outcome-oriented process with an agenda would not have allowed this issue to emerge. Technically, it was off track. Yet this issue (actually, the conflict it represented) was stuck in everyone's craw and until it was aired, resentments on both sides prevented any heartfelt participation in action planning.

Bizarre as it may sound, the group members did not resolve anything about this issue. They just talked about it. Yet something in the group changed. They had all had the opportunity to say their piece. The resentments were dissipated and the air was cleared. At that point they were then ready to move on to an agenda. An e-mail to me three days later confirmed the value dialogue lent to their subsequent action planning sessions. The message said simply, "This is progress!" There are times when a group needs freedom from an agenda.

Then again, there are times when "no agenda" might very well result in waffling and wandering. Jeff Insco, director of quality at a New York catalogue company, says that when the company "tried dialogue for dialogue's sake, it didn't work." His company developed another approach that works better for them. They have been using dialogue for two years to stimulate creativity and accelerate adaptability to change. In Insco's experience, groups need a business topic. He recommends choosing a complex topic but a topic, nonetheless. Insco says it was unproductive to bring people together without a focus. Without a topic, people were confused about the purpose of the meeting.

So for Insco and his group, naming a specific topic works better than a literal interpretation of the "no agenda" rule. He does, however, use the "no decisions" rule and recommends that the group hold "a very long leash on the discussion." He says, "If you end up miles away from the topic, then there is a reason for that." Even when they start with a topic, Insco is conscious to not attempt to control the direction of the discussion. As a facilitator he advises to "let go of the controls" so that the group can find where the problems or opportunities lie. Without interference, the group "seems to go where it needs to go."

One of the most important things to learn about dialogue is how significant seemingly irrelevant issues can become. Some conversations seem irrelevant to a business topic (i.e., the kids' birthday parties, taking care of aging parents, lost career opportunities), yet they have a magical quality of bringing a group together in recognizing our common human experience. These irrelevant issues, preempted by most agendas, can often provide experiences that bond a group more tightly than business issues could ever achieve.

SOMETIMES IT'S NOT A GOOD IDEA TO TELL THE TRUTH

Well, you got me there. If I ask if an outfit makes me look fat, I am not happy to hear, "Kind of makes your butt look barn-size"—true or not! Bella DePaulo of the University of Virginia has done research into the reasons and functional aspects of lying. DePaulo's research points out that some types of "lying" grease the social interactions of daily life. We present our "self" to others in a way that is "characteristically an edited and a packaged one." She and others even developed a "taxonomy of lies" that moves from simple exaggerations to outright lies. Among the distinctions is the difference between lies of kindness and lies of self-interest. That research is fascinating but too complex to discuss here. Suffice it to say that sometimes it isn't a good idea to tell the truth. Being unkind isn't fruitful, nor is being naively vulnerable.

In a strict hierarchy, when someone in power has the reputation for retribution, it would be irresponsible to encourage the discussion of dangerous truths. One time I believed a manager's self-description as "open-minded and empowering." Introducing dialogue to her group was a mistake. She was not open-minded and had a reputation for shooting the messenger. The result was agony—two hours of people squirming in their seats, eyes darting longingly toward the door, and no one daring to tell the truth. The minute the greatly feared manager left, there was a rush to dialogue. The group dialogued for another hour and a half. The dialogue without her was fruitful for the participants (most of them decided to send out resumes), but it was not in the best interests of the company.

Dialogue is not a wholesale license to bare all and tell all. Some truths aren't helpful. In fact, when I ask groups to anonymously rate their levels of honesty and coherence in percentage terms, the ones with high honesty ratings sometimes give low ratings on coherence. Honesty without a sense of shared responsibility for the cause and the effect of that honesty is not the best policy. The idea that dialogue is a "safe place for dangerous truths" does not mean all truths.

Perhaps the best articulation of a facilitator's role around truth comes from Joseph Phelps, a Baptist minister who wrote *More Light, Less Heat* to encourage Christians to use dialogue so they can discuss tough issues like homosexuality and abortion. He says, "A facilitator can serve as a translator to the group and also for the one who is speaking to help him or her understand what he or she is really trying to say—what fears, hopes, and dreams are represented by [his or her] words." When a person's "truth" is explored to reveal a hidden intent, it often reveals a much more productive statement. When someone says, "You are wrong," it can really mean, "If I listen to you, I'm afraid it will shake the foundations of what I believe." That sort of truth invites both sides to make an extra effort to look harder and understand more deeply. These are the truths dialogue encourages us to explore.

RELINQUISHING CONTROL IS DANGEROUS— SOMEONE MIGHT GET HURT

The idea of inviting a group to drop protective communication norms and air dangerous truths without an external "safety control" scares the wits out of many people. They envision scathing personal attacks, scapegoating, or worse, vulnerable honesty rewarded with post-dialogue retributions. This process is definitely out of any one person's control. Control is trusted to the group. Uncontrolled by any individual and sometimes a wild ride, dialogue reveals the secret conversations that are fracturing group effort. To allow those conversations into the room feels dangerous. To allow them into the room without a facilitator who "protects" the participants can seem irresponsible. Many people like the idea of dialogue but fear what a group might do without authoritarian safeguards.

The fact is that this process will mirror the deepest intentions of the people there and the information available to them. You don't know in advance what those are. But if you can trust that intentions are good (underneath fear and distrust, almost everyone's are) and the information, once shared, will help the group build a coherent bigger picture, then the ultimate risk is really quite low. Dialogue trusts a group to control itself in a way that faces dangerous truths without damaging individuals.

On rare occasions a person may choose to leave (i.e., quit), deciding the group is not for her. (More often, individuals who thought they wanted to leave discover they want to stay.) However, if someone does choose to leave, it is almost always an acceleration of a split that would have happened anyway. Dialogue does not create by itself. It simply reveals current thoughts and feelings so group participants can be more conscious about what they are choosing to create. With dialogue, a group has the opportunity to approach issues proactively rather than reactively. Hiding from a dangerous truth only makes things worse. Yet facing it requires a certain amount of skill.

William Isaacs says one of the highest levels of competence for a facilitator is the capacity to evolve a co-inquiry where "no subject is forbidden." This is only one of five levels within Isaacs's "competency cycle" for a dialogue facilitator. The other four include deep skills of noticing where the shared energy (the field) of a group is, the ability to name it, to engage the qualities, and then to evoke an engagement of that field. Isaacs is concerned that any facilitator opening the Pandora's box of dialogue have the maturity and skill to maintain a "dialogic way of being" and to create a "wholesome place" for dialogue to occur. The fact that Isaacs's consulting firm, Dia Logos, offers a training program that takes over a year to complete is testament to the depth of competence he feels is necessary to facilitate dialogue.

When I told Isaacs that many of the people who come to me to be trained to facilitate dialogue decide not to try it, he said that is a good sign—it's a "test" of the quality of instruction given. While I wish I could say anyone can facilitate dialogue, I have to agree. In the hands of an immature facilitator, attempts at dialogue can be risky. Linda Ellinor and Glenna Gerard of The Dialogue Group also advise, "We need to do our own personal work first—to know thyself— because only to the extent that I know myself am I able to be with and know others." So if you know yourself, if you can know others, and if you can maintain a dialogic way of being, then you should be equipped to handle the risks. If you can initiate a dialogue where you do not need to control the group but can instead bring a sense of safety simply through your state of being, the risk of anyone "getting hurt" is very low.

NO LEADER SHOULD MEAN NO FACILITATOR

Opinions on this issue are widely distributed. If you are a manager, you may need to participate in, as well as facilitate, dialogue with your workgroup. The model presented in this book keeps the facilitator on the outside of the group. As a consultant, I keep myself external to the group for two main reasons. The most important reason is that I do not wish to distort the group's collective thinking process. Since I am only there for a short time, I feel that my participating in the dialogue runs the risk of contributing new thinking that may not be sustainable when I am removed from the circle. Being a business consultant, I keep my eye on the shared-action benefits of dialogue. Any ideas stimulated by my thoughts or words may not translate as easily into shared action after I'm gone. However, ideas and insights generated by the group without my input are sure to remain intact and powerful when I leave.

The second reason is that group members get a chance to practice by themselves and experience their own competence. With enough training and modeling beforehand, the members of the group with a natural talent for dialogue will model dialogue skills for the rest of the group, better than I could have. I worry that if I participate, they may think their success in reaching dialogue had something to do with my participation. When I am on the outside of the circle, I can still coach and guide, but the group is essentially doing it without a facilitator (on average, I speak maybe two or three times in two hours). I'd rather the group falter a bit and find its own way to dialogue than follow my lead. When people find their own way, they mark a path that they can travel again later without me.

However, you may not be in a consulting role. If you need (or prefer) to participate as well as facilitate, then you will be interested to hear what other dialogue practitioners in the field recommend. Ellinor and Gerard feel that the facilitator should move into the circle as a "participant/facilitator." They refer to David Bohm's counsel to create an "equal playing field" and feel that a participant/facilitator is better positioned to model the principles of dialogue for the group rather than coach the group as an outside observer. To them, being outside contradicts the idea of an equal playing field. Gerard says, "By being in the circle we are modeling what it is to be a participant/facilitator." This role of participant/facilitator is one they stress for all members of a group who wish to be self-facilitating.

Nancy Dixon is also wary of any method that places emphasis on an external facilitator role. She says, "When I think of dialogue, I never think of it as a facilitated process." She makes the point that using a facilitator can focus participant attention on the facilitator ("Am I doing this right?") when attention should be focused "away from any expert and toward the relationship." To Dixon, what is central about dialogue lies in the relationship among the people, and a facilitator is extraneous to that relationship. On the other hand, she also admits it sets up a "difficult paradox when we tell people dialogue can make a difference—because it begs that we help make that difference."

You can help make a difference either as a facilitator or as a participant/facilitator. Isaacs speaks of "leading from behind." Is that facilitating or participating? The pursuit of dialogue doesn't lend itself to categories. This issue is too complex for easy answers, but your experiments will help to clarify the distinctions you choose to make in your situation. More important than who facilitates is what is going on inside you when you decide to help "make a difference."

BEING MORE THAN DOING

Dialogue gives us an opportunity to balance the emphasis we have placed on doing and blend it with a reflective stage to consider together who we are being and what that means. Much of our contact with other human beings occurs at work, and to pretend that we need only concern ourselves with the doing part is to miss a big piece of the equation. Dialogue brings us back to the important conversations that can dispel the fears, overcome the distrust, and release the passions we want to bring to the work we do together. We discover that what we have together is more powerful and more resilient than the dangerous truths from which we hide. We find that facing those dangerous truths builds an esprit de corps that is not possible with a less courageous group.

As you begin to experiment with dialogue, I encourage you to start big or small, at work or home, in a volunteer group or a workgroup, in a group of peers or subordinates, with lots of time or limited time. Try being a facilitator and participant at the same time, or just be a facilitator. Try the mind-sets and preempts provided (see Chapter 11) and try your own. Try doing it without mind-sets or preempts. Do it with a group of strangers or with people you know. Just try something!

Each experience will teach you something new about dialogue and about facilitating dialogue. As you experiment, you will build your own theories and methods that work for you and your environment. You only learn by trial and error; as long as you reflect on your experience, you will be in good shape. William Isaacs's admonition to reflect on our experiments was beautifully phrased. He said, "If I could place a warning label on the jar of dialogue it would say, 'Do not use without reflection!'"

I encourage you to reflect on the assumptions made in this book, your own assumptions, and your experiences because that is the essence of learning. It means creating a place that is safe enough to revisit the scary notion that we aren't as smart as we'd like to think, and trusting others enough to join forces so we can be smarter as a group than we were alone. Helping ourselves and helping others to find this level of safety and trust is gratifying work. The journey will introduce you to your own dangerous truths. It can be scary, but ultimately you will find that like the groups you serve, what you say and what you do come closer and closer together into one integrated whole. It is from this state of integrity that work requires fewer struggles and offers more experiences of effortless flow. Work and life get easier when you know how to dialogue.

A Recipe for Dialogue

F
acilitating dialogue cannot be reduced to a step-by-step process. Yet it is helpful to observe steps that have worked before. I present an all-too-clear, all-too-directive "recipe" for the setup leading to dialogue. Take it with a grain of salt. Use what you want. And for goodness' sake, don't follow it word for word. Notice the basic structure and then create your own process to fit your own situation.

The recipe follows a linear progression. I never do it in the same order twice, but this order is as good as any:

Before You Begin

What Is Dialogue to You?

"Wants/Don't Wants" Process

Your Role as Facilitator

Building Expectations for Dialogue

Using Icons: Five Stages of Dialogue

Going Slow to Go Fast

Content/Process Model

Positive Intent Model

Comfort Zone Model

Group Escape Strategies

Individual Escape Strategies

Identifying Assumptions With Ladder of Inference (Experiential Exercise)

Choosing the Rules for Dialogue

Begin Dialogue

End Dialogue

Harvesting

To help us communicate in an "online, offline" sort of way, I will make my behind-the-scenes comments in italics. I present a facsimile of a script (Lord save us from people who give scripts and expect us to use them word for word!) in regular type along with a subject description in bold at the beginning of each section. In real life, sections don't have clear distinctions, and the order usually follows the flow of the group. But for our purposes, the distinctions make sense for illustrating the process.

Before You Begin

[Before you begin, try to have a few informal one-on-one conversations to discover the dangerous truths or real problems. (You can also use this time to build expectations.) People will tell you things in a one-on-one conversation that they do not intend to mention in the group. Assure them of anonymity and stick to your agreement. But find out the hidden issues if you can. Use this time to softly encourage individuals to speak truthfully once dialogue begins. As you facilitate, you may have the opportunity to ask questions in a way that gives permission to discuss these dangerous truths. Frequently, as a facilitator you can say things that no one else can say. Use this time to build rapport and to find out what dangerous truths need to find a safe place.]

8:30 A.M. What Is Dialogue to You?

Facilitator: Some of you know me; some don't. I would like to share a little bit about who I am and why I am here. My interest in dialogue began in 1993 when I wrote my thesis on dialogue. Since then, the experience that this process can transform a group to a higher level of understanding and cohesion has fascinated me. I wanted to know how it works and what I could do to help it along. I've studied psychology, sociology, adult education, neurobiology, and even dabbled in quantum physics in my effort to understand this process. Let me explain some of the definitions that people use to describe dialogue.

David Bohm, the quantum physicist who is credited with our renewed interest in the process, said that "a thought observed is transformed" and that "dialogue is the collective way of opening up judgments and assumptions," an "exploration of the shared meanings that constitute our culture."

Edgar Schein said that dialogue is a technology that makes it possible for "people to discover that they use language differently, that they operate from different mental models and the categories we employ are ultimately learned social constructions of reality and thus arbitrary."

Linda Ellinor and Glenna Gerard say, "Dialogue is a powerful communications practice [that] transforms those who engage in it." What do you think they mean by "transform"?

Peter Senge says, "In dialogue, individuals gain insights that simply could not be achieved individually." How might that help this group?

What do you think dialogue means? *[I recommend metaphors like the ones in Chapter 2 to stimulate discussion.]*

[The words you use in the first five minutes are very important. Use words that build your credibility as a facilitator and that simultaneously demonstrate your respect for the intelligence of the group. Avoid setting yourself up as an expert—it will sabotage the group's efforts later. Build a discussion that creates a working definition of dialogue and links it clearly to benefits that make the group think this will be a worthwhile use of its time. This first part can take up to an hour. It is time well spent if group members develop their own compelling vision of dialogue.]

9:00 A.M. "Wants/Don't Wants" Process

Facilitator: So why are you here? What sort of outcome could we achieve today that would make your time "time well spent?" What sort of things would you like to avoid? You have some experience with this group. You already know the sort of things that would take this group off track. Think about it. This is the time to speak, *before* any of those old disruptive patterns begin. I want everyone in the room to come up with at least one "want" and one "don't want." What is it that you want from today? What are you pretty sure you don't want?

> [This is a very important part of your process. You will probably have to milk group members for their wants and don't wants. Some people will say things such as, "I don't know what you are planning, so how can I say what I want?" or "I dunno." This may demonstrate a lack of interest or apathy. Apathetic people can't dialogue. Dialogue only occurs when people deeply care about what they are discussing. Help them mine deeply into their memories and find something they care about or something that they can hope for. Many people feel that they might set themselves up for disappointment. Your energy and enthusiasm will be necessary to get them to hope that today may be different from all the other times they sat in a room and wasted time.]

Use a flip chart and record the wants and don't wants of the group. Make sure everyone says at least one of each. Work with every person to get them to state their desires and fears. This stakes them out at the beginning of the process. Once you can get them to state a want or don't want, you have changed their position in the group. They have gone on record as saying that they have a stake in the outcome of the day. They become engaged and your job just got easier.

Facilitator Probes

- What might you say at the end of the day if this is successful? How would you measure success? What would tell you that you had had a successful dialogue?

- What behaviors do you want to see in yourself and others (particularly the ones you don't usually see)? If you don't want anything, then why are we here? There better be something worthwhile to achieve, or we are wasting a lot of time for a lot of people.

- If you have some bad habits (e.g., dominating, talking too much, talking too little), why not go ahead and use that as your don't want (before someone else does and gives you the "meaningful stare")?

■ What behaviors normally take this group away from dialogue? How can we phrase those into a don't want?

[Once you have a list of wants and don't wants from everyone in the group (with groups larger than twelve people, you can let them "ditto"), you have begun the process for them to create their own expectations and constraints. This list will facilitate the group as much as you will. A sample list from a dialogue session I ran included:

WANTS	DON'T WANTS
People to be open and honest, to tell the truth	Anyone to feel hurt or damaged by this process
Buy in	Waste of time
To understand the different points of view—why people do what they do	To lose the individual in all this "groupness"
Learn something	Vendettas afterward
Respect for everyone's point of view	The same fighting and shutdown we always get

Each group intuitively chooses words that address its most problematic norms. The process not only heightens the group's awareness but gives you valuable information as a facilitator. I use the wants/don't wants process at the beginning of any process I do because it builds shared responsibility right from the start.]

9:30 A.M. *Your Role as Facilitator*

Facilitator: I have some wants and don't wants, too. I want to be a good facilitator and I need to share with you what I think that means. I am not the leader of this dialogue. That would disrupt the process. I am here to facilitate and to share with you the things I know about group process and the unique communication process called dialogue, but I am not here to lead your process.

I want to become unnecessary as soon as possible. My goal is to transfer what I know to you as soon as possible. During the dialogue my goal is to say nothing.

I want to give you tools, not rules. You will impose your own guidelines and I will act as a reminder, only.

I don't want to and won't argue. If you want to argue, I'll let you win. Arguing is counter to dialogue. Sure, debate can be fun, but this isn't the time or place to indulge ourselves.

I don't want to and will not take responsibility for your outcome. The process is completely in your hands. If I take responsibility, that cheats you of the opportunity to learn how to dialogue by yourselves. I trust you to take your dialogue to the level you want and need.

[Use this time to build the group's expectations of you. Correct for any style issues you may have. Preempt any issues you think may cause you problems. For instance, I spend a lot of time on the part about me not taking responsibility. I want them to understand I have a strong commitment to their success, but for me that means not being too directive. This avoids the resentment they may feel later in the afternoon when they are frustrated and I don't seem to be helping them out of that frustration.]

I'd also like to note that I used the word *outcome* without doubling back to explain that dialogue has no outcome—one of the rules is "no outcome." After years of facilitating dialogue, I have learned that you will lose the group and disappear into psychobabble if you try to stay true to the finer points of dialogue too early in the process. Limit yourself to one step at a time. If you were teaching a group to dance, you would only confuse people by focusing on the finer points of posture at the same time you are teaching them the basic steps. Since dialogue is nonlinear and full of polarities to be managed, there are many points where you could disappear into tangents. I've found it to be very helpful to learn to ignore some of the contradictions that occur in the beginning when you must oversimplify the process in order to explain it. If someone calls you on a contradiction (and sooner or later they will), you can use the opportunity to model inquiry and reflection.

9:40 A.M. *Building Expectations for Dialogue*

Facilitator: What is dialogue? Where are we at with our definition?

[Opening the floor for discussion gives you an opportunity to find out where the group is at. If there are people who are suspicious of the process, their comments or body language will tell you. Guide the group to give a definition that is interesting enough to proceed. You will build

your definition from theirs. Tap into the things they say to make a link between dialogue and something that is important to them. No one will (or should) participate in this process unless they believe that they are going to get something out of it that is worth their investment of time. Your first job as a facilitator is to reveal to them the benefits of the process. They need to be sold on the process; the ideal situation is to set it up so that they sell themselves.]

Facilitator: One definition comes from the Latin derivatives:

Dia: Shared   **Logos:** Meaning

I've seen dialogue change a group. I've seen the process, in one day, erase patterns of interaction that were tearing a group apart. One time I was asked to work with a group where trust was very low. People were withholding information, sabotaging projects; it was a big mess. When I went in, I found varying degrees of hostility and apathy—I didn't see much enthusiasm. Soon I discovered that this group represented the survivors of a major downsizing—and it felt a bit guilty about that. Not only that, but they had been individual contributors Ph.D.s (each with an administrative assistant), and now they were being asked to share a pool of support staff. One of them would soon be chosen to head the group and they were all in competition for this important job.

Of course, trust was low! There were many outside dynamics at work that set this group up to feel like a bunch of enemies. There were negative emotions and dangerous truths that—well, there was so much that they couldn't talk about, it left very little room for communication. This happens often—so many subjects become taboo that no one can talk to each other anymore.

They weren't too enthusiastic about this dialogue approach either. Negative comments, sarcastic sidebars, and not a few Ph.D.-like challenges: "Is there any empirical evidence to support the theoretical validity of that statement?" Oi vey! It was rough. So by the time we got to dialogue, I wondered if they would just sit and stare for two hours, tear each other to pieces, or walk out. But they surprised me. I believe that we all have a hunger to stop hiding and deal with reality for better or worse—that somewhere deep inside us is a desire to make things better.

They sat in silence for a long time. Once someone began to speak, it quickly reached a bitter exchange. Each one had secret suspicions that the others had behaved unethically to keep their jobs or to snare the leadership position. As long as their suspicions were secret, they festered and corrupted the relationship. At one point one of the women (the toughest one there, I might add) started to cry. It changed the state of the group. They dropped the tough-guy act, too. The entire group began to speak of their sadness, their dashed hopes, and the guilt they felt when they talked to the ones who hadn't made the cut.

This dialogue gave them the opportunity to test the negative assumptions they had made about themselves and others and to find them false. Instead of a bunch of cutthroats, they discovered that they were all in the same boat. And as the negative assumptions dissipated, their energy began to return. The deadness turned into aliveness and they began to come up with creative solutions. Not the least of which is that they decided that the leader role wasn't worth fighting over. Most of them really didn't even want the headaches that it would entail. They began to design a plan where systems could help them share the support staff equitably without a formal leader.

It was a very different group after dialogue. This is the sort of thing that happens in dialogue. There are stories of union and management in the steel industry finding that they had more in common than they ever suspected. They all loved their families. They all wanted to do a good job—and they all wanted to ensure they weren't exploited. That common ground bound them together to collectively seek out solutions. If dialogue can bring archenemies like union and management together, what can it do for you?

[Tell your own story, feel free to use any of mine, or use one from any of the wonderful books and articles being published on dialogue. But find a compelling story that builds a picture of hope for the group. I always choose a story that addresses the same sort of problems I see in the group.]

9:50 A.M. Using Icons:
Five Stages of Dialogue

Facilitator: A picture is worth a thousand words. I have a visual definition of dialogue that I would like to share with you. Since language is really inadequate to describe this living, moving, transformative process, I use pictures, or icons.

As a picture, dialogue looks something like this:

POLITENESS AND PRETENDING

Politeness and Pretending

In the beginning, no one admits anything is wrong. They blame everyone else or pretend as if the problem is unsolvable. Each of these squiggles in the square is a belief. We all walk in knowing exactly "what needs to happen here." *[Draw a pattern for each of the following statements.]* Marketing thinks we need to do more research (a figure eight). Accounting thinks we need to cut costs (an ellipse). Information technology thinks we need to buy more hardware (a square). Manufacturing thinks we need to fire the salespeople if they don't stop selling what doesn't exist (a triangle). Each one of us has a belief that is a closed system. But no one is going to say anything . . . yet. *[Draw the lines over the patterns.]* Everyone is going to see if they can sniff out what the other one thinks first.

CHAOS

Chaos

Eventually someone speaks her mind —which bumps directly against someone else's point of view—then she speaks out and . . . it's on. When the group finally faces the facts and allows hidden conflicts to surface, it usually looks like chaos. *[Redraw the exposed patterns with collision lines.]* We usually avoid chaos. Some groups stop here and revert right back to the politeness and pretending stage without ever solving the underlying problems. Some dive into chaos and stay there, looping back through the same old arguments they always loop through. However, if the group uses the new norms of dialogue, something different will happen.

    With dialogue, progress continues to the next stage.

DISCARDING AND REDEFINING

If the group addresses its conflict and each group member willingly risks certainty about the "facts" and becomes flexible enough to generate a dialogue about the issues, what you begin to see is a process of discarding and redefining. I give a little bit and you give a little bit. *[Draw patterns opening up.]* The beliefs begin to bend and flex. Old ones don't disappear—they just adapt to new incoming information. When you are here, you know you know it because it feels lousy. It is uncomfortable and risky. Before you were sure and now you aren't. There are long silences as people deconstruct what they thought they knew for sure. There isn't much eye contact as people begin to really think about their thinking.

Discarding and Redefining

RESOLUTION AND COLLECTIVE LEARNING

Eventually, if people keep talking, the belief systems begin to connect into a new belief that is a function of the original ones, pieces of the old, but new. *[Draw the bigger new pattern with the four arrows.]* If each original belief was a piece of the elephant (I've used the blind men and the elephant metaphor by now), then all of a sudden, each member of the group gets a picture of the whole elephant.

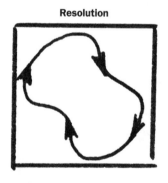

Resolution

This is a new, shared belief that transcends/connects the seemingly contradictory beliefs people started out with. It is higher learning. This is where the group thinks as a collective and builds a bigger picture inclusive of all positions. This new view is big enough to hold the inherent conflicts and to deliver a consensus viewpoint that works for everyone. Everyone doesn't agree on everything, but from this major vantage point on they all see the same things. You know you are here because it feels great. This is the birth of a new, creative group point of view. These ideas, concepts, and beliefs did not exist before dialogue.

CLOSURE

But we can't stay in this heightened state of flexibility for too long. In dialogue nothing is firm or clear or definite. Dialogue is not the state from which action occurs. That is why we make dialogue a special time. Most of the time our beliefs need to be firm and clear. We can't go through life questioning all of our assumptions. We'd never get anything done. Two hours is about as much as we

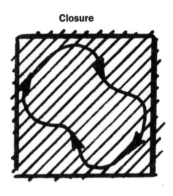

Closure

can take. Dialogue is exhausting, so we need to take time to put habits and norms back in place. *[Begin to draw lines over the new bigger pattern.]*

Part of the reason we can do it is that we all agree that we don't have to be this open and flexible all the time. At the end of a dialogue we need to bring it to closure.

This is the point where we move back to a more stable state of lowered risk and less flexibility. Heretofore, we have avoided solidifying anything. Now, as a part of closure, we can harvest the benefits of dialogue with new agreements and implementation plans.

[I suggest you draw the pictures as you talk. Why? Two reasons: retention and the ability of pictures to target the right brain. Convenience is dramatically overrated in most training. Overheads of beautifully drawn pictures will not be as engaging as watching you draw. (The worse your drawing skills, the more engaging it becomes!) The human mind remembers symbols better than it can remember a long string of words.]

Their minds draw along with your hand. More important, the pictures help you develop the expectations of the group. One of your challenges will be to reframe conflict and discomfort as positive things. That's not going to be easy. Their intuitive right brain will be more receptive to that idea than their logical left brain. Pictures help you start talking to their right brain early.

10:20 A.M. Break

10:35 A.M. Going Slow to Go Fast

Facilitator: So how can we speed this up? Let's find a way to dump a bunch of people in a room, stir them up, and have them emerge transformed by the process in under an hour. *[Pause to let them think about that one.]* Kind of unrealistic, isn't it? This process takes time. We have to go backward before we can go forward.

I have a greyhound named Larry. Larry comes from the rescue shelter. He obviously didn't win too many races because Larry was retired very young. Now, retired greyhounds make wonderful pets, but they grew up in a kennel. When a greyhound comes to live with you, there are certain life skills you need to share with him. Like house-training. They also don't have much road sense. They may have been on a leash before, but going for a walk in the neighborhood presents a few surprises. My Larry, for instance, has not yet figured out—and shows no signs of figuring out—that if he walks on one side of a telephone pole and I walk on the other, we aren't going anywhere. He looks up at me, wonder on his little dog face, asking, "What's your problem?"

Now I can tell myself that I'm the adult here and he is the dog, but he isn't going to back off until I back off. If I back off, he will follow my lead. I don't want to go too far with this metaphor—I suspect there are a few people in this room thinking about a doglike person in your life who is preventing forward movement. The important point is that sometimes you have to back off to go forward. Particularly if they aren't going to back off until you do.

Sometimes you have to go slow to go fast. Dialogue is about slowing it down so we can check for errors.

So the process itself is designed to slow down thinking, to back up and take a look. By noon, some of you will probably be thinking, "I've never in my life talked about talking for so long without actually talking!" The slowness can be frustrating, but it is very useful.

If dialogue spontaneously happened whenever we needed it, we wouldn't have to go to so much trouble to create it, would we? Why don't we just jump right in? Why don't we dialogue right now?

[Open the floor for discussion. Bring out statements such as: Some people dominate, others zone out; we don't all share the same picture of what "it" is; people argue the same old arguments; and so on. This vents frustration with the process early on and preempts negative comments to "just get on with it."]

Facilitator: We will be spending several hours doing other things before you even get to dialogue. This is because dialogue is different from normal conversation, and there are specific skills that, when everyone does them together, dramatically changes the way you communicate as a group. Western culture has a bias to action that prevents us from spending too much time on the basics up front. When that happens, easily preventable mistakes occur, and avoidable problems are not avoided. This morning, we are taking the entire morning to make sure we avoid the pitfalls that normally sabotage conversation. We could take longer, but a half day is a good balance between talking about it and doing it.

[Here you are building an expectation and asking permission. If it sounds plausible enough, they will participate enthusiastically. If not, you will spend more of your time dealing with resistance. Talk about how people spend a week preparing to make a three-minute parachute jump, or other stories about spending up-front planning time so implementation is fast and simple. Your goal here is twofold. You want to build expectations and acceptance for "going slow" during dialogue, and you need to get implicit permission for a few more hours of preparation time.]

10:45 A.M. Content/Process Model

Facilitator: This is one of the most important models I have ever learned as far as helping me get better results when I deal with people and group process. It is also one of the simplest—it is deceptively simple. There are two pieces of any message, and thus any communication or any group interaction. (See Appendix Figure 1) They are:

- Content (what is said)
- Process (how it is said)

Have you ever been in a meeting where, by the end of the meeting, everyone had agreed on the "what"? Maybe there was an action plan with a critical path of tasks, each allocated to someone, and with a date that each task was to be completed. The content was beautiful, perfect—and then three weeks later, what did you find? Nothing had happened, or major pieces hadn't. This is because it is not only the "what" (the content) that is important. Anyone can produce a list of things to do. It is "how" that list is generated (the process) that gets the list done. And the "how" that creates coordinated action usually takes longer than the apparent time needed to generate a list. There is so much more going on than content. If you want coordinated action, you have to pay more attention to process, to the "how." Do the people who are supposed to take these actions feel as if they were a part of the process? Do they think it is a good idea? Does everyone hold the same picture in their mind of what these actions mean?

Appendix Figure 1

In your experience, you've probably run across a situation like this: Two people come to you, angry and upset, and one says, "All I did was ask him where the report is," and the other one says, "It was how you asked." You can ask a question many different ways. You can ask, "Where is the report?" or you can ask, "Where is the report?" *[Ask one sarcastically, implying incompetence, and the other as a genuine question.]* What is the difference between those two comments? Some people ask a question, but it isn't really a question. How you say something is very important in dialogue.

Another important aspect of the content/process model is the distinction it creates for us in understanding dialogue. Have you ever talked something over and felt as if you ended up right back where you started? With dialogue, the idea is to end up in a different place. The difference between a discussion and dialogue is not what you talk about, but how you talk about it. It will look different and it will feel different. It is hard not to rush to content, but the secret to dialogue is to pay attention to process. That gives the content a chance to evolve into something new, something that brings coherence to the group.

Don't worry about the action plan. Experiment with a complete focus on process. I think you will be pleasantly surprised a week from now when you review the impact this process makes on your ability to create coordinated action.

[The purpose here is to build the expectation that everyone will be held responsible for the messages sent by their tone of voice and body language as well as their words. Again, you are building the expectation that this will be different. The expectation that it will be different is as much a part of the process as the skills.]

10:55 A.M. Positive Intent Model

Facilitator: Have you ever gone into a communication with a clear goal—say, to make someone feel better (A)—and ended up getting a very contrary result—making them feel worse (B)? (See Appendix Figure 2 and 3.)

Maybe you've asked what you think is an encouraging question, and instead of being encouraged someone gets all defensive. ("So are you finished yet?") Or with your spouse, you've done everything to create a romantic evening, and instead of gazing into each other's eyes you end up fighting? Why does that happen? How does that happen? There are a thousand different reasons, but the most important thing to remember is that it happens.

Our best intentions don't always translate into reality. We want to do the right thing (A), we try to do the right thing, and yet we end up making people feel bad (B). If it happens to us, it happens to other people, too. We jump to conclusions too often that the people who are making us feel worse intended to do that. The truth is they probably didn't intend that at all. They probably have positive intentions that we just couldn't see. We can never see someone's intention. All we see is behavior and the impact it has on us. A new

Appendix Figure 2   **Appendix Figure 3**

budget program that makes our life hell is often not assumed to come from a sincere desire to help the company, but from some anal retentive manager's control need. The psychologists call it malicious attribution—where we assume that a person has malicious intent. We assume that people are making us crazy, miserable, or inconvenienced on purpose. Usually they aren't.

We see their action and assume we understand their intent. This is a major assumption that I encourage you to explore during dialogue. I'd venture to bet that at least 50 percent of the time (and that is a conservative estimate) you are dead wrong about someone's intent. There is a lightning-flash judgment we rarely notice when something irritates us, looks counterproductive, seems stupid, whatever. All human beings supply an assumption about why other people do whatever they did. If more of us were to test these assumptions about others' intent, we would be amazed at the number of people who want the same things we want.

Think about the person in this room who drives you crazy. Don't look at him for heaven's sake—look somewhere else. Now, try to come up with an alternative explanation in your mind that places a positive intent behind the actions that you find so frustrating. What would be a positive intent behind that person's actions? During dialogue you will have an opportunity to test that hypothesis. I encourage you to go looking for positive intentions that you may have missed before. If you look for them, you may find them.

[*Use this section to get the group members to begin to challenge the assumptions they are making about the other people in the room. This is a good place for a story—maybe a time when you made assumptions and found out you were wrong about another's intent.*]

11:05 A.M. Comfort Zone Model

Facilitator: Why do we hang out in the politeness and pretending stage so much? When we begin to reveal our differences, how does it feel? Being open to change is uncomfortable.

What is the purpose of your mind? [*This question is always good for discussion.*] Basically, it is a survival machine. It was designed to help you survive. Cavemen, once they found a stream that was safe from attacking lions, tigers, and bears, did what? They (a) found a new stream or (b) kept going to the same stream? They kept going to the same stream, didn't they? Sure, and the beliefs you have right now about *x* and *y* [name subjects relevant to the group] represent your favorite streams. You go back to them over and over. You don't need a new belief—it could be dangerous, risky.

Someone in this room knows about a better stream, a better belief, and for you to listen to it—to go try out this new stream—how is it going to feel? Uncomfortable, right? What if that person is wrong?

Okay, if the comfort zone was designed to protect our survival, how does our brain keep us safe? What is our automatic reaction when anyone takes us out of our comfort zone? [Let the group answer.] Fight or flight, right?

Several hundred years ago, these terms were pretty literal. We punched, scratched, and kicked, or we ran like hell. Today we have the same emotional impulses, but we have developed more civilized behaviors to respond to those impulses. What are the 1990s versions of fight and flight that we use whenever we are faced with information that takes us out of our comfort zone?

[Let the group list these. Prompt them only to get them started. This is not about the list you generate. This is a real-time self-awareness process designed to develop a heightened awareness that will last through dialogue.]

FIGHT		FLIGHT	
Argue	Defend	Withdraw	Change subject
Sarcasm	Mocking	Ignore	Shut down
Blame	Belittle	Deny	Get bored or
Attack	Justify	Intellectualize	confused
Explain	Discredit	Patronize	Placate
Confound	Confuse	Pretend to agree	
Launch guerrilla attacks	Check out		

Now, take a few minutes to consider the three defensive patterns that you use most often in group discussions when you feel you might discover you were wrong about something]

[After the members of the group have written them down, ask permission to go around the room and have them read the three items they listed aloud for the group. In my experience, no group has ever said no to this request. They intuitively know it will help. It also allows everyone

to "self-disclose" together—this way no one has to muster the courage
to stand alone and admit they do these sorts of things. This begins to
"build the muscle" for being open and honest. It is an imbedded prompt
to get the ball rolling.]

Now, how do we know when we are in danger? One thing about the fight/flight response is that it is an automatic and mindless reaction. You usually don't know until it is too late. I want to give you an exercise—an experiential exercise—that will develop your skill in recognizing the physical feeling that precedes this sort of behavior.

In a minute, starting with *[name someone introverted]*, I am going to have everyone stand up and sing, individually, the first verse of "The Star-Spangled Banner."

[Natter on about how this will help them understand their comfort zone.
This gives them time to panic. Most will. Then call it off.]

Okay, you don't really have to sing. I just wanted you to notice what the thought of singing did to your body. Did you feel a physiological response to the idea of stepping outside your comfort zone? What was it?

[Encourage people to describe the physical reaction of sweaty palms,
tightness in the gut, a flushed face, and so on.]

You will feel that same response when someone in this room challenges one of your near and dear beliefs. It is different for everyone, so pay attention to what you just learned about yourself and your physiology. The emotions that stimulate these responses give you a physical cue first. If you watch for it, you can learn to feel the discomfort without reacting the way you usually do—and see if there might be something new to learn. Learning always requires a step outside the comfort zone.

Remember, if you are successful in dialogue, you will emerge from this process, each one of you, somewhat changed by the experience. This will inevitably take you to the edge of your comfort zone. If you don't feel uncomfortable, you aren't digging deeply enough.

[In these sections you are teaching the group to monitor itself so you
don't have to. Now is the time to introduce these concepts—while

everything is calm and peaceful, so that when you remind them of it later, they won't feel attacked. This is the secret of good facilitation: the ability to teach group members how to facilitate themselves.]

11:15 A.M. *Group Escape Strategies*

Facilitator: There are a few easily predicted patterns that groups display the minute the going gets tough. This comes straight from group dynamics. Why would you want to study groups? What was the original purpose of group dynamics?

[Open for discussion. Bring out statements such as: to get them to do what you want, to stick with the task, to avoid predictable problems, and so on. Find out what is relevant to them.]

Groups are predictable in the way they collude to avoid getting outside their comfort zone. There are four basic ways that a group will get off course. I introduce them to you so that you can watch out for them. My job as a facilitator will be to help you stay alert, but the main responsibility lies with you. Ultimately, you as a group must monitor yourselves to avoid these escape strategies.

I'm going to draw them as pictures to help you remember. We will post them on the wall as a reminder.

[Again, draw the pictures as you talk. Even if they get a giggle from your drawing abilities, they will remember longer.]

FLIGHT

What does flight look like in a meeting?

[Bring out comments such as: ignoring, looking out the window, zoning out, for example. You will probably have to add: structured decision processes such as splitting into subgroups, majority vote, and calls for the group to go outside to sit in the sun.]

Flight

FIGHT

What does this fight look like?

Fight

[Bring out descriptions of heated inquiry, uproar, sarcasm, "let's you and him fight," for example. Add whatever you have learned about the group's fight patterns. Most groups have one argument over and over and the same people play the same roles. See if you can draw that out so they become aware of the pattern.]

PAIRING

When you have a group of fifteen people and two of those people lean over together *[cup your hand over your mouth and whisper to one of the group members]*, what does that do to the group? How many groups do you have now? What about a raised eyebrow shot across the room? Or the rolling eyes? That is pairing. It is an escape from true dialogue. It is hard to talk with a large group. It decreases the complexity significantly to limit your conversation to one person, but it is not dialogue. Pairing is an escape. How else do people do this escape?

Pairing

[Bring out descriptions of whispers in the back of the room, inside jokes, sidebar comments, for example.]

DEPENDENCY

What does dependency look like? *[Let them guess what the drawing means.]* Dialogue is hard, and with anything that is hard we have a tendency to want to get some help. Problem is, that tendency can turn into dependency. We treat leaders that way all too frequently. We can't

figure out what we should do, so
we go to our leaders and ask
them to tell us. We want them
to do our thinking for us. At
some point you are going to
want me to tell you if you are
doing dialogue "right." I'm
going to do everything in my

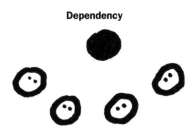

Dependency

power to get you to make that evaluation yourself—to do your own
thinking. If someone emerges as a leader, speaking for the group, that
isn't dialogue, either. One of the rules of dialogue is "No Leader" just
so that everyone is actively involved in the hard work of thinking.
How does this group tend to do dependency?

> [Bring out comments such as: defer to a facilitator, blame the process,
> you didn't say to do x, you didn't get us there, it's your fault we are fight-
> ing, and so on.]

So these are the group escape strategies to watch out for. My
job as a facilitator will be to operate as a highlighter for a period of
time, drawing your attention to these dynamics when they occur so
that you can avoid them. By the fourth or fifth time that we do this
process, my goal is that you won't need me anymore. You will have
developed a new habit of avoiding these counterproductive dynamics
and will monitor yourselves.

11:30 A.M. Individual Escape Strategies

Facilitator: Along with the group escape strategies, there are several individual escape strategies that invariably sabotage a group's
efforts to achieve true dialogue. Expect to see these. Look for them—
because you will find them. And most important, look for them in
your own thinking and speaking. These defense strategies occur
inside your own head. They are frequently invisible to you yet visible
to others. Ideally you want to monitor yourself—but don't be embarrassed if someone else points out that you are doing one of these. It is
only natural and to be expected. Your brain likes to keep things simple and would prefer to stick with its present view of the world rather
than shift over to a newer view that might take some getting used to.

What sort of mental patterns do we use so that we don't have
to reevaluate our position? The common patterns are as follows:

TENACITY

Can you tell what this is? What does it mean mentally when we are "digging our heels in"?

Tenacity

> [Bring out comments such as: shut down, closing off input, prejudice, "that's the way we've always done it," saying the same thing a hundred different ways.]

What's the best way to get someone to dig in her heels? To attack her point of view, maybe? We are all guilty of tightening our grip on a particular belief or position for no other reason than that someone else is trying to get us to change our mind. Or sometimes just the thought of admitting that we were wrong causes us to stick to our guns. Watch out for this one. If you find yourself repeating the same point more than three times, even if you paraphrase it, ask yourself if you are engaging in tenacity.

FACTUMPTIONS

Just the facts, right? What is a fact? Give me some facts, a few "facts of life."

Factumptionism

> [Bring out comments such as time is money, hard work pays off, tell the boss what she wants to hear, and so on.]

Are they facts or are they opinions? We base new opinions on these "facts" until we are several steps away from any semblance of a fact. Dialogue is the opportunity to question assumptions that we have used for so long that our mind thinks they are facts. Real creativity means challenging "common knowledge"—particularly any common knowledge that begins "You can't do x" or "Everyone knows that x won't work or isn't possible." Assumptions about people are escapes, also. If "she is just unreasonable," then you don't have to try so hard to dialogue with her, do you? Think about the assumptions you treat as fact.

REDUCTIONISM

We use imaginary lines and cat-egories to simplify our world into manageable chunks. Our brains can't hold the complexity of reality so we chunk it down into imaginary pieces. Like an organization chart, this is not real. There are no boxes; there are no clear lines where my role stops and yours begins. What is

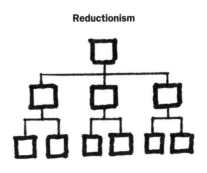

Reductionism

this in comparison to reality? What are some other arbitrary lines that we treat as real?

> [Bring out concepts such as national borders, market segmentation, racial lines, right and wrong, and good and bad as examples.]

The truth is that all of these lines are fuzzy, and for the dura-tion of dialogue we stop pretending that they aren't and see whatever it is that we miss when we pretend the lines are distinct.

DISTANCING

A special form of reductionism is the one that draws a line between me and "the problem," which is over there, where you are. We do that all the time. We gripe about the govern-ment—and I want to know whose government is it? We are a part of it, not separate and distinct from it. Liv-ing overseas helped me see this one. Whenever a problem seems too daunting to solve alone, we will tend

Distancing

to distance ourselves from it. To admit that we are a part of the system that needs fixing begs action of some sort and, well, we are more comfortable putting the problem way over there and us over here. What are some ways that we use the mental defense of distancing?

[Bring out comments such as: it's not my job, that is "your" area, it's "your problem" not "our problem."]

If you do not consider yourself as part of the system, you are powerless and it prevents your participation in dialogue.

So, do you think you can refrain from these escapisms for at least two hours? It is harder than you think. Do I have your permission to point out the times when I see you are engaging in one of these escape strategies?

[One of the most important things you will say as a facilitator is, "Do I have your permission?" Say it up front before you have to point out these escape strategies. Once you are in the middle of the dialogue, the group may be embarrassed or defensive or whatever, and then it is much harder to manage.]

11:45 A.M. Identifying Assumptions With Ladder of Inference

Facilitator: What is the primary cause of miscommunication?

[Let the group list several causes, but you want to end up with something that says: "Assuming you understand when you don't." Resist the urge to get into a deeper discussion here. Save most of your discussion for later; otherwise people will doctor up their left-hand column to look more rational.]

In a way, dialogue is the art of finding assumptions that are deeply embedded in our thinking. In a minute, we are going to do an exercise that will give you some material to work with. We are going to do the left-hand column exercise adapted from the work of Chris Argyris. Has anyone done this exercise before?

[Let people talk about their previous experience to ensure there are no objections that will hamper the process.]

To do this exercise, I want you to think back to an exchange, maybe with a subordinate, a superior, a supplier, or a customer, that didn't turn out like you wanted it to. This is *not* a situation where you and your masterful interpersonal skills saved the day, but a situation where you or someone else ended up unhappy with the result. Everyone has one or two recent ones. Choose one of them. If you need help, think about the one person at work who makes your life difficult and use one of the recent conversations you've had with that person.

Choose a situation where there was just the two of you—a discussion you can remember pretty well, what you said, the other person said, then what you said, and so on. Once you have that in mind, I want you to take a sheet of paper and draw a line vertically down the middle, dividing it into two columns.

Then in the right-hand column—don't worry about the left for now—write out the verbal exchange just like a scriptwriter would write. Make it look like a movie script, complete with stage direction that you'll write in parentheses, such as (pause), (rolled her eyes), or comments on tone: (angrily), (patronizingly), and so on. Don't analyze the words, but do include such things as shrugs, grunts, anything that a scriptwriter would include to re-create the exchange exactly as it happened.

So, to repeat:

1 Choose a recent discussion or argument that didn't turn out right.

2 Divide a clean sheet of paper in two equal columns.

3 On the right side write a script of the exchange: He said, I said, and so on.

[Allow enough time to get at least ten lines of "He said, I said." Then walk around the room and ensure that people are providing the material they will need—take about ten minutes. You will probably need to coach them individually. Use the time to find one of the examples that will be particularly good for the next step. Before you start to walk around, ask if anyone would rather you didn't look over their shoulder. People may choose a personal exchange and, if you forget to ask, they will be offended at your eavesdropping. It's about safety, remember? Everything you do should be moving people toward feeling more and more safe. When you find a "good one," ask the person's permission to use it and start writing it up on the flip chart paper while everyone else is finishing up.]

Now, in the left-hand column we are going to add the thoughts and feelings that were left unspoken. We want to document the assumptions that were behind the words.

Jeff was kind enough to let us use his example. I'd like us all to pretend that we don't know Jeff and that these are two strangers. It helps us remember that there are no "facts" when we are dealing with assumptions. Otherwise we end up badgering Jeff here with questions, and that is not the point.

Okay, this is what was said. *[Read the script.]* What wasn't said? In the left-hand column we are going to fill in the unspoken assumptions and begin to deconstruct the underlying beliefs that were the foundation for the exchange.

First, I'm going to read an example. Listen to what was really said. *[Read the right-hand column of the example given below.]* Pretty polite discussion, huh? Now I'll read it with the left-hand column added. The left-hand column is what wasn't said but was thought—the hidden assumptions behind the polite words.

[Read the following example. Read the right-hand column first, using the cues for tone and nonverbals. Ham it up and have some fun. Then read it with the left-hand column so the participants understand what you are looking for. After this, begin to work the example provided by the volunteer.]

UNSPOKEN THOUGHTS	SCRIPT OF CONVERSATION
I know that I better go easy here. She could go off at any moment.	Bert: Hi, Sally, having a good day, so far? (smirk)
Here he comes again to badger me about those figures.	Sally: (eyes roll) I *was* having a great day.
She is determined to make my life miserable. What did I ever do to her?	Bert: What's up with the report? Got those figures yet? (feigned neutrality)
He must think I don't have anything else to do but make spreadsheets for his department.	Sally: Didn't I tell you I would get them to you by Friday? (still no eye contact)
I didn't believe you, so I'm here to make damn sure you do.	Bert: I just thought you might have them done early. Tomorrow is Friday.
Even if I did have them early, I wouldn't give them to you, you jerk.	Sally: You will have them on Friday. (dismissively)
I better have them you old bag, or you will be sorry.	Bert: That's great. See you tomorrow.

What do you notice about this exchange? Have you ever seen a discussion like this? Ever been in one? What about our own example—what might have been the assumption here?

[Fill in first the left-hand column for one part of the exchange. Leave the other person for later. Shift the group to think in terms of an imaginary person, someone not present in the group. Use probes to build awareness, such as:

■ *What was the assumption this person may have had when he said this?*

■ *Was this person asking a question or making a point here?*

■ *What was the assumption behind the decision to make this point?*

■ *Is this what he really meant? What did he really mean?*

■ *Did he already know the answer to this question? What is the assumption that caused him to ask a question he knew the answer to?*

■ *What did he think he "knew?"*

Document all the hidden thoughts and feelings not communicated. Invite discussion. Then ask the group to document (guessing, of course) the assumptions, thoughts, and feelings not communicated by the other person. Make the point that what we say is usually several steps away from what we think or believe.]

There are two things to learn here. One—we may think our assumptions are hidden, but they have a tendency to communicate themselves through our tone and manner. During dialogue we are more up-front about those assumptions (since people infer them anyway). Two—we regularly, habitually even, do not say what we mean. Particularly when it comes to discussing a dangerous truth. How can we expect to communicate? During dialogue we try to come closer to the real meaning.

It is a wonderful investment of your time to think about your assumptions. Many problems come from faulty assumptions. For the duration of dialogue you have an opportunity to test some of the assumptions you regularly use in talking to your coworkers. If you want different results, you need to do something different. The best place to create that difference is to replace an assumption that is faulty.

Don't worry about correcting assumptions at this point. The hard part is seeing them. Take your piece of paper and begin to fill in the left-hand column, first for yourself and then for the other person.

[Have the rest of the participants fill in the left-hand column for their script. Walk around and make sure they aren't fudging. Let the person who volunteered this script do another one or finish out the rest of his. Allow at least ten minutes.]

Dialogue means that you identify your own assumptions and you are more honest about your hidden beliefs. This can be done tactfully. For instance, Bert could, in a safe environment of dialogue, tell Sally: "I bug you because I figure you don't think my work is important or that I am important enough to listen to—and I want your respect as much as I want the numbers." We are not recommending that you speak from your left-hand column, only that you use it to identify the assumptions you can test.

This exercise is designed to give you an experience of what is beneath the politeness and pretending layer that normally covers all of our discussions. Dialogue delves into your left-hand column and even goes behind that. One of the skills of dialogue is to suspend assumptions. That means you "hold them out for others to see"—not that you review them privately, but that you review them with the group's input.

The skill of deconstructing your own assumptions is a wonderful skill that can enhance your creativity, enable you to think outside the box, and reach consensus with others. It is an individual skill to know how to identify assumptions. The next step requires the skill of the group to review these assumptions as a group without blame, attack, or defensiveness. Let's begin to build the group skill as you each work on your individual skill of identifying assumptions.

One model that can really help you visualize the layers of assumptions that are normally transparent to you is the "Ladder of Inference," also developed by Chris Argyris (see Appendix Figure 4).

LADDER OF INFERENCE

Facilitator: We humans operate with a set of beliefs that helps us choose how to interpret what we see and hear, and what actions to take in response to what we see and hear. Some of those beliefs were put in place based on a series of experiences that weren't a good representation of reality. In fact, most of our beliefs are based on insufficient data. We take a sample of someone's behavior and make judgments about how that person thinks when we don't really know how he thinks. In fact, we can be reasonably sure that for the most part we have about 10 percent of the data we would need to make a firm judgment. Yet we file

Appendix Figure 4

our new belief away and use it as if it were a fact. Take, for instance, a situation where you have scheduled a meeting. You have been waiting there for ten minutes and this is the second time people from "the other department" have kept you waiting. What thoughts start to go through your head?

> [Draw the ladder on your flip chart and start from the bottom rung up. Make sure you have three or four stages. Use the group's words if possible to fill in the layers of assumptions. Present the model with several examples of layered assumptions, like this:
>
>> Corrected my grammar—to—he thinks I'm stupid
>>
>> Missed a deadline—to—he is unreliable
>>
>> Did not give me the data—to—she is withholding information]

A lot of the time the dangerous truth, too dangerous even to discuss, is at the top of this ladder. But it is not the truth at all. If we step back down the ladder and examine each assumption on which it is based, it gets less and less dangerous and easier and easier to discuss.

Some of you think that others in here are lazy, that they don't do their fair share. Well, that is a bit dangerous to say, isn't it? But what if you engaged this person in helping you to examine your assumptions? One powerful example of that happened with a group of bank managers. One guy used to leave the office right at 5:00 P.M. He sometimes came in late and, to top it off, he didn't bother to attend the company picnic. Everyone in the room had climbed right up their ladder to the generalized belief that he "didn't care."

This wasn't the subject of the dialogue, of course, but it was hampering the group's ability to communicate. At one point someone had the courage to say, "My assumption when I see you leave at five is that you are going home to relax while I stay here and work, and I resent that." After about ten minutes of genuine inquiry—he did not initially trust them enough to tell the truth—he told them, "My wife has AIDS from a blood transfusion ten years ago. I'm barely able to care for her and our three kids. She is dying, and when I leave at five, I'm going home to take care of her. On top of everything else, I feel guilty about not pulling my weight at work. I'm so sorry. I've kept it secret because of the stigma attached to AIDS, and I was afraid of losing my job."

Their ladders came tumbling down. They realized he did care, and he realized that not only would he not lose his job, but there was an untapped wealth of support ready to make things easier for him and his family. The examination of assumptions on both sides shifted the paradigm of the group. The tone and pitch of the dialogue deepened. They began to search for other assumptions that were sabotaging their ability to work together.

If you can understand your assumptions and their assumptions, then you can improve communication. What are some common assumptions that screw up your communication? Here are some I can almost guarantee that you have encountered:

COMMON ASSUMPTIONS	REALITY
"I understand the problem."	"I only understand a piece of the problem."
"We need to find the solution."	"We need to understand the problem."
"They can't take or don't want the truth."	"Everyone (including me) usually believes they already know the truth."

[Discuss the cost of unidentified assumptions in communication. Give the group an opportunity to make the link between this exercise and the dialogue process.]

12:30 P.M. Lunch

1:30 P.M. Choosing the Rules for Dialogue

Facilitator: Okay, we are almost ready to do this dialogue thing. Only one more step left. This will take about twenty minutes—and these will be a very important twenty minutes. We could do this quicker, but that would defeat the purpose. I'm about to hand the process back over to you guys, but before I do, I want to help you build a set of agreements that will help you remember to stay on track.

How in the world do we remember all of this stuff and dialogue at the same time? It isn't easy. That's why dialogue takes practice. The best way to keep on track is to make some agreements about how you want this group interaction to be different from usual. You can make up your own rules or use some of the ones I have here. I suggest that you limit yourself to five to seven rules. That's the limit for your short-term memory, anyway. Don't bite off more than you can chew. Start with five to seven and you can add more later.

[Pass out a list of possible dialogue rules. (For more on this see Chapter 6.)]

Facilitator: You get to choose your own rules. Why? Because this is not my process, it is yours. You know your group better. You know the old habits and norms that most need to change in order for you to achieve dialogue. The rules you choose should directly address what you know about yourselves as a group. Which ones do you want? Take a few quiet minutes and individually mark the four rules that you think would be most powerful in shifting this group to a more dialogic style of interaction.

[Give the group three minutes.]

Okay, let's hear what you selected. Would someone like to nominate one of these?

[Let the group struggle a bit with this one. They will take the rules more seriously if they worry over them a bit, rather than just taking the top seven. With each recommendation ask, "How will keeping that rule

make the interaction of this group different from your usual interac-
tions? What will you do differently?" This prompts important discussion
that builds a group definition for each chosen rule. For any of these
rules, the only relevant meaning is the interpretation of the group.]

Know that any rule you recommend will end up feeling more like your rule than their rule. If you choose to influence the group, wait until the discussion of what each rule means is well under way. At that point you may want to say something, like the following comments.

There are several basic rules that have been recommended most often. They include, No Leader, No Task, No Decisions, and Speak Personally.

No Leader . . . I'm not going to be a leader. If I did, it would sabotage your ability to learn to dialogue as a group. I will be a coach for a while and decrease even that activity as much as I can, as soon as I can. You will want to remember that when the going gets tough, there may be someone in the group who wants to step in and "help," or the group may spontaneously begin looking to someone here to be your leader. If that happens, what escape strategy is the group using? (Dependency) You may want to use this rule to help you stay away from dependency. It is a hard one to resist. It is easier to have a leader, but it is not dialogue.

No Task . . . Again, you'll want to rush to agreement. You will want clarity so bad you will ignore the outstanding issues that haven't been resolved yet and try to reach some sort of outcome. This rule keeps you from going that route. You will say things like, "Do we all agree to get x done by Friday?" when either there is no way in hell you can get it done or stopping there prevents you from exploring the next brilliant idea. That is why you have the rule of No Task. It forces you to stay, for the time period of the dialogue, in an exploration phase rather than rushing to closure just for the comfort of having "gotten somewhere."

No Decisions . . . This rule is the same as above, really. Decisions stop exploration. There will be time enough for decisions later, after dialogue.

Speak Personally . . . This is a good one. That means that people are forced to speak only from their position and from their experience. You don't realize how often you speak for others or state an opinion and keep a safe distance from it at the same time. For instance: "I went to the grocery store, and you know how when you are standing in line and the guy in front of you can't seem to get his act together, and it just makes you want to tell him to 'just write the damn check'?" Who is in the grocery line? Every time you use the word *you*, please stop and check if you should be using the word *I* instead. Dialogue works much better if you speak for yourself and let others speak for themselves.

This is only a list of suggested rules. Choose from these or make up your own. You have the opportunity to create this group process to be whatever you want it to be.

[Again, don't let the group rush through this part without taking it seriously. Use comments such as, "Are you sure? Does anyone feel that there is a rule not included that might really benefit the group? If so, which one are you willing to drop to include it?" Slow them down if you need to. If they begin to argue over a rule, it just means they are taking the process seriously; guide them to a resolution, but don't cut off the discussion.]

Okay, these are your chosen rules. *[Reread them.]* Is everyone willing to commit to every single one of them for two hours? It's not forever, remember. If so, let's move to the circle and begin. Let's move away from the tables and make a circle with our chairs. You do not need any writing materials. Just you and a chair.

Beginning Dialogue

[If possible, move to a new room. Otherwise, rearrange the room you are in. Remove tables and writing materials, and arrange the chairs in a circle. Leave yourself enough room to move outside the circle with access to the flip chart pages displaying the stages, defensive strategies, and the group's chosen rules.]

Facilitator: Dialogue will feel awkward at first. You may feel as if you aren't doing it "right." Remember that however you do it is "right enough." It is natural to feel awkward and uncomfortable. That is your best clue that you are doing it "right," whatever that means. As you reach the chaos stage, don't chicken out. The purpose is to find out where you have different beliefs. As you reach discarding and redefining, don't be afraid of the silences. That means people are reconsidering their positions.

[Deliver any remaining mind-sets you think will help the group.]

How would you like me to remind you of the escape strategies? By just pointing to the picture on the wall? Or should I have two steps—should I stand up first and only say something if you don't seem to correct?

[Always ask for guidance on how the group members want you to intervene. Let them choose. There is no one way that works best. They can even make up some method—the point is, they choose. Again, you are shifting power to them. Remind them that they are giving you permission to facilitate. Later, when you have to call their attention to an escape strategy, it will be in their memory that they asked you to remind them just this way. This shifts the power to them and avoids a lot of defensive behavior.]

Is everyone ready to begin? How long are we going to go for? Okay, at 4:00 P.M. we will finish. Until then, my goal is to say as little as possible.

2:00 P.M. Begin Dialogue

Facilitator: Please begin.

[Once they have formed the circle, sit down and be silent. More than likely they will ask you a question. Use your judgment, but if you think they have any chance of figuring it out by themselves, don't answer. Use eye contact to indicate that they should look to someone else in their group for the answer. Remove yourself from the circle. Stand outside. Be separate. You may even want to step outside the room so that they can't see you for a while.

Later on, people may continue to direct comments to you. Try to look at the person they are talking about, so their eyes will follow yours and they will begin communicating with them instead of you. Discourage any interaction directed at you. Intervene only as necessary.]

4:00 P.M. (Approximate) End Dialogue

[Watch the time and monitor the group stage. If they look like they will still be in the chaos or discarding and redefining stages at the wrap-up time, you may want to stop them a little earlier so you can move them to a more stable state before they leave. Don't let them leave "all opened up." They need to bring some closure to the process. You may want to use the "wells and wishes" process:]

Facilitator: Let's take a few minutes to look at what you think that you did "well" and what you "wish" you could do better next time. As we go around the room, I'd like for everyone to give one sentence *[you may want to remind people that this is not the time to make a last positional statement!]* about one thing you think the group did well and one thing you think you could do better next time. This is about process, not content. This will help us bring closure to today, as well as build your collective skills in continuing to improve your ability to dialogue as a group. This is not something you learn how to do in one day. Now is the time to capture your learning.

> *[You can close in any of a thousand different ways. I almost always use some sort of rounds process to close. Refer to the stage of closure and people will make it happen that way. Use your intuition to help you find a way to focus on a positive note during closure. Sometimes you will want to anchor the meaning the group has created. I had one group close with a statement about what keeps them committed to the group.]*

Sometimes the dialogue will end painfully. Facing dangerous truths is not fun stuff. Pain is frequently a price of development. It may be that the best you can do is to acknowledge the pain of the group as a step in the right direction.

4:00 P.M. Harvesting

> *[I usually leave an hour at the end of the day to allow the group to do some kind of outcome-oriented work. They may develop a new set of agreements for daily communication (using the rules of dialogue is too much of a stretch) or develop an action plan. Often gains made during dialogue can be anchored into actions. To return to the familiar ground of "getting things done" is a part of the closure process.]*

That is a doctored example of how I present dialogue to a group. I never do it the same way twice, nor would I recommend you do that, either. Each group will give you cues on how to proceed. The process works much better if you adapt to the group's interests and pace. I give you this script because I want you to get the feeling that you had an opportunity to watch a video sample of the setup. In facilitation, there are thousands of subtleties that are more easily demonstrated than discussed. I hope you will find that reading this script gave you some ideas on what you would like to do and how you would like to be as you facilitate a group to dialogue.

I welcome the opportunity to dialogue with you about dialogue. Feel free to contact me with questions or suggestions at:

Annette Simmons
Group Process Consulting
Phone: 336-275-4404
E-mail: AnnetteGPC@aol.com

Bibliography

Argyris, Chris. *On Organizational Learning.* Malden, MA: Blackwell Publishers, 1992.

Argyris, Chris. *Overcoming Organizational Defenses: Facilitating Organizational Learning.* Needham Heights, MA: Allyn and Bacon, 1990.

Bohm, David. *On Dialogue.* Ojai, CA: David Bohm Seminars, 1990.

Bohm, David, and Mark Edwards. *Changing Consciousness.* New York: Harper Collins, 1991.

Bohm, David, and Peter Garrett. "Dialogue: A Proposal." Unpublished paper.

Brehmer, B. "Social Judgment Theory and the Analysis of Interpersonal Conflict," *Psychological Bulletin*, Vol. 86 (1976), pp. 307–324.

Buber, Martin. *I and Thou by Martin Buber: A New Translation with a Prologue and Notes by Walter Kaufman.* New York: Scribner's, 1970. (Note: Buber's original work was published in 1937.)

Capra, Fritjof. *The Web of Life: A New Scientific Understanding of Living Systems.* New York: Anchor Books, 1996.

Carden, Kara. "The Only Meaning of Story," *Storytelling Magazine*, Vol. 10, No. 3 (July 1998), p. 17.

DePaulo, Bella M., and Deborah A. Kashy. "Everyday Lies in Close and Casual Relationships," *Journal of Personality and Social Psychology*, Vol. 74, No. 1 (1998), pp. 63–79.

DePaulo, Bella M., and Deborah A. Kashy. "Who Lies?" *Journal of Personality and Social Psychology,* Vol. 70, No. 5 (1998), pp. 1037–1051.

DePaulo, Bella M., and Jenny S. Tornqvist. "Deception," *Encyclopedia of Mental Health,* San Diego: Academic Press, 1998.

DePaulo, B. M., et al. "Lying in Everyday Life," *Journal of Personality and Social Psychology,* Vol. 70, No. 5 (1996), pp. 979–995.

Dixon, Nancy. *Perspectives on Dialogue: Making Talk Developmental for Individuals and Organizations.* Greensboro, NC: Center for Creative Leadership, 1996.

Dunnette, M.D., J. Campbell, and K. Jaastad. "The Effect of Group Participation on Brainstorming Effectiveness for Two Industrial Samples," *Journal of Applied Psychology,* Vol. 46 (1963), pp. 30–37.

Eisenberg, Eric M., and H. L. Goodall, Jr. *Organizational Communication: Balancing Creativity and Constraint.* New York: St. Martin's Press, 1993.

Ellinor L., and G. Gerard. *Dialogue: Rediscovering the Transforming Power of Conversation.* New York: John Wiley, 1998.

Friedman, Maurice. *Dialogue and the Human Image: Beyond Humanistic Psychology.* Thousand Oaks, CA: Sage Publications, 1992.

Fritz, Robert. *Corporate Tides.* San Francisco: Berrett–Koehler, 1996.

Hall, J. "Decisions, Decisions, Decisions," *Psychology Today* (November 1971), pp. 50–54.

Hall, J., and W. H. Watson. "The Effects of a Normative Intervention on Group Decision-Making Performance," *Human Relations,* 23, No. 4 (1971), pp. 299–317.

Isaacs, William N. *Dialogue and the Art of Thinking Together.* New York: Doubleday Currency, 1999.

Isaacs, William N. "Dialogue: The Power of Collective Thinking," *The Systems Thinker,* Vol. 4, No. 3 (1993), pp. 1–4.

Isaacs, William N. *Dimensions of Generative Dialogue: MIT Dialogue Project Summary.* Cambridge, MA: Massachusetts Institute of Technology, 1992.

Isaacs, William N. "Taking Flight: Dialogue, Collective Thinking and Organizational Learning," *Organizational Dynamics,* Vol. 22, No. 2 (1993), pp. 24–39.

Isaacs, William N. *The Dialogue Project Annual Progress Report: April 1992–March 1993.* Cambridge, MA: Massachusetts Institute of Technology, 1993.

Kaner, Sam. *Facilitator's Guide to Participatory Decision Making.* Gabriola Island, British Columbia: New Society Publishers, 1996.

Kofman, F., and Peter M. Senge. "Communities of Commitment: The Heart of Learning Organizations," *Organizational Dynamics,* Vol. 22, No. 1 (1993).

Kung, Hans. *Global Responsibility: In Search of a New World Ethic.* New York: Crossroad Publishing, 1991.

Manning, G., K. Curtis, and S. McMillen (eds.). *Building Community: The Human Side of Work.* Cincinnati, OH: Thomson Executive Press, 1996.

Maranhao, Tullio. *The Interpretation of Dialogue.* Chicago: University of Chicago Press, 1990.

Markova, I., C. Graumann, and K. Fopa (eds.). *Mutualities in Dialogue.* Cambridge, United Kingdom: Cambridge University Press, 1995.

McGrath, Joseph E. *Groups: Interaction and Performance.* Englewood Cliffs, NJ: Prentice Hall, 1984.

Mendex-Flohr, Paul. *From Mysticism to Dialogue: Martin Buber's Transformation of German Social Thought.* Detroit, MI: Wayne State University Press, 1989.

Myerson, George. *Rhetoric, Reason and Society: Rationality as Dialogue.* Thousand Oaks, CA: Sage Publications, 1994.

Nisbett, R. E., and T. D. Wilson. "Telling More Than We Can Know: Verbal Reports on Mental Processes," *Psychological Review,* Vol. 84, No. 3 (1977).

Osburn, J. D., et al. *Self-Directed Work Teams: The New American Challenge.* Homewood, IL: Business One Irwin, 1990.

Patterson, James, and Peter Kim. *The Day America Told the Truth.* Englewood, NJ: Prentice Hall, 1991.

Peck, M. Scott. *The Different Drum: Community Making and Peace.* New York: Simon & Schuster, 1987.

Phelps, Joseph, *More Light, Less Heat: How Dialogue Can Transform Christian Conflict into Growth.* San Francisco: Jossey-Bass, 1998.

Rollins, E. William, and Henry Zohn (eds.). *Men of Dialogue: Martin Buber and Albrecht Goes.* New York: Funk & Wagnalls, 1969.

Sallis, John. *Being and Logos: Reading the Platonic Dialogues.* Bloomington and Indianapolis: Indiana University Press, 1996.

Schein, Edgar H. "On Dialogue, Culture and Organizational Learning," *Organizational Dynamics,* Vol. 22, No. 2 (1993), pp. 40–51.

Schein, Edgar H., with I. Schneier and C. Barker. *Coercive Persuasion: A Socio-Psychological Analysis of American Civilian Prisoners by the Chinese Communists.* New York: W.W. Norton & Co., 1961.

Schmidt, Lawrence K. (ed.). *The Specter of Relativism: Truth, Dialogue, and Phronesis in Philosophical Hermeneutics.* Evanston, IL: Northwestern University Press, 1995.

Senge, Peter M. *The Fifth Discipline: The Art and Practice of the Learning Organization.* New York: Doubleday Currency, 1990.

Senge, P., et al. *The Fifth Discipline Fieldbook: Strategies and Tools for Building a Learning Organization.* New York: Doubleday Currency, 1994.

Spear, Stephanie. "The Emergence of Learning Communities," *The Systems Thinker,* Vol. 4, No. 5 (1993), pp. 1–4.

Taylor, D. W., P. C. Berry, and C. H. Block. "Does Group Participation When Using Brainstorming Facilitate or Inhibit Creative Thinking?" *Administrative Sciences Quarterly,* Vol. 3 (1958), pp. 23–47.

Taylor, Talbot J., and Deborah Cameron. *Analyzing Conversation: Rules and Units in the Structure of Talk.* New York: Pergamon Press, 1987.

Tedlock, Dennis, and Bruce Mannheim. *The Dialogic Emergence of Culture.* Urbana and Chicago: University of Illinois Press, 1995.

Teurfs, Linda, and Glenna Gerard. "A Practice Field for Creating Community at Work," *At Work: Stories of Tomorrow's Workplace,* Vol. 2, No. 2 (1993), pp. 21–24.

Teurfs, Linda, and Glenna Gerard. "Dialogue . . . Something New, Something Simple and Profound." Unpublished paper, 1993.

Teurfs, Linda, and Glenna Gerard. *Reflection on Building Blocks and Guidelines of Dialogue.* Murrietta, CA: The Dialogue Group, 1993.

Tesser, Abraham. "Self-Generated Attitude Change," *Advances in Experimental Social Psychology,* Vol. 11 (1978), pp. 289–338.

Wardhaugh, Ronald. *How Conversation Works.* Oxford, England: Basil Blackwell Publisher, 1985.

Weisbord, Marvin. *Productive Workplaces: Organizing and Managing for Dignity, Meaning and Community.* San Francisco: Jossey-Bass, 1989.

Wheatley, Margaret J. "Chaos and Complexity: What Can Science Teach?" *OD Practitioner,* Vol. 25, No. 3, pp. 2–10.

Wilson T. D., et al. "Introspection, Attitude Change, and Attitude-Behavior Consistency: The Disruptive Effects of Explaining Why We Feel the Way We Do," *Advances in Experimental Social Psychology,* Vol. 22 (1989), pp. 287–343.

Index